THE SOUL
THE QUALITY OF LIFE

D1602398

THE SOUL
THE QUALITY OF LIFE

Compiled by a student who has imposed his
own punctuation on the original text

From the Writings of
Alice A. Bailey
and
The Tibetan Master, Djwhal Khul

LUCIS PUBLISHING COMPANY
New York

LUCIS PRESS, Ltd.
London

First Printing, 1974
Second Printing, 1979 (1st Paperback Edition)
Fifth Printing, 2006

ISBN: 0-85330-132-8

It has been translated into Danish, Dutch and Russian.

LUCIS PUBLISHING COMPANY
120 Wall Street
New York, NY 10005

LUCIS PRESS, Ltd.
Suite 54
3 Whitehall Court
London SW1A 2EF

MANUFACTURED IN THE UNITED STATES OF AMERICA

REFERENCE INDEX

Books by The Tibetan (Djwhal Khul), through Alice A. Bailey

BOOKS BY ALICE A. BAILEY

The Consciousness of the Atom
The Soul and its Mechanism
From Intellect to Intuition
From Bethlehem to Calvary
The Light of The Soul
The Unfinished Autobiography

NOTE

Reference Example: A reference number, such as for instance (12 – 135/6) at the end of a quotation, would refer to a quotation taken from "*Education in the New Age*" (12) starting on page 135, and continued on page 136.

CONTENTS

EXTRACT FROM A STATEMENT BY THE TIBETAN

Published August 1934

Suffice it to say, that I am a Tibetan disciple of a certain degree, and this tells you but little, for all are disciples from the humblest aspirant up to, and beyond, the Christ Himself. I live in a physical body like other men, on the borders of Tibet, and at times (from the exoteric standpoint) preside over a large group of Tibetan lamas, when my other duties permit. It is this fact that has caused it to be reported that I am an abbot of this particular lamasery. Those associated with me in the work of the Hierarchy (and all true disciples are associated in this work) know me by still another name and office. A.A.B. knows who I am and recognises me by two of my names.

I am a brother of yours, who has travelled a little longer upon the Path than has the average student, and has therefore incurred greater responsibilities. I am one who has wrestled and fought his way into a greater measure of light than has the aspirant who will read this article, and I must therefore act as a transmitter of the light, no matter what the cost. I am not an old man, as age counts among the teachers, yet I am not young or inexperienced. My work is to teach and spread the knowledge of the Ageless Wisdom wherever I can find a response, and I have been doing this for many years. I seek also to help the Master M. and the Master K.H. whenever opportunity offers, for I have been long connected with Them and with Their work. In all the above, I have told you much; yet at the same time I have told you nothing which would lead you to offer me that blind obedience and the foolish devotion which the emotional aspirant offers to the Guru and Master whom he is as yet unable to contact. Nor will he make that desired contact until he has transmuted emotional devotion into unselfish service to humanity—not to the Master.

The books that I have written are sent out with no claim for their acceptance. They may, or may not, be correct, true and useful. It is for you to ascertain their truth by right practice and by the exercise of the intuition. Neither I nor A.A.B. is the least interested in having them acclaimed as inspired writings, or in having anyone speak of them (with bated breath) as being the work of one of the Masters. If they present truth in such a way that it follows sequentially upon that already offered in the world teachings, if the information given raises the aspiration and the will-to-serve from the plane of the emotions to that of the mind (the plane whereon the Masters *can* be found) then they will have served their purpose. If the teaching conveyed calls forth a response from the illumined mind of the worker in the world, and brings a flashing forth of his intuition, then let that teaching be accepted. But not otherwise. If the statements meet with eventual corroboration, or are deemed true under the test of the Law of Correspondences, then that is well and good. But should this not be so, let not the student accept what is said.

THE GREAT INVOCATION

From the point of Light within the Mind of God
Let light stream forth into the minds of men.
Let Light descend on Earth.

From the point of Love within the Heart of God
Let love stream forth into the hearts of men.
May Christ return to Earth.

From the centre where the Will of God is known
Let purpose guide the little wills of men—
The purpose which the Masters know and serve.

From the centre which we call the race of men
Let the Plan of Love and Light work out
And may it seal the door where evil dwells.

Let Light and Love and Power restore the Plan on Earth.

"The above Invocation or Prayer does not belong to any person or group, but to all Humanity. The beauty and the strength of this Invocation lies in its simplicity, and in its expression of certain central truths which all men, innately and normally, accept—the truth of the existence of a basic Intelligence to Whom we vaguely give the name of God; the truth that behind all outer seeming, the motivating power of the universe is Love; the truth that a great Individuality came to earth, called by Christians, the Christ, and embodied that love so that we could understand; the truth that both love and intelligence are effects of what is called the Will of God; and finally the self-evident truth that only through *humanity* itself can the Divine Plan work out."

ALICE A. BAILEY

1. PREFACE

1. We have here received much upon which to ponder, to think and to meditate. Let us search for the thread of gold which will lead us, in waking consciousness, into the treasure house of our own souls, and there to learn to be at-one with all that breathes, to sense the vision for the whole, as far as we can, and to work in unison with God's Plan as far as it has been revealed to us by Those Who know. (15-242/3)

2. Nothing under heaven can arrest the progress of the human soul on its long pilgrimage from darkness to light, from the unreal to the real, from death to immortality, and from ignorance to wisdom. . . . Nothing can keep the spirit of man from God. (7-124), (8-159)

2. LIMITATION OF WORDS

Words fail to express and language handicaps rather than aids the objective that I have in view. Human thought is now entering a field for which there exists, as yet, no true language-form, for we have no adequate terms, and in which word-symbols mean but little. Just as the discovery of the automobile, and the radio have necessitated the formulation of an entirely new set of terms, phrases, nouns and verbs, so in the years that are coming the discovery of the fact of the soul will necessitate a new language approach. It is true, is it not, that a man of the Victorian age, listening to the technical jargon of the present radio laboratory or the ordinary garage, would be completely in the dark? So the psychologist of today is in the dark very often and understands not what we are trying to convey, for the new language is not yet evolved and the old terms are inadequate. I am, therefore, unable to do more than employ the terms which seem to me to be the most suitable, knowing that I am failing to express the true significance of my ideas, and you are consequently gaining only an approximate understanding and conception of the concepts I am endeavouring to expound. (15-425)

3. KNOW THYSELF

1. Only as a man understands himself can he arrive at an understanding of that which is the sum total that we call God. This is a truism and an occult platitude, but when acted upon leads to a revelation which makes the present "Unknown God" a recognised reality. (4-29)

2. The spiritual man is he who having been both a man of the world and an occult student, has reached the conclusion that behind all those causes with which he has been hitherto engaged, is a CAUSE; this causal unity then becomes the goal of his search. This is the mystery lying behind all mysteries; this is the secret of which all that has hitherto been known and conceived is but the veil; this is the heart of the Unknown which holds hid the purpose and the key to all that IS, and which is only put into the hands of those exalted Beings Who—having worked their way through the manifold web of life—know Themselves indeed and in truth to be Atma, or Spirit itself, and veritable sparks in the one great Flame.

Three times the cry goes out to all the Pilgrims upon the Path of Life: *"Know thyself"* is the first great injunction, and long is the process of attaining that knowledge. *"Know the Self"* comes next, and when that is achieved, man knows not only himself but all selves; the soul of the universe is to him no longer the sealed book of life, but one with the seven seals broken. Then, when the man stands adept, the cry goes forth *"Know the One"*, and the words ring in the adept's ears: "Search for that which is the responsible Cause, and having known the soul, and its expression —form—search for THAT which the soul reveals." (3-1237)

3. In the rigid disciplining of yourself comes eventual perfection. To the disciple naught is too small to undertake, for in the rigid adjustment of the details of the lower world life comes, at the end, attainment of the goal. The life of the disciple becomes not easier as the Gate is neared, but ever the watch must be more thorough, ever right action must be taken with no regard to result, and ever each body, in all its aggregate of detail, must be wrestled with and subjugated. Only in the thorough comprehension of the axiom "Know Thyself" will come that understanding that enables man to wield the law and know the inner working of the system from the centre to the periphery. Struggle, strive, discipline, and rejoicingly serve, with no reward save the misunderstanding and the abuse of those who follow *after*—this is the role of the disciple. (2-310)

4. THE CONSTITUTION OF MAN

The constitution of man, as considered in the following pages, is basically threefold, as follows:

I. *The Monad, or pure Spirit, the Father in Heaven.*
   This aspect reflects the three aspects of the Godhead:
   1. Will or Power .... The Father.
   2. Love-Wisdom .... The Son.
   3. Active Intelligence ...... The Holy Spirit.
   and is only contacted at the final initiations, when man is nearing the end of his journey and is perfected. The Monad reflects itself again in

II. *The Ego, Higher Self, or Individuality.*
    This aspect is potentially
    1. Spiritual Will .... Atma
    2. Intuition .... Buddhi, Love-Wisdom, the Christ
       principle.
    3. Higher or Abstract Mind   Higher Manas.
    The Ego begins to make its power felt in advanced men, and increasingly on the Probationary Path, until by the third initiation the control of the lower self by the higher is perfected, and the highest aspect begins to make its energy felt.

III. *The Personality, or lower self, physical plane man.*
     This aspect is also threefold:
     1. A Mental body .... lower manas.
     2. An Emotional body ...... astral body.
     3. A Physical body .... the dense physical and the etheric
        body.
     The aim of evolution is therefore to bring man to the realisation of the Egoic aspect and to bring the lower nature under its control.
     (1-xv)

5. THE NATURE OF MAN

When the public mind has apprehended, even cursorily, the following briefly stated facts, the trend of popular education, the object of political science, and the goal of economic and social endeavour, will take a new and better direction. These facts might be summed up in the following postulates:

1. Man is *in essence* divine. This has ever been enunciated throughout the ages, but remains as yet a beautiful theory or belief, and not a proven scientific fact, nor is it universally held.

2. Man is a fragment of the Universal Mind, or world soul, and as a fragment is thus partaker of the instincts and quality of that soul, as it manifests through the human family. Therefore, unity is only possible upon the plane of the mind. This, if true, must lead to the tendency to develop within the physical brain a conscious realisation of group affiliations on the mental plane, a conscious recognition of group relationships, ideals and goal, and a conscious manifestation of that continuity of consciousness which is the object of evolution at this time. It will further produce the transference of the race consciousness from the physical plane to the mental, and a consequent solving through "knowledge, love and sacrifice" of all present problems. This will bring about emancipation from the present physical plane disorder. It must lead to the education of the public as to the nature of man, and the development of the powers latent within him—powers which will set him free from his present limitations, and which will produce in the human family a collective repudiation of the present conditions. When men everywhere recognise themselves and each other, as divine self-conscious units, functioning primarily in the causal body, but utilising the three lower vehicles only as a means of contact with the three lower planes, we will have government, politics, economics and the social order readjusted upon sound, sane and divine lines.

3. Man in his lower nature, and in his three vehicles, is an aggregate of lesser lives, dependent upon him for their group nature, for their type of activity, and collective response, and who—through the energy or activity of the solar Lord—will themselves later be raised and developed to the human stage.

When these three facts are understood, then and only then will we have a right and just comprehension of the nature of man. (3-809/11)

4

6. SPIRIT

1. The nature of Spirit can only be intelligibly revealed to the higher grades of the initiates, that is, to those who (through the medium of the work effected in the third Initiation) have been put in conscious contact with their "Father in Heaven", the Monad. Esoteric students, disciples and the initiates of lower degree are developing contact with the soul, or the second aspect, and only when this contact is firmly established, can the higher concept be entertained.   (3-1229)

2. The goal of realisation for man is consciousness of the nature of the Soul, the medium through which the Spirit aspect ever works. More it is not possible for him to do. Having learnt to function as the soul, detached from the three worlds, man then becomes a conscious corporate active part of that Soul which permeates and pervades all that is in manifestation. Then, and only then, the pure light of Spirit *per se* becomes visible to him through a just appreciation of the Jewel hidden at the heart of his own being; then only does he become aware of that greater Jewel which lies hidden at the heart of solar manifestation. Even then, at that advanced stage, all that he can be aware of, can contact and visualise, is the light which emanates from the Jewel and the radiance which veils the inner glory.

. . . Needless it is, therefore, for us to study and consider that which the initiate of high degree can only dimly sense; useless it is for us to seek for terms to express that which lies safely hidden behind all ideas and all thought, when thought itself is not perfectly understood, and the machinery for comprehension is not perfected. Man himself—a great idea and a specific one—knows not the nature of that which he is seeking to express.

All that we can do is to apprehend the fact that there exists THAT which may not as yet be defined, to realise that a central Life persists which permeates and animates the Soul, and which seeks to utilise the form through which the soul expresses itself. This can be stated to be true for all forms, of all souls, human, subhuman, planetary and solar. (3-1231/2)

3. All that tends to lift the status of humanity on any plane of manifestation, is religious work and has a spiritual goal, for matter is but spirit on the lowest plane, and spirit, we are told, is but matter on the highest. All is spirit and these differentiations are but the products of the finite mind. Therefore, all workers and knowers of God, in or out of fleshly bodies,

5

and working in any field of divine manifestation, form part of the planetary hierarchy, and are integral units in that great cloud of witnesses who are the "onlookers and observers". They possess the power of spiritual insight or perception as well as objective or physical vision.   (4-56)

4. The word "spiritual" does not refer to religious matters, so-called. All activity which drives the human being forward towards some form of development—physical, emotional, mental, intuitional, social—if it is in advance of his present state, is essentially spiritual in nature and is indicative of the livingness of the inner divine entity. The spirit of man is undying; it forever endures, progressing from point to point, and stage to stage upon the Path of Evolution, unfolding steadily and sequentially the divine attributes and aspects.   (12-1)

7.   THE MONAD

1. *Monad*: The One. The threefold spirit on its own plane. In occultism it often means the unified triad—Atma, Buddhi, Manas; Spiritual Will, Intuition and Higher Mind—or the immortal part of man which reincarnates in the lower kingdoms, and gradually progresses through them to man and thence to the final goal.   (1-221/2)

2. *Atma*: The Universal Spirit; the divine Monad; the seventh Principle; so called in the septenary constitution of man.   (1-216)

3. Just as it is not possible upon the physical plane for the physical vehicle fully to express the total point of development of the Ego or higher self, so it is not possible even for the Ego fully to sense and express the quality of Spirit. Hence the utter impossibility for human consciousness justly to appraise the life of the Spirit or Monad.   (3-50)

4. The evolution of the Monad is a much more intricate thing than appears in the books as yet given to the public. In those books the development of consciousness and its transition through the kingdoms of nature are the points dwelt upon. Yet there have been earlier cycles, which it will be only possible to comprehend as the history and evolution of the planetary Logoi become gradually revealed. They are parts of His body of manifestation, cells within that greater vehicle, and thus vitalised by His life, qualified by His nature, and distinguished by His characteristics.

This will take the history, therefore, of a Monad back to the earlier kalpas. Such history it is not possible to reveal, and no purpose would be served by such a revelation. The fact only can be touched upon, as it must be considered along general lines if the true nature of the Self is to be accurately known. . . .

The Monad has cycles analogous, though on a miniature scale, to those of the One Life Who permeates and animates all lesser lives. Certain of these cycles cover periods of time so vast, and so long past, that their history can only be conveyed to the investigating Adepts through the medium of sound and symbol. The details of that development are lost in the night of other kalpas, and all that can be seen are the *results*—the cause must be accepted as existing, though for us remaining inexplicable until the higher initiations are taken. (3-1087/9)

5. Groups of Monads come into incarnation according to which centre in a Heavenly Man of a particular planetary scheme, or which centre of the solar Logos, is in process of vivification or cyclic activity. (3-1090)

6. The Monad is the source of light, not only to the human family, but it is the receiver of light from the threefold Sun; it is the lens through which the light of the solar Logos can flow to the planetary Logos, preserving and holding steady in that light the vision, the purpose, the will and the creative intention of the planetary Logos. (6-400)

7. In the earlier stage upon the evolutionary path, the Monad is the source of the exhalation or of the expiration which brought the soul into being upon the physical plane: upon the Path of Return . . . the Monad is the source of inhalation or of inspiration. (15-322)

8. THE SPIRITUAL TRIAD

1. *Triad* : The Spiritual Man; the expression of the Monad. It is the germinal spirit containing the potentialities of divinity. These potentialities will be unfolded during the course of evolution. This Triad forms the individualised or separated Self, or Ego. (1-225)

2. (The Triad) is literally Atma-Buddhi-Manas, the expression of the Monad, just as the personality is the expression of the Ego. The Monad expresses itself through the Triad, and its lowest or third Aspect forms

the Egoic or Causal body, the infant or germinal Ego. Similarly, the Ego express itself through the threefold lower man, mental, emotional, and etheric (these being the reflection of the higher Triad), and these three give rise to the dense physical manifestation.   (3-69)

9.   THE LIFE PRINCIPLE IN MAN

This life principle in man (Spirit, soul and body) manifests in a triple manner:

1. As the directional will, purpose, basic incentive. This is the dynamic energy which sets the being functioning, brings him into existence, sets the term of his life, carries him through the years, long or short, and abstracts itself at the close of his life cycle. This is the *spirit in man*, manifesting as the will to live, to be, to act, to pursue, to evolve. In its lowest aspect this works through the mental body or nature, and in connection with the dense physical, makes itself felt through the brain.

2. As the coherent force. It is that significant essential quality which makes each man different, which produces that complex manifestation of moods, desires, qualities, complexes, inhibitions, feelings and characteristics, which produce a man's peculiar psychology. This is the result of the interplay between the spirit or energy aspect, and the matter or body nature. This is the distinctive subjective man, his colouring, or individual note; this it is which sets the rate of vibratory activity of his body, produces his particular type of form, is responsible for the condition and nature of his organs, his glands, and his outer aspect. This is *the soul* and—in its lowest aspect—it works through the emotional or astral nature, and in connection with the dense physical, through the heart.

3. As the activity of the atoms and cells of which the *physical body* is composed. It is the sum total of those little lives of which the human organs, comprising the entire man, are composed. These have a life of their own and a consciousness which is strictly individual and identified. This aspect of the life principle works through the etheric or vital body, and in connection with the solid mechanism of the tangible form, through the spleen.   (4-452/3)

10.   INDIVIDUALISATION

1. Back in the dim past of history (hinted at through symbolism and in the Bibles of the world) there was a first major Approach when God took notice of man and something happened—under the action and will of God the Creator, God transcendent—which affected primeval man, and he "became a *living soul*". As the yearning urge towards an undefined and unrealised good made itself felt in the inchoate longings of unthinking man (literally unthinking at that stage), it evoked a response from Deity; God drew near to man and man became imbued with that life and energy which, as time went by, would enable him to recognise himself as a son of God, and eventually to express that sonship perfectly. This Approach was signalised by the appearance of the faculty of mind in man. In man was planted the embryonic power to think, to reason and to *know*. The Universal Mind of God was reflected in the tiny mind of man.   (7-149/50)

2. What . . . is *individualisation* from the standpoint of the psychological unfoldment of man? It is the focussing of the lowest aspect of the soul, which is that of the creative intelligence, so that it can express itself through the form nature. It will eventually be the first aspect of divinity thus to express itself. It is the emergence into manifestation of the specific quality of the solar angel through the appropriation, by that angel of a sheath or sheaths, which thus constitute its appearance. It is the initial imposition of an applied, directed energy upon that triple force aggregation which we call the form nature of man. The individual, on the way to full co-ordination and expression, appears upon the stage of life. The self-aware entity comes forth into physical incarnation. The actor appears in process of learning its part; he makes his debut and prepares for the day of full personality emphasis. The soul comes forth into dense form and on the lowest plane. The self begins the part of its career which is expressed through selfishness, leading finally to an ultimate unselfishness. The separative entity begins his preparation for group realisation. A God walks on earth, veiled by the fleshly form, the desire nature and the fluidic mind. He is a prey temporarily to the illusion of the senses, and dowered with a mentality which primarily hinders and imprisons, but which finally releases and liberates.

. . . Individualisation . . . can be simply defined as the process whereby forms of life in the fourth kingdom in nature arrive at:

1. Conscious individuality, through experiencing the life of the senses.

9

2. The assertion of individuality through the use of the discrimininating mind.

3. The ultimate sacrifice of that individuality to the group.

$$(15-9/10)$$

11. THE MIND (MANAS)

1. *Manas, or Manasic Principle*: Literally, the Mind, the mental faculty; that which distinguishes man from the mere animal. It is the individualising principle; that which enables man to know that he exists, feels, and knows. It is divided in some schools into two parts, higher or abstract mind, and lower or concrete mind.   (1-220)

2. *Fifth Principle*: The principle of mind; that faculty in man which is the intelligent thinking principle, and which differentiates man from the animals.   (1-218)

3. *The Fire or Spark of Mind* . . . shows as that intelligent will which links the Monad or Spirit with its lowest point of contact, the personality, functioning through a physical vehicle.

It likewise demonstrates, as yet imperfectly, as the vitalising factor in the thought-forms fabricated by the Thinker. As yet but few thought-forms, comparatively, can be said to be constructed by the centre of consciousness, the Thinker, the Ego. Few people as yet are in such close touch with their Higher Self, or Ego, that they can build the matter of the mental plane into a form which can be truly said to be an expression of the thoughts, purpose or desire of their Ego, functioning through the physical brain.   (3-46)

4. This quality of manas may be somewhat apprehended if the student regards it as the intelligent will, the active purpose, and the fixed idea of some Entity which brings about existence, utilises form, and works out effects from causes through discrimination in matter, separation into form, and the driving of all units within His sphere of influence to the fulfilment of that set purpose. Man is the originating source of mind as regards the matter of his vehicles, and their latent manasic impulse. So again with a Heavenly Man and His larger sphere of influence, and so with the solar Logos. Each discriminated, and thus formed His ring-pass-not; each has

a purpose in view for every incarnation; each is actively following and intelligently working to effect certain ends, and thus each is the originator of manas to His scheme; each is the animating fire of intelligence to His system; each, through this very manasic principle individualises, expands gradually this self-realisation till it includes the ring-pass-not of the Entity through Whom the fifth principle comes to him; and each attains initiation, and eventually escapes from form. . . .

To all intents and purposes, manas is the active will of an Entity working itself out through all the lesser lives who go to the content of the ring-pass-not or sphere of influence of the indwelling Existence. Therefore—as concerning man on this chain—he is but expressing the purpose and the will in action of the planetary Logos in Whose body he is a cell or lesser life. (3-354/5)

5. *Discrimination*: . . . All students recognise the discriminative quality of manas and its selective capacity; all recognise the faculty in man which enables him to distinguish intelligently between the Self and the Not-Self. What we are apt to forget is that this faculty persists on all planes, and is threefold in manifestation:

First. Discrimination between the I-consciousness, and that which is cognised in the external world. This is the ability to distinguish between oneself and all other forms extant. It is universally developed and has reached a fairly high stage of evolution.

Second. Discrimination between the Ego and the Personality. This narrows the concept down to the sphere of a man's own consciousness, and enables him to differentiate between his subjective self or soul, and the bodies which hold that soul enshrined. This is not by any means so universally developed. Most men do not as yet distinguish with accuracy between themselves as the Thinker, persistent in time and space, and the vehicle through which they think, which is ephemeral and transient. The real recognition of this essential duality, and the scientific appreciation of it is to be seen in the mystics, the advanced thinkers of the race, the conscious aspirants, and those nearing the Portal of Initiation.

Third. Discrimination between soul and Spirit, or the realisation by the man that not only can he say, *"I am"*; not only can he realise that *"I am That"*, but that he can advance to a still further realisation, and say *"I am That I am"*.

In all these expansions and appreciations the discriminative faculty of manas is utilised. . . .

Broadly (in relation to man) it might be stated that:

"I am" refers to the *personality* consciousness on the three lower planes, or to all that is considered as inferior to the causal body. It concerns a man's realisation of his place upon the *globe* within a chain.

"I am That" refers to his *egoic* consciousness, and to the planes of the Triad. It concerns a man's realisation of his place within the *chain* and his relationship to the group of which he forms a part.

"I am That I am" refers to a man's *monadic* consciousness, and his relationship to the planes of abstraction. It concerns his realisation of his position in the *scheme.* (3-418/20)

6. In our planetary development, the emphasis of the entire evolutionary process is on the MIND and on the various aspects of the mind—intelligence, mental perception, the Son of Mind (the soul), the lower mind, the abstract mind, the mind as will, the Universal Mind. The three which are of major importance and which form an esoteric triangle, requiring to be brought into a vital interrelation, are the Son of Mind, the abstract mind, and the Universal Mind. They are, when fully related and active, the factors which engineer divine Purpose and step it down into such form that we call it the hierarchical Plan and can act upon it. Only when the initiate has attained, through monadic contact, a touch of the Universal Mind, can the Purpose be sensed by him; this involves also the development of the abstract mind, plus the residue of mental perception which the Son of Mind has bequeathed to him; through all this unfoldment he can join the group who are the Formulators of the Plan. We are dealing here with most difficult and complex matters, inherent in the initiate consciousness, and for which we have as yet no correct terminology. Also the average aspirant has no idea what is the nature of the awareness or the reactions to contact of Those Who have passed beyond the third initiation; these limitations of the average student must constantly be borne in mind. . . . The light and futile talk of certain writers and thinkers anent the cosmic consciousness, and their flippant use of such phrases as "tuning in with the Infinite" or "tapping the Universal Mind", serve only to show how very little is known in reality about the responses and the reactions of those of high initiate rank, or of those on the highest levels of hierarchical life. (11-71/2)

7. In the esoteric philosophy we are taught . . . that on the mental plane there are three aspects of the mind, or of that mental creature we call a man. These three aspects constitute the most important part of his nature:

1. His lower concrete mind, the reasoning principle. It is with this aspect of the man that our educational processes profess to deal.

2. That Son of Mind, which we call the Ego or Soul. This is the intelligence principle, and is called by many names in the esoteric literature, such as the Solar Angel, the Agnishvattas, the Christ principle, etc. With this, religion in the past has professed to deal.

3. The higher abstract mind, the custodian of ideas, and that which is the conveyor of illumination to the lower mind, once that lower mind is en rapport with the soul. With this world of ideas philosophy has professed to deal.

We might call these three aspects:

The receptive mind, the mind as dealt with by the psychologists.

The individualised mind, the Son of Mind.

The illuminating mind, the higher mind.

. . . The gap between the lower mind and the soul has to be bridged, and curiously enough humanity has always realised this and has talked therefore in terms of "achieving unity" or "making the at-one-ment" or "attaining alignment". These are all attempts to express this intuitively realised truth.   (12-4/5)

8. When the right method of training is instituted, the mind will be developed into a reflector or agent of the soul, and so sensitised to the world of true values, that the lower nature—emotional, mental and physical or vital—will become simply the automatic servant of the soul. The soul will then function on earth through the medium of the mind, thereby controlling its instrument, the lower mind. Yet at the same time, the mind will remain the recorder and reflector of all information coming to it from the world of the senses, from the emotional body, and will register also the thoughts and the ideas current in its environment. At present, it is alas true, the trained mind is regarded as the highest expression of which humanity is capable; it is viewed entirely as a personality, and the possibility of there being something which can use the mind, as the mind in its turn uses the physical brain, is overlooked.   (12-17)

9. *The Higher Mind.* Practically speaking, except in rare and highly evolved souls, the higher mind does not manifest in children any more than it did in infant humanity. It can only truly make its presence felt when soul and mind and brain are aligned and co-ordinated. Flashes of insight and vision, when seen in the young, are frequently the reaction of

their very sensitive response apparatus to group ideas and the dominant thoughts of their time and age, or of someone in their environment. (12-13)

10. Let (the disciple) learn to control and consciously employ the mind; let him train his mind to receive communications from three sources:

1. The three worlds of ordinary living, thus enabling the mind to act as the "common-sense".

2. The soul, and thus consciously become the disciple, the worker in an Ashram, illumined by the wisdom of the soul, and superseding gradually the knowledge gained in the three worlds. That knowledge, rightly applied, becomes wisdom.

3. The Spiritual Triad, acting as the intermediary between the Monad and the brain of the personality. This can eventually take place, because the soul and personality are fused and blended into one functioning unit, this superseding again what we mean when we use the erroneous phrase *"the* soul". Duality then takes the place of the original triplicity. (18-432/3)

12. THE FIVE SENSES AND THE SELF

1. What are the senses? How many are there? And what is their connection with the Indwelling Man, the Thinker . . . ? These are questions of vital moment, and in their due comprehension comes the ability wisely to follow the path of knowledge.

The senses might be defined as those organs whereby man becomes aware of his surroundings. We should perhaps express them not so much as organs (for after all, an organ is a material form, existent for a purpose) but as media whereby the Thinker comes in contact with his environment. They are the means whereby he makes investigation on the plane of the gross physical, for instance; the means whereby he buys his experience, whereby he discovers that which he requires to know, whereby he becomes aware, and whereby he expands his consciousness. We are here dealing with the five senses as used by the human being. In the animal these five senses exist but, as the thinking correlating faculty is lacking, as the "relation between" the self and the not-self is but little

developed, we will not concern ourselves with them at this juncture. . . .
The senses in man are his individual asset, and demonstrate:

(a) As the separate realisation of self-consciousness.

(b) As ability to assert that individualisation.

(c) As a valuable means to self-conscious evolution.

(d) As a source of knowledge.

(e) As the transmuting faculty towards the close of life in the three
worlds.

As we know, the senses are five in number, and in order of development are as follows: (a) Hearing, (b) Touch, (c) Sight, (d) Taste, and (e)
Smell.   (3-186)

2. In time, and in the three worlds, each sense on each plane is employed
to convey to the Thinker some aspect of the not-self, and by the aid of
mind, the Thinker can then adjust his relationship thereto:

Hearing gives him an idea of relative direction, and enables a man to
fix his place in the scheme, and to locate himself.

Touch gives him an idea of relative quantity, and enables him to fix
his relative value as regards other bodies, extraneous to himself.

Sight gives him an idea of proportion, and enables him to adjust his
movements to the movements of others.

Taste gives him an idea of value, and enables him to fix upon that
which to him appears best.

Smell gives him an idea of innate quality, and enables him to find that
which appeals to him as of the same quality or essence as himself.

In all these definitions it is necessary to bear in mind that *the whole
object of the senses is to reveal the not-self, and to enable the Self therefore to differentiate between the real and the unreal.*

In the evolution of the senses, *hearing* is the first vague something which
calls the attention of the apparently blind self

(a) To another vibration.

(b) To something originating outside of itself.

(c) To the concept of externality. When sound is first contacted, the
consciousness for the first time becomes aware of that which is without.

But all that is grasped by the dormant consciousness (by means of this one sense of hearing) is the fact of something extraneous to itself, and of the direction in which that something lies. This apprehension, in course of time, calls into being another sense, that of *touch*. The Law of Attraction works, the consciousness moves slowly outwards towards that which is heard, and when contact is made with the not-self, it is called touch. This touch conveys other ideas to the groping consciousness, ideas of size, of external texture, and of surface differences; the concept of the Thinker is thus slowly enlarged. He can hear and feel, but as yet knows not enough to correlate nor name. When he succeeds in naming, he has made a big stride forward. . . .

Sight follows on this, the third sense, and the one definitely marking the correlation of ideas, or the relation between; it parallels the coming of the Mind, both in time and function. We have hearing, touch or feeling, and then sight. In connection with the correspondence it is to be noted that sight came in with the third root-race in this round, and that the third race saw also the coming of the Mind. The Self and the not-self were immediately correlated, and co-ordinated. Their close partnership became an accomplished fact, and evolution hastened forward with renewed impetus. . . .

As regards *taste* and *smell,* we might call them minor senses, for they are closely allied to the important sense of touch. They are practically subsidiary to that sense. (3-193/6)

3. In all these perfections (of the senses) is seen the *awareness* of the Self, and the graded process of identification, utilisation, manipulation and final rejection of the not-self by that Self who is now consciously aware. He hears the note of nature and that of his Monad; he recognises their identity, utilises their vibration, and passes rapidly through the three stages of Creator, Preserver and Destroyer.   (3-200)

4. The whole object of the senses is to reveal the not-self, and to enable the Self therefore to differentiate between the real and the unreal. (15-562)

13. THE UNIVERSAL SOUL

(*The Anima Mundi*)

1. There exists in our manifested universe the expression of an Energy of Life which is the responsible cause of the diverse forms and the vast hierarchy of sentient beings who compose the sum total of all that is. . . .

One life pervades all forms and those forms are the expressions, in time and space, of the central universal energy. Life in manifestation produces existence and being. It is the root cause, therefore, of duality. This duality which is seen when objectivity is present and which disappears when the form aspect vanishes, is covered by many terms, of which for the sake of clarity, the most usual might here be listed:

Spirit		*Matter*
Life	....	Form
Father	....	Mother
Positive	....	Negative
Darkness	....	Light

Students must clearly have this essential unity in mind e'en when they talk (as they needs must) in finite terms of that duality which is everywhere, cyclically, apparent. . . .

The one Life, manifesting through matter, produces a third factor, which is consciousness. This consciousness, which is the result of the union of the two poles of spirit and matter, is the soul of all things; it permeates all substance or objective energy; it underlies all forms, whether it be the form of that unit of energy which we call an atom, or the form of man, a planet, or a solar system.   (4-8)

2. The soul of matter, the *anima mundi,* is the sentient factor in substance itself. It is the responsiveness of matter throughout the universe and that innate faculty in all forms, from the atom of the physicist, to the solar system of the astronomer, which produces the undeniable intelligent activity which all demonstrate. It can be called attractive energy, coherency, sentiency, aliveness, awareness or consciousness, but perhaps the most illuminating term is that *the soul is the quality which form manifests.* It is that subtle something which distinguishes one element from another, one mineral from another. It is the intangible essential nature of the form which in the vegetable kingdom determines whether a rose or a

cauliflower, an elm or a watercress shall come into being; it is a type of energy which distinguishes the varying species of the animal kingdom, and makes one man different from another in his appearance, nature and character. . . . The problem of life itself still eludes the wisest, and until the understanding of the "web of life" or the body of vitality, which underlies every form and links every part of a form with every other part is recognised and known to be a fact in nature, the problem will remain unsolved. (4-33/4)

3. The *anima mundi* is that which lies back of the web of life. The latter is but the physical symbol of that universal soul; it is the outer and visible sign of the inner reality, the concretion of the sensitive responsive entity which links spirit and matter together. This entity we call the Universal Soul, the middle principle from the standpoint of the planetary life. When we narrow the concept down to the human family, and consider the individual man, we call it the mediating principle, for the soul of mankind is not only an entity linking spirit and matter, and mediating between Monad and personality, but the soul of humanity has a unique function to perform in mediating between the higher three kingdoms in nature, and the lower three. (4-47)

4. Arguing as one ever should, from the universal to the particular, it is essential that humanity relate its own mechanism to the greater mechanism (our entire planetary life) and view what is called "one's own soul" as an infinitesimal part of the world soul. It is necessary also for man to relate his soul to his personality, viewing both as aspects and integral parts of the human family. This will be increasingly the case. This process is beginning to demonstrate in the steadily expanding group, national, and racial consciousness which humanity is today demonstrating. (9-95)

5. Let us, talking necessarily in symbols, consider the universal Soul, or the consciousness of the Logos Who brought our universe into being. Let us regard the Deity as pervading the form of His solar system with life, and as being conscious of His work, or His project and His goal. This solar system is an appearance, but God remains transcendent. Within all forms God is immanent, yet persists aloof and withdrawn. Just as a thinking, intelligent human being functions through his body but dwells primarily in his mental consciousness or in his emotional processes, so God dwells withdrawn in His mind nature; the world that He has created and pervaded with His life, goes forward towards the goal for which He has created it. Within, however, the radius of His appearing form, greater

activities are going forward; varying states of consciousness and stages of awareness are to be seen; developing degrees of sentiency emerge, and even in the symbolism of the human form we have such differing states of sentiency as are registered by the hair, by the internal organisms in the body, by the nervous system, by the brain, and by the entity we call the Self (who registers emotion and thought). In the same way does the Deity, within the solar system, express as wide a divergence of consciousness. (14-57/8)

6. It is wise to remember that on the plane of soul existence there is no separation, no "my soul and thy soul". It is only in the three worlds of illusion and of maya that we think in terms of souls and bodies. This is an occult platitude and well known, but the re-emphasis of the well-known truth will sometimes serve to bring home to you its exactitude. (15-116)

7. We find in the Bible the words: "In Him we live and move and have our being". This is the statement of a fundamental law in nature, and the enunciated basis of the relation which exists between the unit soul, functioning in the human body, and God. It determines also, *in so far as it is realised,* the relation between soul and soul. We live in an ocean of energies, and all these energies are closely interrelated and constitute the one synthetic energy body of our planet. (15-184)

14. THE SOUL

1. We shall, from the outset, accept the fact of the soul. We shall not consider the arguments for or against the hypothesis of there being a soul—universal, cosmic, and divine, or individual and human. For our purposes of discussion, the soul exists, and its intrinsic reality is assumed as a basic and proven principle. Those who do not admit this assumption can, however, study (this) book from the angle of a temporarily accepted hypothesis, and thus seek to gather those analogies and indications which may substantiate the point of view. To the aspirant, and to those who are seeking to demonstrate the existence of the soul because they believe in its existence, this expression of its laws and tradition, its nature, origin and potentialities will become a gradually deepening and experienced phenomenon. (14-xxii)

2. I shall seek to make this treatise upon the soul relatively brief. I shall seek to express these abstract truths in such a way that the general public, with its profound interest in the soul, may be intrigued and won to a deeper consideration of what is as yet a veiled surmise. The Aquarian Age will see the fact of the soul demonstrated. This is an attempt, carried forward in the difficulties of a transition period which lacks even the needed terminology, to aid that demonstration.   (14-xxiv)

3. The soul is as yet an unknown quantity. It has no real place in the theories of the academic and scientific investigators. It is unproven and regarded by even the more open-minded of the academicians as a possible hypothesis, but lacking demonstration. It is not accepted as a fact in the consciousness of the race. Only two groups of people accept it as a fact; one is the gullible, undeveloped, childlike person who, brought up on a scripture of the world, and being religiously inclined, accepts the postulates of religion—such as the soul, God, and immortality—without questioning. The other is that small but steadily growing band of Knowers of God and of reality, who know the soul to be a fact in their own experience, but are unable to prove its existence satisfactorily to the man who admits only that which the concrete mind can grasp, analyse, criticise and test.   (4-17)

4. Back of the outer form of a human being, responsible for its creation, its maintenance and its use, lies . . . the soul. Back of all activity for the furthering of human evolution as well as of other evolutionary processes, stands the Hierarchy. Both represent centres of energy; both work under Law creatively; both proceed from subjective activity to objective manifestation, and both are responsive (in the great sequence of graded lives) to vitalisation and stimulation from higher centres of energy.   (4-281)

5. The soul is *not* a twelve-petalled lotus (symbolically) floating around in mental substance, but is in reality a vortex of force or twelve energies held together by the Will of the spiritual entity (the Monad on its own plane).   (6-193)

6. "Soul . . . is a word used to express the sum total of the psychic nature —the vital body, the emotional nature and the mind stuff. But it is also more than that, once the human stage is reached. It constitutes the spiritual entity, a conscious psychical being, a son of God, possessing life, quality and appearance—a unique manifestation in time and space of the three expressions of the soul as we have just outlined them :

1. The soul of all the atoms, composing the tangible appearance.

2. The personal soul or the subtle coherent sum total which we call the Personality, composed of the subtle bodies—etheric or vital, astral or emotional, and the lower mental apparatus. These three vehicles humanity shares with the animal kingdom as regards its possession of vitality, sentiency, and potential mind; with the vegetable kingdom as regards vitality and sentiency; and with the mineral kingdom as regards vitality and potential sentiency.

3. The soul is also the spiritual being, or the union of life and quality. When there is the union of the three souls, so called, we have a human being.

Thus in man you have the blending or fusion of life, quality and appearance, or spirit, soul and body, through the medium of a tangible form.

In the process of differentiation, these various aspects have attracted attention, and the underlying synthesis has been overlooked or disregarded. Yet all forms are differentiations of the soul, but that soul is one Soul, when viewed and considered spiritually. When studied from the form side, naught but differentiation and separation can be seen. When studied from the consciousness or sentiency aspect, unity emerges. When the human stage is reached and self-awareness is blended with the sentiency of forms and with the tiny consciousness of the atom, some idea of a possible subjective unity begins dimly to dawn on the thinker's mind. When the stage of discipleship is reached, a man begins to see himself as a sentient part of a sentient whole, and slowly reacts to the purpose and intent of that whole. He grasps that purpose little by little, as he swings consciously into the rhythm of the sum total of which he is a part. When more advanced stages and more rarefied and refined forms are possible, the part is lost in the whole; the rhythm of the whole subjects the individual to a uniform participation in the synthetic purpose, but the realisation of individual self-awareness persists and enriches the individual contribution, which is now intelligently and willingly offered, so that the form not only constitutes an aspect of the sum total (which has always and inevitably been the case, even when unrealised), but the conscious thinking entity knows the *fact* of the unity of consciousness and of the synthesis of life. Thus we have three things to bear in mind as we read and study:

1. The synthesis of life ....   Spirit.
2. The unity of consciousness ....   Soul.
3. The integration of forms ....   Body.

These three have always been at-one, but the human consciousness has not known it. It is the realisation of these three factors and their integration into the technique of living, which is for man the objective of his entire evolutionary experience. (14-55/7)

7. Man's form nature reacts in its consciousness to the form nature of Deity. The outer garment of the soul (physical, vital and psychic) is part of the outer garment of God.

Man's self-conscious soul is en rapport with the soul of all things. It is an integral part of the universal Soul, and because of this can become aware of the conscious purpose of Deity; can intelligently co-operate with the Will of God, and thus work with the Plan of Evolution.

Man's spirit is one with the life of God and is within him, deep-seated in his soul, as his soul is seated within the body.

The spirit will in some distant time put him en rapport with that aspect of God which is transcendent, and thus each son of God will eventually find his way to that centre—withdrawn and abstracted—where God dwells beyond the confines of the solar system. (14-58/9)

8. Men will know, and know soon, that the soul is not an imaginary fiction, that it is not just a symbolic way of expressing a deep-seated hope, and is not man's method of building a defence mechanism; nor is it an illusory way of escape from a distressing present. They will know that the soul is a Being, a Being that is responsible for all that appears upon the phenomenal plane. (14-109)

(a) SOME SYNONYMS FOR THE "SOUL"

1. The terms, Lower Self, Higher Self, Divine Self, are apt to be confusing, until the student apprehends the various synonyms connected with them. The following table may be found helpful:

Father	Son	Mother
Spirit	Soul	Body
Life	Consciousness	Form
Monad	Ego	Personality
Divine Self	Higher Self	Lower Self
Spirit	Individuality	Personal Self
The Point	The Triad	The Quarternary
Monad	Solar Angel	Lunar Lords

(3-48/9)

2. (The following are some synonyms that are being used for "the Soul". These synonyms already give some indication as to some of the characteristics and qualities of the Soul):

The Soul; the Ego; the Self; the One Self; the Higher Self; the Spiritual Self; the One; the Inner Ruler; the God Within; the Inner Reality; the Divine Inner Ruler; the Inner Spiritual Sun; the Divine Indweller; the Master Within the Heart; the Indwelling Flame; the Inner God; the Christ Within; the Christ Principle; the Individuality; the Divine Reality; the Real Man; the Thinker; the Spiritual Thinker; the Solar Angel; the Angel; the Angel of the Presence; the Jewel; the Son of the Father; the Flame of Spirit; the Developing Point; the Agnishvattas; the Son of Mind; the Mediating Principle; the Triangles; the Director; the Onlooking Unity; the Observer; the Onlooker; the Divine Perceiver; the Beholder; the Watcher; the Interpreter.

(b) RECOGNITION OF THE SOUL

1. The first step towards substantiating the fact of the soul, is to establish the fact of survival, though this may not necessarily prove the fact of immortality. It can nevertheless be regarded as a step in the right direction. That something survives the process of death, and that something persists after the disintegration of the physical body, is steadily being proved. If that is not so, then we are the victims of a collective hallucination, and the brains and minds of thousands of people are untrue and deceiving, are diseased and distorted. Such a gigantic collective insanity is more difficult to credit than the alternative of an expanded consciousness. This development along psychic lines does not prove the fact of the soul, however; it only serves to break down the materialistic position.

It is among the thinkers of the race that the first assured recognition of the soul will come, and this event will be the result of the study and analysis by the psychologists of the world, of the nature of genius and the significance of creative work. (14-98/9)

2. Science . . . gives no place to the electrical force of the soul, which is steadily growing in potency. A few of the scientists among the most advanced are beginning to do this. The next step ahead for science is the discovery of the soul, a discovery which will revolutionise, though not negate, the majority of their theories. (17-368)

(c) DEFINITION OF THE SOUL

1. 1. The soul, macrocosmic and microcosmic, universal and human, is that entity which is brought into being when the spirit aspect and the matter aspect are related to each other.

(a) The soul therefore, is neither spirit nor matter, but is the relation between them.

(b) The soul is the mediator between this duality; it is the middle principle, the link between God and His form.

(c) Therefore the soul is another name for the Christ principle, whether in nature or in man.

2. The soul is the attractive force of the created universe and (when functioning) holds all forms together so that the life of God may manifest or express itself through them.

(a) Therefore the soul is the form-building aspect, and is that attractive factor in every form in the universe, in the planet, in the kingdoms of nature and in man (who sums up in himself all the aspects) which brings the form into being, which enables it to develop and grow so as to house more adequately the indwelling life, and which drives all God's creatures forward along the path of evolution, through one kingdom after another, towards an eventual goal and a glorious consummation.

(b) The soul is the force of evolution itself and this was in the mind of St. Paul when he spoke of the "Christ in you, the hope of glory".

3. This soul manifests differently in the various kingdoms of nature, but its function is ever the same, whether we are dealing with an atom of substance and its power to preserve its identity and form, and carry forward its activity along its own lines, or whether we deal with a form in one of the three kingdoms of nature, held coherently together, demonstrating characteristics, pursuing its own instinctual life, and working as a whole towards something higher and better.

(a) Therefore the soul is that which gives distinctive characteristics and differing form manifestations.

(b) The soul plays upon matter, forcing it to assume certain shapes, to respond to certain vibrations and to build those specified phenomenal forms which we recognise in the world of the physical plane as mineral, vegetable, animal, and human—and for the initiate certain other forms as well.

4. The qualities, vibrations, colours, and characteristics in all the kingdoms of nature, are soul qualities, as are the latent powers in any form seeking expression and demonstrating potentiality. In their sum total, at the close of the evolutionary period, they will reveal what is the nature of the divine life and of the world soul—that over-soul which is revealing the character of God.

(a) Therefore the soul, through these qualities and characteristics, manifests as conscious response to matter, for the qualities are brought into being through the interplay of the pairs of opposites, spirit and matter, and their effect upon each other. This is the basis of consciousness.

(b) The soul is the conscious factor in all forms, the source of that awareness which all forms register and of that responsiveness to surrounding group conditions which the forms in every kingdom of nature demonstrate.

(c) Therefore the soul might be defined as that significant aspect in every form (made through this union of spirit and matter) which feels, registers awareness, attracts and repels, responds or denies response, and keeps all forms in a constant condition of vibratory activity.

(d) The soul is the perceiving entity produced through the union of Father-Spirit and Mother-Matter. It is that which in the vegetable world, for instance, produces response to the sun's rays and the unfolding of the bud; it is that in the animal kingdom which enables it to love its master, hunt its prey, and follow out its instinctual life; it is that in man which makes him aware of his environment and his group, which enables him to live his life in the three worlds of his normal evolution as the onlooker, the perceiver, the actor. This it is which enables him eventually to discover that this soul in him is dual and that part of him responds to the animal soul, and part of him recognises his divine soul. The majority however, at this time will be found to be functioning fully as neither purely animal nor purely divine, but can be regarded as human souls.

. . . The Soul therefore may be regarded as the unified sentiency and the relative awareness of that which lies back of the form of a planet and of a solar system. These latter are the sum total of all forms, organic or

inorganic, as the materialist differentiates them. The soul, though constituting one great total, is however, limited in its expression by the nature
and quality of the form in which it is found, and there are consequently
forms which are highly responsive to and expressive of the soul, and
others which—owing to their density and the quality of the atoms of
which they are composed—are incapable of recognising the higher aspects
of the soul or of expressing more than its lower vibration, tone or colour.
(4-34/9)

2. What is the soul? Can we define it? What is its nature?

Here I shall give but four definitions which will serve as a basis for all
that follows :

1. The soul can be spoken of as the Son of the Father and of the
Mother (Spirit-Matter) and is therefore the embodied life of God, coming
into incarnation in order to reveal the quality of the nature of God,
which is essentially love. This life, taking form, nurtures the quality of
love within all forms, and ultimately reveals the purpose of all creation. . . .
(14-36)

2. The soul can be regarded as the principle of intelligence—an intelligence whose characteristics are mind and mental awareness, which in turn
demonstrate as the power to analyse, to discriminate, to separate, and to
distinguish, to choose or to reject, with all the implications conveyed in
these terms. . . .   (14-38)

I seek in various ways to convey through the symbol of words the significance of the soul. The soul is therefore the Son of God, the product
of the marriage of spirit and matter. The soul is an expression of the mind
of God, for mind and intellect are terms expressing the cosmic principle
of intelligent love—a love which produces an appearance through the nature of mind, and thus is the builder of the separate forms or appearances.
The soul also, through the quality of love, produces the fusion of appearance and of quality, of awareness and of form.

3. The soul is (and here words limit and distort) a unit of light,
coloured by a particular ray vibration, it is a vibrating centre of energy
found within the appearance or form of its entire ray life. It is one of
seven groups of millions of lives which in their totality constitute the One
Life. From its very nature, the soul is conscious or aware in three directions. It is God-conscious; it is group-conscious; it is self-conscious. This
self-conscious aspect is brought to fruition in the phenomenal appearance

of a human being; the *group-conscious* aspect retains the human state of consciousness, but adds to it awareness of its ray life, progressively unfolded; its awareness then is the awareness of love, of quality, of spirit in its relationships; it is *God-conscious* only potentially, and in that unfoldment lies, for the soul, its own growth upward and outward after its self-conscious aspect is perfected and its group-awareness is recognised.... (14-40/1)

4. The soul is the principle of sentiency, underlying all outer manifestation, pervading all forms, and constituting the consciousness of God Himself. When the soul, immersed in substance, is simply sentiency, it produces through its evolutionary interplay an addition, and we find emerging quality and capacity to react to vibration and to environment. This is the soul as it expresses itself in all the subhuman kingdoms in nature.

When the soul, an expression of sentiency and quality, adds to these the capacity of detached self-awareness, there appears that self-identified entity which we call a human being.

When the soul adds to sentiency, quality and self-awareness, the consciousness of the group, then we have identification with a ray-group, and there appears the disciple, the initiate and the master.

When the soul adds to sentiency, quality, self-awareness and group consciousness, a consciousness of divine synthetic purpose (called by us the Plan), then we have that state of being and knowledge which is distinctive of all upon the Path of Initiation, and includes those graded Lives, from the more advanced disciple up to the planetary Logos Himself.

But forget not that when we make these distinctions, it is nevertheless one Soul that is functioning, acting through vehicles of varying capacities, of differentiated refinements, and of greater and lesser limitations, in just the same sense as a man is one identity, working sometimes through a physical body and sometimes through a feeling body, or a mental body, and sometimes knowing himself to be the Self—a rare and unusual occurrence for the majority. (14-53/4)

(d) THE CHRIST WITHIN

1. When humanity is assured of divinity and of immortality, and has entered into a state of knowledge as to the nature of the soul and of the kingdom in which that soul functions, its attitude to daily life and to current affairs will undergo such a transformation, that we shall verily and indeed see the emergence of a new heaven and a new earth. Once the

central entity within each human form is recognised and known for what it essentially is, and once its divine persistence is established, then we shall necessarily see the beginning of the reign of divine law on earth— a law imposed without friction and without rebellion. This beneficent reaction will come about because the thinkers of the race will be blended together in a general soul awareness, and a consequent group consciousness will permit them to see the purpose underlying the working of the law.

Let us put this a little more simply. We are told in the New Testament that we must endeavour to let the mind which was in Christ also be manifest in us. We are working towards the perfecting of the rule of Christ on earth; we are aiming at the development of the Christ consciousness and at the bringing in of the rule or Law of Christ, which is Love. This will come to fruition in the Aquarian Age, and we shall see brotherhood established on earth. The rule of Christ is the dominance of the basic spiritual laws. The mind of Christ is a phrase conveying the concept of the rule of divine intelligent love, which stimulates the rule of the soul within all forms, and brings in the reign of the Spirit. It is not easy to express the nature of the revelation which is on the way. It involves the recognition by men everywhere that the "mind-stuff", as the Hindus call it, to which their own minds are related and of which their mental bodies are an integral part, is also part of the mind of Christ, the cosmic Christ, of Whom the historical Christ is—upon our planet—the ordained representative. When man, through meditation and group service, have developed an awareness of their own controlled and illumined minds, they will find themselves initiated into a consciousness of true being, and into a state of knowledge which will prove to them the fact of the soul beyond all doubt or questioning.

The Mystery of the Ages is on the verge of revelation, and through the revelation of the soul, that mystery which it veils will stand revealed. The scriptures of the world, we know, have ever prophesied that at the end of the age we shall see the revelation of that which is secret, and the emergence into the light of day of that which has hitherto been concealed and veiled. This, our present cycle, is the end of the age, and the next two hundred years will see the abolition of death, as we now understand that great transition, and the establishing of the fact of the soul's existence. The soul will be know as an entity, as the motivating impulse, and the spiritual centre back of all manifested forms. The next few decades will see certain great beliefs substantiated.   (14-94/6)

2. Individual man and his soul are also attempting to come together, and when that event is consummated, the Christ is born in the cave of the heart, and Christ is seen in the daily life with increasing power.   (14-288)

3. *Manifestation of the Subjective Aspect in Man*: One of the objects of evolution is that the subjective reality should eventually be brought forward into recognition. This can be expressed in several symbolic ways, all of them dealing with the same one fact in nature :

The bringing to the birth of the Christ within.

The shining forth of the inner radiance or glory.

The demonstration of the second or Love aspect.

The manifestation of the solar Angel.

The appearing of the Son of God, the Ego or the Soul within.

The full expression of buddhi, as it utilises manas.

This emergence into manifestation is brought about through what is understood by the following terms :

The refining of the bodies which form the casket or sheath hiding the reality.

The process of "unveiling" so that one by one those bodies which veil the Self are brought to a point where they are simply transparencies, permitting the full shining forth of the divine nature.

An expansion of consciousness, which is brought about through the ability of the Self to identify with its real nature as the Onlooker, and no longer regarding itself as the organ of perception.   (18-6)

(e)   THE ETHERIC BODY, THE SYMBOL OF THE SOUL

The great symbol of the soul in man is his vital or etheric body, and for the following reasons :

1. It is the physical correspondence to the inner light body, we call the soul body, the spiritual body. It is called the "golden bowl" in the Bible and is distinguished by :

(a) Its light quality.

(b) Its rate of vibration, which synchronises always with the development of the soul.

(c) Its coherent force, linking and connecting every part of the body structure.

2. It is the microcosmic "web of life" for it underlies every part of the physical structure and has three purposes:

(a) To carry throughout the body the life principle, the energy which produces activity. This it does through the medium of the blood, and the focal point for this distribution is the heart. It is the conveyor of physical vitality.

(b) To enable the soul, or human yet spiritual man to be en rapport with his environment. This is carried forward through the medium of the entire nervous system and the focal point of that activity is the brain. This is the seat of conscious receptivity.

(c) To produce eventually, through life and consciousness, a radiant activity, or manifestation of glory which will make of each human being a centre of activity for the distribution of light and attractive energy to others in the human kingdom, and through the human kingdom, to the subhuman kingdoms. This is a part of the Plan of the planetary Logos for the vitalising and renewing of the vibration of those forms which we designate subhuman.

3 This microcosmic symbol of the soul not only underlies the entire physical structure and thus is a symbol of the *anima mundi,* or the world soul, but is indivisible, coherent and a unified entity, thereby symbolising the unity and homogeneity of God. There are no separated organisms in it, but it is simply a body of freely flowing force. . . .

4. This coherent unified body of light and energy is the symbol of the soul in that it has within it seven focal points . . .

5. The symbolism is carried forward when one remembers that the etheric body links the purely physical, or dense body with the purely subtle, the astral or emotional body. In this is seen the reflection of the soul in man which links the three worlds (corresponding to the solid, liquid and gaseous aspects of the strictly physical body of man) to the higher planes in the solar system, linking thus the mental to the buddhic and the mind to the intuitional states of consciousness. (4-48/50)

(f) EMERGENCE AND PROGRESS OF THE SOUL

1. The life at the heart of the solar system is producing an evolutionary unfoldment of the energies of that universe which it is not possible for finite man as yet to vision. Similarly the centre of energy which we call the spiritual aspect in man is (through the utilisation of matter or sub-

stance) producing an evolutionary development of that which we call the soul, and which is the highest of the *form* manifestations—the human kingdom. Man is the highest product of existence in the three worlds. By man, I mean the spiritual man, a son of God in incarnation. The forms of all the kingdoms of nature—human, animal, vegetable and mineral—contribute to that manifestation. The energy of the third aspect of divinity tends to the revelation of the soul, or the second aspect, which in turn reveals the highest aspect. It must ever be remembered that *The Secret Doctrine* of H. P. Blavatsky expresses this with accuracy in the words "Life we look upon as the one form of existence, manifesting in what is called Matter; or what, incorrectly separating them, we name spirit, soul and matter in man. Matter is the vehicle for the manifestation of soul on this plane of existence, and soul is the vehicle on a higher plane for the manifestation of spirit, and these three are a trinity synthesised by life, which pervades them all".

Through the use of matter the soul unfolds and finds its climax in the soul of man.   (4-13/4)

2. Through . . . creation, existences come into manifestation, participate in the experience of their particular cycle, whether it is ephemeral, like the life of a butterfly, or relatively permanent like the ensouling life of the planetary Deity, and vanish. The two aspects concerned, spirit and matter, are brought thus into a close rapport, and necessarily exert an effect upon each other. Matter, so-called, is energised or "lifted up" in the occult sense of the term by its contact with spirit so-called. Spirit, in its turn, is enabled to enhance its vibration through the medium of its experience in matter. The bringing together of these two divine aspects results in the emergence of a third, which we call the soul, and through the medium of the soul, spirit develops a sentiency and a conscious awareness and capacity to respond, which remains its permanent possession when the divorce between the two comes around eventually and cyclically. (4-522)

3. (There are) the three great divisions which mark the soul's progress towards its goal. Through the process of *Individualisation*, the soul arrives at a true self-consciousness and awareness in the three worlds of its experience. The actor in the drama of life masters his part. Through the process of *Initiation*, the soul becomes aware of the essential nature of divinty. Participation in full conciousness with the group and the absorption of the personal and individual into the Whole, characterise this stage on the path of evolution. Finally comes that mysterious process

wherein the soul becomes so absorbed into that supreme Reality and Synthesis through *Identification* that even the consciousness of the group fades out (except when deliberately recovered in the work of service). Naught is then known save Deity—no separation of any part, no lesser syntheses, and no divisions or differentiations. During these processes it might be stated that three streams of energy play upon the consciousness of the awakening man:

(a) The energy of matter itself, as it affects the consciousness of the inner spiritual man, who is using the form as a medium of expression.

(b) The energy of the soul itself, or of the solar angel, as that energy pours forth upon the vehicles and produces reciprocal energy in the solar form.

(c) The energy of life itself, a meaningless phrase, and one that only initiates of the third initiation can grasp, for even the discoveries of modern science give no real idea as to the true nature of life. (15-19)

4. Such is the program for humanity, as it concerns the unfoldment of the human consciousness. The whole emphasis of the entire evolutionary process is, in the last analysis, placed upon the development of conscious, intelligent awareness in the life animating the various forms. The exact state of awareness is contingent upon the age of the soul. Yet the soul has no age from the standpoint of time, as humanity understands it. It is timeless and eternal. Before the soul there passes the kaleidoscope of the senses, and the recurring drama of outer phenomenal existence; but throughout all these occurrences in time and space, the soul ever preserves the attitude of the Onlooker and of the perceiving Observer. It beholds and interprets. In the early stages, when the "Lemurian consciousness" characterises the phenomenal man, that fragmentary aspect of the soul which indwells and informs the human form, and which gives to the man any real human consciousness which may be present, is inert, inchoate and unorganised; it is devoid of mind as we understand it, and is distinguished only by a complete identification with the physical form and its activities. This is the period of slow tamasic reactions to suffering, joy, pain, to the urge and satisfaction of desire, and to a heavy subconscious urge to betterment. Life after life passes, and slowly the capacity for conscious identification increases, with a growing desire for a larger range of satisfactions; the indwelling and animating soul becomes ever more deeply hidden, the prisoner of the form nature. The entire forces of the life are concentrated in the physical body, and the desires then

expressed are physical desires; at the same time there is a growing tendency towards more subtle desires, such as the astral body evokes. Gradually, the identification of the soul with the form shifts from the physical to the astral form. There is nothing present at this time which could be called a personality. There is simply a living, active physical body, with its wants and its desires, its needs and its appetites, accompanied by a very slow yet steadily increasing shift of the consciousness out of the physical into the astral vehicle.

When this shift, in course of time, has been successfully achieved, then the consciousness is no longer entirely identified with the physical vehicle, but it becomes centred in the astral-emotional body. Then the focus of the soul's attention, working through the slowly evolving man, is in the world of desire, and the soul becomes identified with another response apparatus, the desire or astral body. His consciousness then becomes the "Atlantean consciousness". His desires are no longer so vague and inchoate; they have hitherto been concerned with the basic urges or appetites—first his urge to self-preservation; then to self-perpetuation through the urge to reproduce; and next, to economic satisfaction. At this stage we have the state of awareness of the infant and the raw savage. Gradually, however, we find a steadily growing inner realisation of desire itself, and less emphasis upon the physical satisfactions. The consciousness slowly begins to respond to the impact of the mind and to the power to discriminate and choose between various desires; the capacity to employ time somewhat intelligently begins to make its presence felt. The more subtle pleasures begin to make their appeal; man's desires become less crude and physical; the emerging desire for beauty begins to appear, and a dim sense of aesthetic values. His consciousness is becoming more astral-mental, or kama-manasic, and the whole trend of his daily attitudes, or his modes of living, and of his character begins to broaden, to unfold, and to improve. Though he is still ridden by unreasoning desire most of the time, yet the field of his satisfactions and of his sense-urges are less definitely animal, and more definitely emotional. Moods and feelings come to be recognised, and a dim desire for peace and the urge to find that nebulous thing called "happiness" begin to play their part. This corresponds to the period of adolescence and to the state of consciousness called Atlantean. It is the condition of the masses at this present time. The bulk of human beings are still Atlantean, still purely emotional in their reactions and in their approach to life. They are still governed predominantly by selfish desires and by the calls of the instinctual life. Our earth humanity is still in the Atlantean stage, whereas the intelligentsia of the world, and the disciples and aspirants, are passing rapidly out of this stage, for they reached individualisation on the moon chain, and were the Atlanteans of past history. . . .

In the more advanced people of the world today, we have the functioning of the mind-body; this is to be found in a large scale in our Western civilisation. The energy of the ray of the mental body begins to pour in, and slowly to assert itself. As this happens, the desire nature is brought under control, and consequently the physical nature can become more definitely the instrument of mental impulses. The brain consciousness begins to organise and the focus of energies begins to shift gradually out of the lower centres into the higher. Mankind is developing the "Aryan consciousness" and is reaching maturity. In the more advanced people of the world, we have also the integration of the personality and the emergence into definite control of the personality ray, with its synthetic, coherent grip of the three bodies and their fusing into one working unit. Later, the personality becomes the instrument of the indwelling soul. (15-23/6) See also : (15-342/4)

(g) THE ANGEL OF THE PRESENCE

1. It is said that "thoughts are things" and produce tangible results. It is also said that "as a man thinketh in his heart, so is he" and that therefore, these tangible thought manifestations definitely produce effects in him. In these ancient platitudes lie . . . much instruction, much light and understanding. . . . You, a soul in incarnation, are consciously aware of the fact—subjectively and ofttimes dimly sensed—of your real Self, of the solar Angel, who is the Angel of the Presence. Your problem is to deepen this realisation, and to *know* yourself to be the Angel, standing between you, the physical plane man, and the Presence. It might elucidate matters if we considered for a moment what reality is represented by that word Presence.

The mystic is ever aware of duality; of the lower man and the indwelling soul; of the tired disciple and the Angel; of the little self and the real Self; of human life expression and of spiritual life expression. Many other qualities stand for the same expression of reality. But, behind them all looms—immanent, stupendous, and glorious—that of which these dualities are but the aspects: the Presence, immanent yet transcendent, of Deity. In the nature of this *One,* all dualities are absorbed, and all distinctions and differences lose their meaning.

When you are told to develop the consciousness of the Presence, it indicates, first of all, that you are at this time somewhat aware of the Angel and can now begin to respond, dimly and faintly, to that great Whole which lies behind the subjective world of being, as that world lies behind the physical, tangible world of every day life.

A symbol of this can be seen in the knowledge that the entire planet lies outside of the room in which you are pondering my words, and is only separated from you by the window and the extent of your conscious awareness. The outer universe of the planet, the solar system and the starry heavens, lies revealed to you through that sheet of glass which reveals, if clean and unveiled, but which acts as a barrier to vision, if soiled or hidden by a blind. This and your ability to project yourself into the immensity of the universe, governs the extent of your knowledge at any given time. Think this out, my brother, and look through the window of the mind to that Light which reveals the Angel which, in its turn, veils and hides the vast unknown, yet alive and vibrant, Deity. (5-390/1)

2. Every human being is, in reality, like a miniature whirlpool in that great ocean of Being in which he lives and moves—ceaselessly in motion until such time as the soul "breathes upon the waters" (or forces) and the Angel of the Presence descends into the whirlpool. Then all becomes still. The waters stirred by the rhythm of life, and later stirred violently by the descent of the Angel, respond to the Angel's healing power and are changed "into a quiet pool into which the little ones can enter and find the healing which they need". So says the *Old Commentary*. (17-140)

15. GROUP SOUL

1. As in all else in manifestation, there is a group personality and a group soul; you must learn clearly to distinguish between the two and to throw the entire weight of your influence, desire and pressure, on the side of the Group Angel. In this way there might occur that stupendous recognition for which all initiation prepares the applicant—the revelation of the PRESENCE. (10-160)

2. Just as certain human beings have, through meditation, discipline and service, most definitely made a contact with their own souls, and can therefore become channels for soul expression, and mediums for the distribution into the world of soul energy, so men and women who are

oriented to soul living in their aggregate, *form a group of souls, en rapport* with the source of spiritual supply. They have, as a group, and from the angle of the Hierarchy, established a contact, and are "in touch" with the world of spiritual realities. Just as the individual disciple stabilises this contact and learns to make a rapid alignment and then, and only then, can come into touch with the Master of his group and intelligently respond to the Plan, so does this group of aligned souls come into contact with certain greater Lives and Forces of Light, such as the Christ and the Buddha. The aggregated aspiration, consecration and intelligent devotion of the group carries the individuals of which it is composed to greater heights than would be possible alone. The group stimulation and the united effort sweep the entire group to an intensity of realisation that would otherwise be impossible. Just as the Law of Attraction, working on the physical plane, brought them together as men and women into one group effort, so the Law of Magnetic Impulse can begin to control them when, again as a group and only as a group, they unitedly constitute themselves channels for service in pure self-forgetfulness.

This thought embodies the opportunity immediately before all groups of aspirants and allied men of goodwill in the world today. If they work together as a group of souls, they can accomplish much. This thought illustrates also the significance of this law which *does produce polar union.* What is needed to be grasped is that in this work, there is no personal ambition implied, even of a spiritual nature and no personal union sought. This is not the mystical union of the scriptures or of the mystical tradition. It is not alignment and union with a Master's group, or fusion with one's inner band of pledged disciples, nor even with one's own Ray life. All these factors constitute preliminary implications, and are of an individual application. Upon this sentence I ask you to ponder. This union is a greater and more vital thing *because it is a group union.*

What we are seeking to do is to carry forward a group endeavour which is of such moment that, at the right time, it could produce, in its growing momentum, such a potent, magnetic impulse that it will reach those Lives Who brood over humanity and our civilisation, and Who work through the Masters of the Wisdom and the assembled Hierarchy. This group endeavour will call forth from Them a responsive and magnetic impulse, which will bring together, through the medium of all the aspiring groups, the overshadowing beneficent *Forces.* Through the concentrated effort of these groups in the world today (who constitute subjectively *One* Group) light and inspiration and spiritual revelation can be released in such a flood of power that it will work definite changes in the human consciousness and help to ameliorate conditions in the needy world. It will open men's eyes to the basic realities, which are, as yet, only dimly sensed by the thinking public.   (15-112/4)

16.   THE SOUL OF HUMANITY

1. The sense of responsibility is one of the first indications that the soul of the individual is awakened. The soul of humanity is also at this time awakening en masse, and hence the following indications:

1. The growth of societies, organisations, and mass movements for the betterment of humanity everywhere.

2. The growing interest of the mass of the people in the common welfare. Hitherto the upper layer of society has been interested, either for selfish, self-protective reasons, or because of innate paternalism. The intelligentsia and the professional classes have investigated and studied the public welfare from the angle of mental and scientific interest, based upon a general material basis, and the lower middle class has naturally been involved in the same interest, from the point of view of financial and trade returns. Today this interest has reached down to the depths of the social order, and all classes are keenly alive and alert to the general, national, racial or international good. This is very well and a hopeful sign.

3. Humanitarian and philanthropic effort is at its height, alongside of the cruelties, hatreds, and abnormalities which separativeness, over-stressed national ideologies, aggressiveness, and ambition, have engendered in the life of all nations.

4. Education is rapidly becoming mass effort, and the children of all nations, from the highest to the lowest, are being intellectually equipped as never before. The effort is, of course, largely to enable them to meet material and national conditions, to be of use to the State, and no economic drag upon it. The general result is, however, in line with the divine Plan and undoubtedly good.

5. The growing recognition by those in authority that the man in the street is becoming a factor in world affairs. He is reached on all sides

by the press and the radio, and is today intelligent enough and interested enough, to be making the attempt to form his own opinions and come to his own conclusions. This is embryonic as yet, but the indications of his effort are undoubtedly there; hence the press and radio control which is found in all countries in some form or another. (12-106/7)

2. Much, if not all that can be seen going on in the world today, is caused by a greatly increased soul stimulation, to which the entire human family is reacting, even though, as individuals, they have not made a soul contact. This increased stimulation is due to two things:

1. A great many men, and the number is rapidly increasing, are making contact with their souls through an intense aspiration and—in many cases—very real desperation.

2. The Hierarchy of Masters is exceedingly active today, and this is due to two things:

(a) The demand on the part of humanity which has reached Their attention continuously for the past few decades, and which is calling out an inevitable response.

(b) A stimulation of the planetary Hierarchy itself. This leads many in the ranks of the Hierarchy to pass through one of the higher initiations. They therefore become much more potent and their influence is much more magnetic and radiating. (15-709)

3. In the many strands of light, woven by the aspirants, disciples and initiates of the world, we can see the group antahkarana gradually appearing—that bridge whereby humanity as a whole will be able to abstract itself from matter and form. This building of the antahkarana is the great and ultimate service which all true aspirants can render. (18-497)

4. The whole goal of normal evolution is to bring humanity to the point where a direct line of contact is established between the personality and the Spiritual Triad, via the soul—or rather, through the medium of using the soul consciousness to achieve this awareness. This is consummated at the time of the third initiation. (18-497)

5. The race *as a whole* stands now at the very entrance to the Path of Discipleship. The racial gaze is forward to the vision, whether it is the vision of the soul, a vision of a better way of life, of an improved economic situation, or of better interracial relationship. That this vision is oft distorted, that it is materially oriented or only partially seen, is sadly true;

but in some form or another there exists today an appreciable grasp of the "new and desirable" by the masses—a thing hitherto unknown. In the past, it was the intelligentsia or the elect who were privileged to have the vision. Today, it is the mass of men. Humanity, therefore, as a whole stands ready for a general alignment process, and that is the *spiritual* reason which lay behind the world war. The "sharp shears of sorrow must separate the real from the unreal; the lash of pain must awaken the sleepy soul to exquisite life; the wrenching away of the roots of life from the soil of selfish desire must be undergone, and then the man stands free". So runs the *Old Commentary* in one of its more mystical stanzas. Thus it points prophetically to the close of the Aryan Race—not to a close in the sense of completion, but a closing of a cycle of mental perfecting, preparatory to a cycle wherein the mind will be rightly used as an instrument of alignment, then as the searchlight of the soul, and as the controller of the personality.

For the masses—under the slow processes of evolution—the next step forward is the aligning of the soul and the form, so that there can be a blending in consciousness, following on a mental appreciation, of the Christ principle and its deep expression in the life of the race. This is something which can be seen quite clearly emerging, if you have the eyes to see. It is evident in the universal interest in goodwill, leading eventually to peace; this desire for peace may be based on individual or natural selfishness, or upon a true desire to see a happier world wherein man can lead a fuller spiritual life and base his efforts on truer values; it can be seen in all the planning which is going on for a new world order, based on human liberty, belief in human rights and right human relations; it is demonstrating also in the work of the great humanitarian movements, the welfare organisations, and the widespread evocation of the human mind through the network of educational institutions throughout the world. The Christ spirit *is* expressively present, and the failure to recognise this fact has been largely due to the prevalent human effort to explain and interpret this phrase solely in terms of religion, whereas the religious interpretation is but one mode of understanding Reality. There are others of equal importance. All the great avenues of approach to Reality are spiritual in nature, and interpretative of divine purpose, and whether the religious Christian speaks of the Kingdom of God, or the humanitarian emphasises the brotherhood of man, or the leaders against evil head the fight for the new world order or for the Four Freedoms or the Atlantic Charter, they all express the emergence of the love of God in its form of the spirit of Christ.

Humanity in the mass has therefore reached a point of emergence from darkness; it has itself evoked the reaction of the powers of evil, and hence their attempt to arrest the progress of the human spirit and to stop the onward march of the good, the true and the beautiful. (18-498/500)

17.   THE CAUSAL BODY

"The Temple of the Soul"

1. (The Causal Body) is, from the standpoint of the physical plane, no body, either subjective or objective. It is, nevertheless, the centre of the egoic consciousness, and is formed of the conjunction of buddhi and manas. It is relatively permanent and lasts throughout the long cycle of incarnations, and is only dissipated after the fourth initiation, when the need for further rebirth on the part of a human being no longer exists. (1-217)

2. In the due comprehension of the subject of the Ego functioning in the causal body, comes the ability to work scientifically with the problem of one's own evolution, and to do good work in aiding the evolution of one's brother.   (3-505)

3. In considering the causal body, we are dealing specifically with the vehicle of manifestation of a solar Angel who is its informing life, and who is in process of constructing it, perfecting it, and of enlarging it, and thus reflecting on a tiny scale the work of the Logos on His own plane. (3-1110)

(a)   THE CONTENT OF THE CAUSAL BODY

Just what do you mean when you speak of the causal body? Say not glibly, the body of causes, for words thus spoken are oft nebulous and vague. Let us now consider the causal body and find out its component parts.

On the involutionary path you have what is termed the Group Soul, aptly described (as far as earth words permit) as a collection of triads, enclosed in a triple envelope of monadic essence. On the evolutionary path, groups of causal bodies correspond and are similarly composed, three factors entering in.

The causal body is a collection of permanent atoms, three in all, enclosed in an envelope of mental essence. . . . What happens at the moment
when animal-man becomes a thinking entity, a human being? The
approximation of the Self and not-self by means of mind, for man is
"that being in whom highest spirit and lowest matter are linked together
by intelligence". What do I mean by this phrase? Just this: that when
animal-man had reached a point of adequacy, when his physical body was
sufficiently co-ordinated, when he had an emotional or desire nature
sufficiently strong to form a basis for existence, and to guide it by means
of instinct, and when the germ of mentality was sufficiently implanted to
have donated the instinctive memory and correlation of ideas that can be
seen in the average domesticated animal, then the descending Spirit
(which had taken to itself an atom on the mental plane) judged the time
ripe for taking possession of the lower vehicles. The Lords of the Flame
were called in and they effected the transfer of polarisation from the
lower atom of the Triad to the lowest atom of the Personality. Even then,
the indwelling Flame could come no lower than the third subplane of
the mental plane. There the two met and became one, and the causal
body was formed. All in nature is interdependent, and the indwelling
Thinker cannot control in the three lower worlds without the aid of the
lower self. *The life of the first Logos must be blended with that of the
second Logos and based on the activity of the third Logos.*

Therefore, you have at the moment of individualisation, which is the
term used to express this hour of contact, on the third sub-plane of the
mental plane a point of light, enclosing three atoms, and itself enclosed
in a sheath of mental matter. The work then to be done consists of:

1. Causing that point of light to become a flame, by steadily fanning
the spark and feeding the fire.

2. Causing the causal body to grow and expand from being a colourless ovoid, holding the Ego like a yoke within the egg-shell, to a thing
of rare beauty, containing within itself all the colour of the rainbow.
This is an occult fact. The causal body will palpitate in due course of
time with an inner irradiation, and an inner glowing flame that will
gradually work its way from the centre to the periphery. It will then
pierce through that periphery, using the body (that product of millen-
nia of lives of pain and endeavour) as fuel for its flames. It will burn
all up, it will mount upward to the Triad, and (becoming one with
that Triad) will be reabsorbed into the spiritual consciousness, will

carry with it—using heat as the symbol—an intensity of heat, or quality of colour or vibration, that before were lacking.

Therefore the work of the Personality—for we have to view all from that angle until egoic vision may be ours—is first to beautify, build and expand the causal body; secondly to withdraw within it the life of the personality, sucking the good out of the personal life and storing it in the body of the Ego. We might term this the Divine Vampirism, for always evil is but the other side of good. Then, having accomplished this, comes the application of the flame to the causal body itself, and the joyous standing by whilst the work of destruction goes on, and the Flame—the live inner man and the spirit of divine life—is set free and mounts to its source.

The specific gravity of the causal body fixes the moment of emancipation, and marks the time when the work of beautifying and building is completed, when the Temple of Solomon is erected, and when the *weight* (occultly understood) of the causal body measures up to the standard looked for by the Hierarchy, then the work of destruction supervenes, and liberation approaches. Spring has been experienced, the full verdure of summer has succeeded, now must be felt the disintegrating force of autumn—only this time it is felt and applied on mental levels and not on physical. The axe is laid to the root of the tree, but the life essence is garnered into the divine storehouse.

The content of the causal body is the accumulation, by slow and gradual process, of the good in each life. The building proceeds slowly at first, but towards the end of incarnation—on the Probationary Path and on the Path of Initiation—the work proceeds more rapidly. The structure has been reared, and each stone quarried in the personal life. On the Path, in each of its two divisions, the work of completing and beautifying the Temple proceeds with greater rapidity. . . .   (2-29/32)

(b) BUILDING OF THE CAUSAL BODY

1. The Probationary Path precedes the Path of Initiation or Holiness, and marks that period in the life of a man when he definitely sets himself on the side of the forces of evolution, and works at the building of his own character. He takes himself in hand, cultivates the qualities that are lacking in his disposition, and seeks with diligence to bring his personality under control. He is building the causal body with deliberate intent, filling any gaps that may exist, and seeking to make it a fit receptacle for the Christ principle.   (1-63)

2. The permanent atoms are enclosed within the periphery of the causal body, yet that relatively permanent body is built and enlarged, expanded and wrought into a central receiving and transmitting station (using inadequate words to convey an occult idea) by the direct action of the centres, and *of the centres above all.* Just as it was spiritual force, or the will aspect, that built the solar system, so it is the same force in the man that builds the causal body. . . . By the bringing together (in microcosm) of Spirit and matter, and their coherence by means of force (or the spiritual will) that objective system, the causal body, is being produced. . . . The causal body is but the sheath of the Ego.   (3-178/9)

(c) SPIRITUAL LIBERATION

1. (The causal body) is the vehicle of the higher consciousness, the temple of the indwelling God, which seems of a beauty so rare and of a stability of so sure a nature that, when the final shattering comes of even that masterpiece of many lives, bitter indeed is the cup to drink, and unutterably bereft seems the unit of consciousness. Conscious then only of the innate Divine Spirit, conscious only of the Truth of the Godhead, realising profoundly and to the depths of his being the ephemeral nature of the form and of all forms, standing alone in the vortex of initiatory rites, bereft of all on which he may have leant (be it friend, Master, doctrine or environment), well may the Initiate cry out: "I am that I am, and there is naught else". Well may he then figuratively place his hand in that of his Father in Heaven, and hold the other out in blessing on the world of men, for only the hands that have let slip all within the three worlds are free to carry the ultimate blessing to struggling humanity. Then he builds for himself a form such as he desires—a new form that is no longer subject to shattering, but suffices for his need, to be discarded or used as occasion warrants.   (4-264/5)

2. (The mind stuff, abstract mind, and intuition or pure reason) have to be unified in the consciousness of the aspirant. When this has happened, the disciple has built the bridge (the antahkarana) which links:

1. The Spiritual Triad.

2. The causal body.

3. The personality.

When this is done the egoic body has served its purpose, the solar Angel has done its work, and the form side of existence is no longer needed, as we understand and utilise it, as a medium of experience. The man enters into the consciousness of the Monad, the ONE. The causal body disintegrates; the personality fades out, and illusion is ended. This is the consummation of the Great Work, and another Son of God has entered into the Father's home. That he may go out from there into the world of phenomena in order to work with the Plan is probable, but he will not need to undergo the processes of manifestation as humanity does. He can then construct, for the work, his body of expression. He can work through and with energy as the Plan dictates. Note these last words, for they hold the key to manifestation.   (4-387/8)

3. It is only possible to touch very briefly upon the effect of the application of the Rod (of Initiation) to the causal body of the initiate. . . . There are just two ways in which some idea of the fundamental truth will be conveyed to the mind of the student, which we might now consider.

First, the student should bear in mind the interesting significance of the fact that he, on the physical plane, is a functioning personality, with known and realised characteristics, and yet withal, that he is a subjective Life, who uses that personality as a medium of expression, and who—through the agency of the physical, emotional, and mental bodies, which comprise the threefold lower man—makes his contacts with the physical plane and thus develops. The same general idea of development must be now extended to the higher Self, the Ego on its own plane. This Ego is a great solar Angel, who is the medium of expression for the Monad or pure Spirit, just as is the personality for the Ego on the lower level. From the point of view of man in the three worlds, this Ego, or Solar Lord, is eternal; he persists throughout the entire cycle of incarnation, just as the personality persists during the tiny physical life cycle. Nevertheless, this period of existence is only relatively permanent, and the day dawns when the life which expresses itself through the medium of the Ego, the Thinker, the Solar Lord or Manasadeva, seeks to loose itself from even this limitation, and to return to the source from which it originally emanated.

The life then, which manifested as a solar angel, and which through inherent energy, held together through long ages the form egoic, withdraws itself gradually, and the form slowly dissipates; the lesser lives of which it has been constituted, return to the general fount of deva substance, plus the increased consciousness and activity which is theirs through the experience of being built into a form, and utilised by a still higher aspect of existence. Similarly, in the case of the personality, when the life egoic withdraws, the threefold lower self dissipates; the little lives which form the body of what has been called the lunar self (in contra-distinction to the solar self, being but its reflection) are absorbed into the general reservoir of deva substance of a lower vibration to that which composed the body egoic. Similarly also, their evolution has been furthered through having been built into a form for the use of the higher Self.

Through the application of the Rod of Initiation, the work of separat-ing the spiritual self from the higher self is furthered, and the imprisoned life gradually escapes, whilst the causal body is slowly absorbed or dis-sipated.

This has led to the expression, sometimes used in occult books, of "the cracking of the causal body" at each initiation, and to the idea of the inner central fire gradually breaking through and destroying the con-fining walls, and also of the destruction of the Temple of Solomon through the withdrawal of the Shekinah. All these phrases are symbolic wordings, and are attempts to convey to the mind of man fundamental truth from different angles.

By the time the fourth initiation has been reached, the work of destruc-tion is accomplished, the solar angel returns to his own place, having per-formed his function, and the solar lives seek their point of emanation. The life within the form mounts up then in triumph to the bosom of its "Father in Heaven", just as the life within the physical body at the moment of death seeks its source, the Ego, and this likewise in four stages :

1. By the withdrawal from the dense physical body.

2. By the withdrawal from the etheric body.

3. By a later vacating of the astral body.

4. A final leaving of the mental body.

Another way of emphasising the same truth is to regard the egoic body as a centre of force, a wheel of energy, or a lotus, and to picture it as a lotus with nine petals, hiding within these petals a central unit of three petals; these in their turn secrete the central life, or the "jewel in the lotus". As evolution proceeds, these three circles of three petals gradually unfold, having a simultaneous effect on one or other of the central three. These three circles are called respectively the petals of Sacrifice, Love, and Knowledge. At initiation the Rod is applied to the petals in a scientific manner, and regulated according to ray and tendency. This brings about the opening of the central bud, the revelation of the jewel, the withdrawal of that jewel from the casket which has so long shielded it, and its transference to "the crown", as it is occultly called, meaning its return to the Monad whence it came.

We must clearly recognise that all the above is but an attempt, through the limiting agency of words, to describe the method and the rites whereby spiritual liberation is finally achieved in this cycle; first, through the method of evolutionary unfoldment, or gradual development, and then in the final stages through the Rod of Initiation.   (1-135/8)

4. When the "will to live" vanishes, then the "Sons of Necessity" cease from objective manifestation. This is logically inevitable, and its working out can be seen in every case of *entified objectivity.* When the Thinker on his own plane withdraws his attention from his little system within the three worlds, and gathers within himself all his forces, then physical plane existence comes to an end, and all returns within the causal consciousness. . . . This demonstrates on the physical plane in the withdrawing from out of the top of the head of the radiant etheric body, and the consequent disintegration of the physical. The framework goes and the dense physical form falls apart; the pranic life is abstracted bodily from out of the dense sheath, and the stimulation of the fires of matter ceases to be. The latent fire of the atom remains; it is inherent, but the form is made by the action of the two fires of matter—active and latent, radiatory and inherent—aided by the fire of the second Logos, and when they are separated the form falls apart. This is a picture in miniature of the essential duality of all things acted upon by Fohat.

. . . When a man starts to live his own life of conscious desire, when a man is born into a new world of a subtler form of life, that interlaced cord of etheric matter (which has united him to his physical body) is broken; the "silver cord is loosed" and the man severs his connection with the dense physical body and passes out through the highest centre of the body instead of the lowest, to life in a higher world and of another dimension. So it will be found in all the bodies and sheaths of the microcosm, for the analogy will persist on all planes during manifestation. (3-85/6)

18. THE EGOIC LOTUS

1. Symbolic Description:

All these modes of expression (of the Egoic Lotus) are but pictures which serve to convey some small idea of the beauty, and the intricacy of the divine process as it is carried on in the microcosm and in the macrocosm. They all serve to limit and circumscribe the reality, but to the man who has the divine eye in process of opening, and to him who has the faculty of the higher intuition awakened, such pictures serve as a clue or key to the higher interpretation. They reveal to the student certain ideas as to the nature of fire.   (3-1119)

2. We have seen that on the third level of the mental plane, the egoic lotus is found, and the student should picture it to himself as follows:

Concealed at the very centre or heart of the lotus is a brilliant point of electric fire of a blue-white hue (the jewel in the lotus) surrounded, and completely hidden, by three closely folded petals. Around this central nucleus, or inner flame, are arranged the nine petals in circles of three petals each, making three circles in all. These petals are formed out of the substance of the solar angels, as are the central three—substance which is not only sentient as is the substance of the forms in the three worlds and the lunar bodies, but which has an added quality of "I-ness" or of self-consciousness, enabling the spiritual unity at the centre (by means of it) to acquire knowledge, awareness, and self-realisation. These nine petals are of a predominant orange hue, though the six other colours are found as secondary colours in a varying degree. The inner three petals are of a lovely lemon-yellow hue. At the base of the lotus petals are the three points of light which mark the position of the permanent atoms, and which are the medium of communication between the solar Angels and the lunar Pitris. By means of these permanent atoms the Ego, according to its state of evolution can construct his lunar bodies, acquire knowledge on the lower three planes, and thus buy his experience, and become *aware.* On a higher turn of the spiral, the Monad through the egoic petals, and thus with the aid of the solar Angels, acquires knowledge and equally, on more exalted levels, becomes aware.

The light within these permanent atoms has a dull red glow and we have, therefore, all the three fires demonstrating in the causal body—*electric fire* at the centre, *solar fire* enclosing it as the flame encloses the central nucleus or essence in a candle flame, and *fire by friction,* this

47

latter fire resembling the glowing red wick which lies at the base of the higher flame.

These three types of fire on the mental plane—meeting and unified in the egoic body—produce in time a radiation or warmth which streams out from all sides of the lotus, and forms that spheroidal shape noted by investigators. The more fully developed the Ego may be, and the more the petals are unfolded, the greater the beauty of the surrounding sphere, and the more refined its colouring.

At the early stages after individualisation the egoic body has the appearance of a bud. The electric fire at the centre is not apparent, and all the nine petals are closed down upon the inner three; the orange colour has a dead aspect and the three points of light at the base are just points and nothing more; the triangle which is later seen connecting the points is not demonstrated. The surrounding sphere is colourless and is only to be appreciated as undulatory vibrations (like waves in the air or ether) reaching barely beyond the petal outline.

By the time the *third Initiation* is reached, a wondrous transformation has transpired. The outer sphere is palpitating with every colour in the rainbow, and is of wide radius; the streams of electrical energy circulating in it are so powerful that they are escaping beyond the periphery of the circle, resembling the rays of the sun. The nine petals are fully unfolded, forming a gracious setting for the central jewel, and their orange hue is now of a gorgeous translucence, shot with many colours, that of the egoic ray predominating. The triangle at the base is now quickened and scintillating, and the three points are small blazing fires, showing to the eye of the clairvoyant as sevenfold whorls of light, circulating their light from point to point of a rapidly moving triangle.

By the time the *fourth Initiation* is reached, the activity of this triangle is so great that it looks more like a wheel in rapid revolution. It has a fourth dimensional aspect. The three petals at the centre are opening up, revealing the "blazing jewel". At this initiation, through the action of the Hierophant wielding the electric Rod of Power, the three fires are suddenly stimulated by a downflow of electric, or positive force, from the Monad, and their blazing out in response produces that merging which destroys the entire sphere, dissipates all appearance of form, and produces a moment of equilibrium, or of suspension, in which the "elements are consumed with fervent heat". The moment of highest radiation is known. Then—through the pronouncement of a certain Word of Power—the great solar Angels gather back into themselves the solar fire, thus producing the final dissipation of the form, and hence the separation of the life from the form; the fire of matter returns to the general reservoir, and the permanent atoms and the causal body are no more. The central electric fire becomes centralised in atma-buddhi. The Thinker or spiritual entity stands free of the three worlds, and functions consciously on the buddhic plane. Between these two stages of quiescent (though self-conscious) inertia and of that radiant activity which produces a balancing of forces, is a long series of lives.   (3-761/4)

3. It is not possible to give students an adequate idea of the beauty of the egoic lotus when it has reached the stage of complete unfoldment. The radiancy of its colour is not here referred to, but the brilliancy of the fires, and the rapid scintillation of the ceaselessly moving streams and points of energy. Each petal pulsates with quivering fire "points", and each tier of petals vibrates with life, whilst at the centre glows the Jewel, raying forth streams of energy from the centre to the periphery of the outermost circle.

The fires of living energy circulate around each individual petal and the method of interweaving and the circulation of the fires is (as may be well realised) sevenfold in nature according to the sevenfold nature of the Logos involved. Each circle of petals becomes, as evolution proceeds, likewise active, and revolves around the central Jewel, so that we have, not only the activity of the living points or the deva lives within the petal circumference, but likewise the unified activity of each tier of the threefold lotus. At a specific stage in evolution, prior to the opening of the central veiling bud, the three tiers of petal, considered as a unit, begin to revolve, so that the entire lotus appears to be in motion. At the final stages the central circle of petals opens, revealing that which is hid, and revolves around the Jewel, only in a contrary direction to the rapidly circulating outer lotus. The reason may not here be revealed, for it is hid in the nature of the electric Fire of Spirit itself.

The Jewel remains occultly static, and does not circulate. It is a point of peace; it pulsates rhythmically as does the heart of man, and from it ray forth eight streams of living fire which extend to the tips of the four *love petals* and the four *sacrifice petals*. This eightfold energy is atma-buddhi. It is this final raying forth which produces the eventual disintegration of the body of the Ego. The *knowledge petals,* not being the subject of the attention of this central fire, in due time cease to be active; knowledge is superseded by divine wisdom and the love petals have their forces equally absorbed. Naught is eventually left but the desire to "sacrifice", and as the vibratory impulse is akin to the nature of the living Jewel,

it is synthesised in the central living unit, and only the Jewel of fire remains. When all the petals have merged their forces elsewhere, the process of revelation is completed. The lower fires die out; the central fire is
absorbed, and only the radiant point of electric fire persists. Then a
curious phenomenon is to be seen at the final Initiation. The Jewel of fire
blazes forth as seven jewels within the one, or as the sevenfold electric
spark, and in the intensity of the blaze thus created, is reabsorbed into
the Monad or the One.   (3-1118/9)

4. The Jewel, or diamond concealed by the egoic lotus, is the window
of the Monad or Spirit whereby he looks *outward* into the three worlds.
The *third eye* is the window of the Ego or soul functioning on the physical plane, whereby he looks *inward* into the three worlds.   (3-1130)
   See also: (3-539/44)

19.   EVOLUTION OF THE EGOIC BODY

1. In studying the subject (of egoic unfoldment) with due personal application, the student should bear in mind the following facts:

   First, that according to the Ray of the Monad, so will the petals unfold. For instance, if the Ray of Monad is the second Ray, the knowledge
petal will be the first to open, but the second petal of love will almost
parallel its development, being for that particular type of Ego the line
of easiest unfoldment; the knowledge petal will be for it the most difficult
to open.

   Second, that the effects of one circle of petals opening will be felt within the next circle at an early stage and will cause a vibratory response,
hence the greater rapidity of the later stages of unfoldment as compared
with the first.

   Third, that there exist many cases of uneven or unequal unfoldment.
Quite frequently people are found with perhaps two petals unfolded in
the first circle and one still in latency, while a petal within the central or
second ring may be in full development. This is the explanation frequently of the power in service along certain lines displayed by some, coupled
with a comparatively low stage of development or of consciousness
(egoically speaking). This is due to varying causes, such as the karma of

the Monad itself on its high plane, and the strength of the monadic grip upon the ego; many lives given to a particular line of action, resulting in the setting up of a strong vibration—one so strong that it renders the development of response to subsidiary vibrations difficult of attainment; certain peculiar conditions hidden in the evolution of any particular Lord of a Ray, and the effect of that condition upon a particular group of cells; the group karma of a collection or congery of causal bodies, and their mutual interplay. Every egoic unit or monadic force centre has a definite effect upon the group or community of Egos in which it may have a place, and as the interaction proceeds, results are sometimes produced of a temporarily unexpected nature. (3-546/7)

2. We could divide the (evolutionary) process into three periods:

First. The period wherein the fire of matter (the heat of mother) hides, nourishes and brings to birth the infant Ego. This is the period of purely personality life, when the third aspect dominates, and man is in the veil of illusion.

Second. The period wherein the Ego, or subjective life within the form, passes through certain stages of unfoldment, and comes to an even fuller consciousness. This is the period of egoic development, and is produced by the gradual merging and blending of the two fires. It is the life of service and of the Path.

Third. The period wherein the egoic consciousness itself is superseded by spiritual realisation, and the fire of Spirit blends with the other two.

At first the personality acts the part of mother, or of material aspect, to the germ of the inner life. Then the Ego manifests its life within the personal life, and produces a shining forth which "groweth ever more and more until the perfect day". (Proverbs IV, 18). At that perfect day of revelation it is seen what man in essence is, and the Spirit within is revealed. (3-610/1)

3. Evolution affects (the egoic) body also, and not only man's forms in the three worlds. The effects of the process are interdependent, and as the lower self develops, or the personality becomes more active and intelligent, results are produced in the higher body. As these effects are cumulative, and not ephemeral as are the lower results, the egoic body becomes equally more active and its manifestation of energy is increased. Towards the close of the evolutionary period in the three worlds a constant interchange of energy is seen to be taking place; the lower forms become irradiated with light, and reflect the higher radiance; the egoic body is the

Sun of the lower system, and its bodies reflect its rays, as the moon reflects the light of the solar sun. Similarly the egoic Sun—through the
interaction—shines with ever greater intensity and glory. (3-764/5)

20. PHYSICAL DEATH AND THE SOUL

1. Death is undertaken at the direction of the ego, no matter how unaware
a human being may be of that direction. The process works automatically
with the majority, for when the soul withdraws its attention the inevitable
reaction on the physical plane is death, either by the abstraction of the
dual threads of life and reason energy, or by the abstraction of the thread
of energy which is qualified by mentality, leaving the life stream still
functioning through the heart, but no intelligent awareness. The soul is
engaged elsewhere and occupied on its own plane with its own affairs.

In the case of highly developed human beings we often find a sense of
pre-vision as to the death period; this is incident upon egoic contact and
awareness of the wishes of the ego. It involves sometimes a knowledge of
the very day of death, coupled to a preservation of self-determination up
to the final moment of withdrawal. In the case of initiates there is much
more than this. There is an intelligent understanding of the laws of abstraction, and this enables the one who is making the transition to withdraw consciously and in full waking awareness out of the physical body,
and so to function on the astral plane. This involves the preservation of
continuity of consciousness so that no hiatus occurs between the sense
of awareness on the physical plane and that of the after death state. The
man knows himself to be as he was before, though without an apparatus
whereby he can contact the physical plane. He remains aware of the states
of feeling and of the thoughts of those he loves, though he cannot per-
ceive or contact the dense physical vehicle. He can communicate with
them on the astral plane or telepathically through the mind if they and he
are *en rapport,* but communication that involves the use of the five
physical senses of perception lies necessarily out of his reach. (4-497/8)

2. Death is now the result of the will of the soul. Eventually it has to
be the result of the united will of the soul and the personality, and when
that happens, there will be no fear of death. Ponder on this. (5-669)

3. The intent is for men to die, as every man has to die, *at the demand of his own soul*. When man has reached a higher stage in evolution, with deliberation and definite choice of time, he will consciously withdraw from his physical body. It will be left silent and empty of the soul; devoid of light, yet sound and whole; it will then disintegrate, under the natural process, and its constituent atoms will pass back into the "pool of waiting units", until they are again required for the use of incarnating souls. Again, on the subjective side of life, the process is repeated, but many have already learnt to withdraw from the astral body without being subject to that "impact in the fog", which is the symbolic way of describing the death of a man upon the astral plane. He then withdraws on to the mental level, and leaves his astral carcass to swell the fog and increase its density.   (17-29)

4. It might be desirable, (and it often is) that the disease be permitted to do its work and death open the door to escape of the soul from imprisonment. The time comes inevitably to all incarnated beings when the soul demands liberation from the body and from form life, and nature has her own wise ways of doing this. Disease and death must be recognised as liberating factors when they come as the result of right timing by the soul. It must be realised by students that the physical form is an aggregate of atoms, built into organisms and finally into a coherent body, and that this body is held together by the will of the soul. Withdraw that will on to its own plane or (as it is occultly expressed) "let the soul's eye turn in another direction" and, in this present cycle, disease and death will inevitably supervene. This is not mental error, or failure to recognise divinity, or succumbing to evil. It is, in reality, the resolution of the form nature into its component parts and basic essence. Disease is essentially an aspect of death. It is the process by which the material nature and the substantial form prepares itself for separation from the soul. (17-111)

5. The life span will eventually be shortened or lengthened at will by souls who consciously serve, and use the mechanism of the body as the instrument whereby the Plan is served. Frequently, today, lives are preserved in form—both in old age and in infancy—that could be well permitted liberation. They serve no useful purpose and cause much pain and suffering to forms which nature (left to herself) would not long use, and would extinguish. Note that word. Through our over-emphasis on the value of form life, and through the universal fear of death—that great transition which we must all face—and through our uncertainty as to the

fact of immortality, and also through our deep attachment to form, we arrest the natural processes and hold the life, which is struggling to be free, confined to bodies quite unfitted to the purposes of the soul.

Misunderstand me not. I desire to say naught that could place a premium on suicide. But I do say, and I say with emphasis, that the Law of Karma is oft set aside when forms are preserved in coherent expression which should be discarded, for they serve no useful purpose. This preservation is, in the majority of cases, enforced by the subject's group and not by the subject himself—frequently an unconscious invalid, an old person whose response apparatus of contact and response is imperfect, or a baby who is not normal. These cases constitute definite instances of an offsetting of the Law of Karma. (17-350/1)

6. Two major thoughts will serve to clarify the issue of death with which we are now concerned:

First, the great dualism ever present in manifestation. Each of the dualities has its own expression, is governed by its own laws, and seeks its own objectives. But—in time and space—they merge their interests for the benefit of both, and together produce the appearance of a unity. Spirit-matter, life-appearance, energy-force—each have their own emanating aspect; they each have a relation to each other; each have a mutual temporary objective, and thus in unison produce the eternal flux, the cyclic ebb and flow of life in manifestation. In this process of relationship between Father-Spirit and Mother-Matter, the son (the soul) comes into being, and during the child stage carries on his life processes within the aura of the mother, identified with her yet forever seeking to escape from her domination. As maturity is reached, the problem intensifies, and the "pull" of the Father begins slowly to offset the possessive attitude of the mother, until finally the hold of matter, or of the mother, over her son is finally broken. The son, the Christ-child, released from the guardianship and clinging hands of the mother, comes to know the Father. I am talking to you in symbols.

Second. All the processes of incarnation, of life in form and of restitution (by the activity of the principle of death), of matter to matter, and soul to soul, are carried forward under the great universal Law of Attraction. Can you picture the time when the process of death, clearly recognised and welcomed by the man, could be described by him in the simple phrase, "The time has come when my soul's attractive force requires that I relinquish and restore my body to the place from whence it came"?

Imagine the change in the human consciousness when death comes to be regarded as an act of simple and conscious relinquishing of form. (17-426/7)

7. One thought emerges as we (consider) . . . the death of the physical body in its two aspects: that thought is the integrity of the inner man. *He remains himself.* He is untouched and untrammelled; he is a free agent as far as the physical plane is concerned, and is responsive now to only three predisposing factors:

  1. The quality of his astral-emotional equipment.

  2. The mental condition in which he habitually lives.

  3. The voice of the soul, often unfamiliar, but sometimes well known and loved.

Individuality is not lost; the same person is still present upon the planet. Only that has disappeared which was an integral part of the tangible appearance of our planet. That which has been loved or hated, which has been useful to humanity or a liability, which has served the race or been an ineffectual member of it, still persists, is still in touch with the qualitative and mental processes of existence, and will forever remain— individual, qualified by ray type, part of the kingdom of souls, and a high initiate in his own right. (17-478)

8. Disease and death are essentially conditions inherent in substance; just as long as a man identifies himself with the form aspect, so will he be conditioned by the Law of Dissolution. This law is a fundamental and natural law governing the life of the form in all the kingdoms of nature. When the disciple or the initiate is identifying himself with the soul, and when the antahkarana is built by means of the life principle, then the disciple passes out of the control of this universal, natural law and uses or discards the body at will—at the demand of the spiritual will or through recognition of the necessities of the Hierarchy or the purposes of Shamballa. (17-501)

9. Incarnation succeeds incarnation, and the familiar process of death, intervening between cycles of experience, goes on. However, all the three deaths—physical, astral and mental—are carried out with a steadily awakening state of awareness, as the lower mind develops; the man no longer drifts—asleep and unknowing—out of the etheric, astral and mental vehicles, but each of them becomes as much an event as is physical death.

  Finally the time comes when the disciple dies with deliberation and in full consciousness, and with real knowledge relinquishes his various vehicles. Steadily the soul takes control, and then the disciple brings about death through an act of soul-will and knows exactly what he is doing. (17-514)

10. Life can and often is prolonged after the will of the soul is towards the withdrawal of the soul life; the life of the atoms of the lunar lords can be fostered for a long time, and this greatly distresses the spiritual man who is aware of the process and the intent of his soul. What is kept alive is the physical body, but the interest of the true man is no longer focussed there.   (17-652)

21.   CREMATION AND SOUL RELEASE

1. Occultly speaking, cremation is needed for two main reasons. It hastens the release of the subtle vehicles (still enshrouding the soul) from the etheric body, thus bringing about the release in a few hours instead of a few days; it also is a much needed means for bringing about the purification of the astral plane, and for arresting the "downward moving" tendency of desire which so greatly handicaps the incarnating soul. (17-470/1)

2. By the use of fire, all forms are dissolved; the quicker the human physical vehicle is destroyed, the quicker is its hold upon the withdrawing soul broken. A great deal of nonsense has been told in current theosophical literature about the time equation in relation to the sequential destruction of the subtle bodies. It should be stated, however, that the moment that *true* death is scientifically established (by the orthodox doctor in charge of the case), and it has been ascertained that no spark of life remains in the physical body, cremation is then possible. This complete or true death eventuates when the thread of consciousness and the thread of life are completely withdrawn from the head and the heart. . . . There is no etheric need for delay. When the inner man withdraws from his physical vehicle, he withdraws simultaneously from the etheric body. It is true that the etheric body is apt to linger for a long time on the "field of emanation" when the physical body is interred, and it will frequently persist until complete disintegration of the dense body has taken place. The process of mummifying, as practised in Egypt, and of embalming, as

practised in the West, have been responsible for the perpetuation of the etheric body, sometimes for centuries. . . .

When cremation is the rule, there is not only the immediate destruction of the physical body and its restitution to the fount of substance, but the vital body is also promptly dissolved and its forces swept away by the current of flame into the reservoir of vital energies. . . . If delay is necessary from family feeling or municipal requirements, cremation should follow death within thirty-six hours; where no reason for delay exists, cremation can be rightly permitted in twelve hours. It is wise, however, to wait twelve hours in order to ensure *true* death.   (17-483/5)

22. REINCARNATION

1. The appearance of the incarnating jivas (lives) on the physical plane, will be governed by three things :

First of all, on impulse based on the will-purpose of the Life animating the aggregate of groups on any subray, or one of the seven larger groups.

Second, on impulse based on the will, tinged by desire, of the Life animating a man's egoic group.

Third, on impulse, based on the desire of the Ego for physical plane manifestation.

As identification of a man with his group becomes matured, the desire impulse becomes modified until it is eventually superseded by group will. If these facts are pondered upon, it will be apparent that Egos come into incarnation therefore not singly, but according to group urge, and thus collectively.   (3-770)

2. You have established a thought rhythm which naught can change and which will be a powerful incentive in deciding the time of your return when this incarnation comes to an end, the type of vehicle which you will, as a soul, construct, and the nature of the race, nation and type of service to which the overshadowing soul will commit the personality. (6-477)

3. *The theory of reincarnation* . . . is becoming increasingly popular in the Occident; it has always been accepted (though with many foolish additions and interpretations) in the Orient. This teaching has been as much

distorted as have the teachings of the Christ or the Buddha or Shri Krishna by their narrow-minded and mentally limited theologians. The basic facts of a spiritual origin, of a descent into matter, of an ascent through the medium of constant incarnations in form, until those forms are perfect expressions of the indwelling spiritual consciousness, and of a series of initiations at the close of the cycle of incarnation, are being more readily accepted and acknowledged than ever before.   (17-402)

4. Advanced souls and those whose intellectual capacity is rapidly developing, come back with great rapidity, owing to their sensitive response to the pull of obligations, interests and responsibilities already established upon the physical plane....

   Man reincarnates under no time urge. He incarnates under the demands of karmic liability, under the pull of that which he, as a soul, has initiated, and because of a sensed need to fulfil instituted obligations; he incarnates also from a sense of responsibility and to meet requirements which an earlier breaking of the laws governing right human relations, have imposed upon him. When these requirements, soul necessities, experiences and responsibilities have all been met, he enters permanently "into the clear cold light of love and life" and no longer needs (as far as he himself is concerned) the nursery stage of soul experience on earth. He is free from karmic impositions in the three worlds, but is still under the impulse of karmic necessity, which extracts from him the last possible ounce of service that he is in a position to render to those still under the Law of Karmic Liability.   (17-403/5)

(a)   THE LAW OF REBIRTH

1. This Law is the major corollary of the Law of Evolution. It has never been grasped or properly understood in the West, and in the East, where it is acknowledged as a governing principle of life, it has not proved useful because it has been soporific in its effect, and a detriment to progress. The Eastern student regards it as giving him plenty of time; this has negated the driving effort to achieve a goal. The average Christian confuses the Law of Rebirth with what he calls "the transmigration of souls", and frequently believes that the Law of Rebirth signifies the passing of human beings into the bodies of animals or of lower forms of life. Such is by no means the case. As the life of God progresses onwards through form after form, that life in the subhuman kingdoms of nature proceeds progressively from mineral forms into vegetable forms, and from these vegetable forms into animal forms; from the animal form stage, the life

of God passes into the human kingdom, and becomes subject to the Law of Rebirth and *not* the Law of Transmigration. To those who know something of the Law of Rebirth or of Reincarnation, the mistake seems ridiculous.

The doctrine or theory of reincarnation strikes the orthodox Christian with horror; yet if one asks him the question which the disciples asked Christ about the blind man, "Master, did this man sin, or his fathers, that he was born blind?" (John IX: 2), they refuse the implications; or they express amusement or dismay as the case may be. . . .

If the goal of right human relations will be taught universally by the Christ, the emphasis of His teaching *must* be laid upon the Law of Rebirth. This is inevitably so, because in the recognition of this law will be found the solution of all the problems of humanity, and the answer of human questioning.

This doctrine will be one of the keynotes of the new world religion, as well as the clarifying agent for a better understanding of world affairs. When Christ was here in person, before, He emphasised the fact of the soul and the value of the individual. He told men that they could be saved by the life of the soul, and of the Christ within the human heart. He said also that "except a man be born again, he cannot see the King-dom of God". (John III: 3). Only *souls* can function as citizens of that kingdom, and it was this privileged functioning that He held for the first time before humanity, thus giving men a vision of a divine possibility and an unalterable conclusion to experience. He told them to "Be ye therefore perfect, even as your Father which is in Heaven is perfect." (Matt. V: 48)

This time He will teach men the method whereby this possibility can become accomplished fact—through the constant return of the incarnat-ing soul to the school of life on earth, there to undergo the perfecting process of which He was the outstanding example. That is the meaning and teaching of reincarnation. . . .

It should be remembered that practically all the occult groups and writings have foolishly laid the emphasis upon *past* incarnations and upon their recovery; this recovery is incapable of any reasonable checking —anyone can say and claim anything they like; the teaching has been laid upon imaginary rules, supposed to govern the time equation and the interval between lives, forgetting that time is a faculty of the brain-con-sciousness, and that, divorced from the brain, time is non-existent; the emphasis has always been laid upon a fictional presentation of relation-ships. The teaching (hitherto given out on reincarnation) has done more harm than good. Only one factor remains of value: the existence of a Law of Rebirth is now discussed by many and accepted by thousands.

Beyond the fact that there is such a law, we know little, and those who know from experience the factual nature of this return, reject earnestly the foolish and improbable details, given out as fact by the theosophical and occult bodies. *The Law exists; of the details of its working we know as yet nothing.* Only a few things can be said with accuracy about it, and these few warrant no contradiction:

1. The Law of Rebirth is a great natural law upon our planet.

2. It is a process, instituted and carried forward under the Law of Evolution.

3. It is closely related to, and conditioned by, the Law of Cause and Effect.

4. It is a process of progressive development, enabling men to move forward from the grossest forms of unthinking materialism to a spiritual perfection and an intelligent perception which will enable a man to become a member of the Kingdom of God.

5. It accounts for the differences among men and—in connection with the Law of Cause and Effect (called the Law of Karma in the East)—it accounts for differences in circumstances and attitudes to life.

6. It is the expression of the will aspect of the soul and is not the result of any form decision; it is the soul in all forms which reincarnates, choosing and building suitable physical, emotional and mental vehicles through which to learn the next needed lessons.

7. The Law of Rebirth (as far as humanity is concerned) comes into activity upon the soul plane. Incarnation is motivated and directed from soul level, upon the mental plane.

8. Souls incarnate in groups, cyclically, under law and in order to achieve right relations with God and with their fellow men.

9. Progressive unfoldment under the Law of Rebirth, is largely conditioned by the mental principle, for "as a man thinketh in his heart, so is he". These few brief words need most careful consideration.

10. Under the Law of Rebirth, man slowly develops mind, then mind begins to control the feeling, emotional nature, and finally reveals the soul and its nature and environment to man.

11. At that point in his development, the man begins to tread the Path of Return, and orients himself gradually (after many lives) to the Kingdom of God.

12. When—through a developed mentality, wisdom, practical service, and understanding—a man has learnt to ask nothing for the separated self, he then renounces desire for life in the three worlds and is freed from the Law of Rebirth.

13. He is now group conscious, is aware of his soul group and of the soul in all forms, and has attained—as Christ had requested—a stage of Christlike perfection reaching unto the "Measure of the stature of the fulness of the Christ". (Eph. IV : 13)

Beyond this generalisation, no intelligent person will attempt to go. When Christ reappears, our knowledge will become more true and realistic; we shall know that we are eternally related to the souls of all men, and that we have a definite relationship to those who reincarnate with us, who are learning with us the same lessons, and who are experiencing and experimenting with us. This proven and accepted knowledge will regenerate the very sources of our human living. We shall know that all our difficulties and all our problems are caused by our failure to recognise this fundamental law, with its responsibilities and obligations; we shall then gradually learn to govern our activities by its just and restraining power. The Law of Rebirth embodies the practical knowledge which men need today to conduct rightly and correctly their religious, political, economic, communal and private lives, and thus establish right relations with the divine life in all forms. (8-115/20)

2. The first postulate which must be laid down, and to which the general public must be educated, is that all souls incarnate and re-incarnate under the Law of Rebirth. Hence each life is not only a recapitulation of life experience, but an assuming of ancient obligations, a recovery of old relations, an opportunity for the paying of old indebtedness, a chance to make restitution and progress, an awakening of deep-seated qualities, the recognition of old friends and enemies, the solution of revolting injustices, and the explanation of that which conditions the man and makes him what he is. Such is the law which is crying now for universal recognition, and which, when understood by thinking people, will do much to solve the problems of sex and marriage. (14-300)

3. The foundation of the new psychology must inevitably be built upon the premise that this one life is not man's sole opportunity in which to

achieve integration and eventual perfection. The great Law of Rebirth must be accepted and it will then be found to be, in itself, a major releasing agent in any moment of crisis or any psychological problem case. The recognition of further opportunity and a lengthened sense of time, are both quieting and helpful to many types of mind; its interpretative value will be found illuminating as the patient grasps the fact that behind him lie points of crisis wherein it can be demonstrated by his present equipment that he achieved integration, thus guaranteeing to him victory in his present point of crisis and of difficult conflict. The light which this throws on relationships and environment will serve to stabilise his purpose and make him comprehend the inevitability of responsibility. When this great law is understood in its true implications and not interpreted in terms of its present childish presentation, then man will shoulder the responsibility of living with a daily recognition of the past, an understanding of the purpose of the present, and with an eye to the future. This will also greatly lessen the growing tendency towards suicide which humanity is showing. (15-431)

4. Psychology has to recognise eventually:

1. The fact of the soul, the integrating agent, the self.

2. The Law of Opportunity or Rebirth.

3. The nature of the inner structure of man and its relation to the outer tangible form.

It is interesting to note that practically all the teaching given anent rebirth or reincarnation, has emphasised the material phenomenal side, though there has always been a more or less casual reference to the spiritual and mental gains acquired in the school of life upon this planet, from incarnation to incarnation. The true nature of the unfolding awareness and the growth in the inner consciousness of the true man, have been little noted; the gain of each life in added grasp of the mechanism of contact, and the result of increased sensitivity to the environment (which are the only values with which the self concerns itself), are seldom if ever stressed.   (15-432/3)

5. It would appear that as yet only two rules are posited in connection with the return of an ego to physical incarnation. The first is that if perfection has not been achieved, then the soul must return and continue the perfecting process upon the Earth. The second is that the impulse predisposing the ego to such action, is some form of unsatisfied de-

sire. Both these statements are true in part and generic in effect, but they are only partial truths and incident to larger truths which have not yet been sensed or noted accurately by esotericists; they are secondary in nature and are expressed in terms of the three worlds of human evolution, of personality intent, and of time-space concepts. Basically, it is not desire which prompts return, but will and knowledge of the Plan. It is not the need for achieving an ultimate perfection which goads the ego on to experience in form, for the ego is already perfect. The main incentive is sacrifice and service to those lesser lives that are dependent upon the higher inspiration (which the spiritual soul can give) and the determination that they too may attain planetary status equivalent to that of the sacrificing soul. . . . Bear this always in mind as you study the subject of rebirth. In themselves, rebirth and reincarnation are misleading terms, and "cyclic impulsion", "intelligent purposeful repetition", and "conscious inbreathing and out-breathing" would describe more accurately this cosmic process. It is, however, difficult for you to grasp this idea, for it necessitates the ability to identify oneself with the One Who thus breathes— the planetary Logos—and the entire theme must therefore remain relatively obscure until initiation has been taken.

Esoterically speaking, the point of greatest interest lies in the fact that it is *group rebirth* which is taking place all the time, and that the incarnation of the individual is only incidental to this greater happening. This has been largely ignored and forgotten because of the intense and selfish interest in personal experience and living, evidenced in the speculative details anent individual return given in the current so-called occult books, most of which are largely inaccurate and certainly unimportant. (16-324/5)

6. (There are three major processes) under the Law of Rebirth. They are:

1. *The Process of Restitution,* governing the period of withdrawal of the soul from the physical plane and from its two phenomenal aspects, the dense physical body and the etheric body. This concerns the Art of Dying.

2. *The Process of Elimination.* This governs that period of the life of the human soul after death, and in the two other worlds of human evolution. It concerns the elimination of the astral-mental body by the soul, so that it is "ready to stand free in its own place".

3. *The Process of Integration,* dealing with the period wherein the liberated soul again becomes conscious of itself as the Angel of the

Presence and is reabsorbed into the world of souls, thus entering into a state of reflection. Later, under the impact of the Law of Karmic Liability or Necessity, the soul again prepares itself for another descent into form. (17-407/8)

7. When the two phases of the Art of Dying are over, the discarnate soul stands free from the control of matter; it is purified (temporarily by the phases of Restitution and Elimination) from all contamination by substance. This is achieved, not through any activity of the soul in form, the human soul, but as a result of the activity of the soul on its own plane, abstracting the fraction of itself which we call the human soul. It is primarily the work of the overshadowing soul which effects this; it is not carried forward by the soul in the personality. The human soul, during this stage, is only responsive to the pull or the attractive force of the spiritual soul as it—with deliberate intent—extracts the human soul from its imprisoning sheaths. Later on, as the evolutionary processes proceed and the soul increasingly controls the personality, it will be the soul *within* the imprisoning sheaths, which will bring about—consciously and with intention—the phases of dying. In the earlier stages, this release will be brought about with the aid of the overshadowing spiritual soul. Later on, when the man is living upon the physical plane as the soul, he will himself—with full continuity of consciousness—carry out the processes of abstraction, and will then (with directed purpose) "ascend to the place from whence he came". This is the reflection in the three worlds of the divine ascension of the perfected Son of God. (17-409/10)

(b) IMMORTALITY

1. The spirit of man is undying; it forever endures, progressing from point to point, and stage to stage, upon the Path of Evolution, unfolding steadily and sequentially the divine attributes and aspects. This truth involves necessarily the recognition of two great natural laws: the *Law of Rebirth* and the *Law of Cause and Effect.* The churches in the West have refused officially to recognise the Law of Rebirth, and have thereby wandered into a theological impasse and into a cul-de-sac from which there is no possible exit. The churches in the East have over-emphasised these laws so that a negative, acquiescent attitude to life and its processes, based on continuously renewed opportunity, controls the people. Christianity has emphasised immortality but has made eternal happiness dependent upon the acceptance of a theological dogma: Be a true professing Christian and live eternally in a somewhat fatuous heaven, or refuse to

be an accepting Christian and go to an impossible hell—a hell growing out of the theology of *The Old Testament* and its presentation of a God full of hate and jealousy. Both concepts are today repudiated by all sane, sincere, thinking people. No one of any true reasoning power or with any true belief in a God of Love accepts the heaven of the churchmen, or has any desire to go there. Still less do they accept the "lake that burneth with fire and brimstone" (Rev XIX: 20) or the everlasting torture to which a God of love is supposed to condemn all who do not believe in the theological interpretations of the Middle Ages, of the modern fundamentalists, or of the churchmen who seek—through doctrine, fear and threat —to keep people in line with the obsolete old teaching.

The essential truth lies elsewhere. "Whatsoever a man soweth that shall he also reap" (Gal. VI: 7) is the truth which needs re-emphasising. In these words, St. Paul phrases for us the ancient and true teaching of the Law of Cause and Effect called in the Orient, the Law of Karma. To that, he adds in another place the injunction to "work out your own salvation" and—as that contradicts the theological teaching and above all else is not possible to do in any one life—he implicitly endorses the Law of Rebirth, and makes the school of life a constantly recurring experience, until man has fulfilled the command of the Christ (and this refers to every man) "Be ye therefore perfect, even as your Father in Heaven is perfect". Through recognition of the results of action—good or bad—and through constant reliving upon the earth, man eventually attains "unto the measure of the stature of the fulness of the Christ".

The fact of this innate divinity explains the urge at the heart of every man for betterment, for experience, for progress, for increasing realisation and for his steady moving on towards the distant height which he has visioned. There is no other explanation of the capacity of the human spirit to emerge out of darkness, out of evil and death into life and goodness. This emergence has been the unfailing history of man. Something is always happening to the human soul which projects him nearer to the Source of all good and nothing on earth can arrest this progress nearer to God.   (7-142/4), (8-145/7)

2. The fact of immortality is today on the verge of scientific proof; the fact of the survival of some factor has already been proved, though what has been demonstrated as surviving is apparently not in itself intrinsically immortal. The factual nature of the soul, and the fact of soul survival and of its eternal livingness, go hand in hand and have not yet been scientifically proven; they are, however, known and recognised as truths

today by such countless millions and by so many intellectuals that—unless mass hysteria and mass deception is posited—their existence is already correctly surmised. (8-105)

3. (From) the heaven and hell complexes of the present religious faiths . . . grew, automatically, the idea of a persistent entity called the soul, which could enjoy heaven or suffer hell at the will of God, and as the result of actions done whilst in the human form. As the forms of man grew in sensitivity; as they became more and more refined under the influence of the law of selection and of adaptation; as the group life grew closer and the group integration was improved; as the heritage of history, of tradition and of the arts grew richer and made its impress, so that ideas of God grew, and likewise ideas of the soul and of the world, man's concepts of reality grew richer and deeper, so that today we are faced with the problem of a thought inheritance which testifies to a world of concepts, ideas and intuitions which deal with the immaterial and the intangible, and which testify to an age-long belief in a soul and its immortality, for which there is no true justification. At the same time we have demonstrated to us by science that all we can really know with certainty is the tangible world of phenomena, with its forms, its mechanisms, its test tubes and its laboratories, and the bodies of men "fearfully and wonderfully made", diverse and different. These in some mysterious way produce thoughts and dreams and imaginings, and which in their turn, find expression in the formulated schemes of the past, the present and the future, or in the fields of literature, art and of science itself, or in the simple everyday life of the ordinary human being who lives and loves and works and plays and bears children, and eats food and earns money and sleeps.

And then what? Does man disappear into nothingness, or does somewhere, a part of him (hitherto unseen) live on? Does this aspect survive for a time and then in its turn disappear, or is there an immortal principle, a subtle intangible entity which has an existence either in the body or out of the body, and which is the undying immutable Being, belief in Whom has sustained countless millions down the ages? Is the soul a fiction of the imagination and has science satisfactorily disproved its existence? Is consciousness a function of the brain and of the allied nervous system, or shall we accept the idea of a conscious dweller in the form? Does our power to become aware of and react to our surroundings find its source in the body-nature, or is there an entity who beholds and takes action? Is this entity different to and separable from the body, or is it the result of the body type and life, and so either persists after the body disappears, or disappears with it and is lost? Is there nothing but matter or energies in constant movement which produce the appearances of men who react in their turn and express the energy that is pouring through them blindly and unconsciously, having no individual existence? Or are all these theories partially true, and shall we really comprehend the nature and being of man only in the synthesis of all of them and in the acceptance of the general premises? Is it not possible that the mechanically minded and scientific investigators are right in their conclusion anent the mechanism and the form nature, and that the spiritually minded thinkers who posit an immortal entity are also right? As yet perhaps something is lacking which would bridge the gap between the two positions. Is it possible that we may discover a something which will link the intangible world of true being with the tangible world (so-called) of form life?

When humanity is assured of divinity and of immortality, and has entered into a state of knowledge as to the nature of the soul and of the kingdom in which that soul functions, its attitude to daily life and to current affairs will undergo such a transformation that we shall verily and indeed see the emergence of a new heaven and a new earth. Once the central entity within each human form is recognised and known for what it essentially is, and once its divine persistence is established, then we shall necessarily see the beginning of the reign of divine law on earth—a law imposed without friction and without rebellion. This beneficent reaction will come about because the thinkers of the race will be blended together in a general soul awareness, and a consequent group consciousness will permit them to see the purpose underlying the working of the law. (14-93/5)

See also: "The Problem of Immortality." (14-183/4)

(c) DEVACHAN

1. *Devachan*: A state intermediate between two earth lives into which the Ego enters after its separation from its lower aspects or sheaths. (Footnote: 3-737)

2. Devachan is a state of consciousness, reflecting, in the life of the Personality, that higher state which we call nirvanic consciousness, and which is brought about by egoic action. It is but a dim reflection in the separated units (and therefore tinged with selfishness and separative pleasure) of the group condition called nirvanic. In this high state of

consciousness each separate identity, though self-realising, shares in the group realisation, and therein lies bliss for the unit. Separation is no longer felt, only unity and essential oneness is known. Therefore, as might be naturally deduced, there is no devachan for the savage or little evolved man, as they merit it not, and have not the mentality to realise it; hence, therefore, the rapidity of their incarnations, and the brevity of the pralayic period. There is little in their case for the Ego, on its own plane, to assimilate in the residue of incarnations, and hence the life principle withdraws rapidly from out of the mental form, with the resulting impulse of the Ego to reincarnate almost immediately.

When the life of the personality has been full and rich, yet has not reached the stage wherein the personal self can *consciously* co-operate with the Ego, periods of personality nirvana are undergone, their length depending upon the interest of the life, and the ability of the man to meditate upon experience. Later, when the Ego dominates the personality life, the interest of the man is raised to higher levels, and the nirvana of the soul becomes his goal. He has no interest in devachan. Therefore, those upon the Path (either the probationary Path, or the Path of Initiation) do not, as a rule, go to devachan, but immediate incarnation becomes the rule in the turning of the wheel of life; this time it is brought about by the conscious co-operation of the personal Self with the divine Self or Ego.   (3-736/8)

3. There has been a great deal of misunderstanding of (the *devachan*) experience. The general idea has been that, after the process of ridding himself of the astral and mental bodies, the man enters into a sort of dream state wherein he re-experiences and reconsiders past events in the light of the future, and undergoes a sort of rest period, a kind of digestive process, in preparation for the undertaking of renewed birth. This somewhat erroneous idea has arisen because the concept of time still governs theosophical presentations of truth. If, however, it is realised that time is not known apart from physical plane experience, the entire concept of devachan clarifies. From the moment of complete separation from the dense physical and etheric bodies, and as the eliminative process is undertaken, the man is *aware of past and present*; when elimination is complete and the hour of soul contact eventuates, and the manasic vehicle is in process of destruction, he becomes immediately *aware of the future*, for prediction is an asset of the soul consciousness and in this the man temporarily shares. Therefore, past, present and future are seen as one; the recognition of the Eternal Now is gradually developed from incarna-

tion to incarnation and during the continuous process of rebirth. This constitutes a state of consciousness (characteristic of the normal state of the advanced man) which can be called devachanic. (17-496/7)

(d) APPROPRIATION OF THE SHEATHS BY THE EGO

1. The manifestation of the etheric body in time and space has in it what has been esoterically called "two moments of brilliance". These are, first, the moment prior to physical incarnation, when the descending light (carrying life) is focussed in all its intensity around the physical body and sets up a rapport with the innate light of matter itself, to be found in every atom of substance. This focussing light will be found to concentrate itself in seven areas of its ring-pass-not, thus creating seven major centres, which will control its expression and its existence upon the outer plane, esoterically speaking. This is a moment of great radiance; it is almost as if a point of pulsating life burst into flame, and as if within that flame seven points of intensified light took shape. This is a high point in the experience of taking incarnation, and precedes physical birth by a very short period of time. It is that which brings on the birth hour. The next phase of the process, as seen by the clairvoyant, is the stage of interpenetration, during which "the seven become the twenty-one and then the many"; the light substance, the energy aspect of the soul, begins to permeate the physical body, and the creative work of the etheric or vital body is completed. The first recognition of this upon the physical plane is the "sound" uttered by the newborn infant. It climaxes the process. The act of creation by the soul is now complete; a new light shines forth in a dark place. (17-469/70)

2. In all the work of form-building, certain very vital occasions occur which concern the Ego even more than the sheaths themselves, though the reflex action between the lower personal self and the higher is so close as to be well nigh inseparable....

It is often overlooked that the path of incarnation is not a quick one, but that the Ego descends very slowly and takes possession gradually of his vehicles; the less evolved the man, the slower is the process. We are dealing here with the period of time which transpires after the Ego has made the first move towards descent, and not with the time which elapses between two incarnations. This work of passing on to a plane for purposes of incarnation, marks a definite crisis, and is characterised by the exertion of the will in sacrifice, the appropriation of the substance in love, and its energising into activity.

. . . The Ego ceases from his work of overshadowing, and at some period between the fourth and seventh year makes his contact with the physical brain of the child. A similar occurrence takes place in connection with the etheric vehicle, the astral, and the mental.   (3-787)

3. At seven years we are told the Ego "takes hold", and again at adolescence; at twenty-one that hold may be made still firmer. Again, as lives are passed, the Ego (in connection with a human being) grips its vehicles and so sways them to his purpose with more effect and fullness. (3-366)

4. The term of the life cycle may be long or short, according to the purposes involved; it may cover only a very few short years, or a century. Prior to the seventh year, the vitality of the physical elemental is largely the determining factor. The soul is then focussed in the etheric body, but is not fully utilising all the centres; it has simply a gently pulsating control and a gentle impulsive activity—sufficient to preserve consciousness, to vitalise the various physical processes, and to initiate the demonstration of character and of disposition. These become increasingly marked until the twenty-first year, when they stabilise into what we call the personality. In the case of disciples, the grip of the soul upon the etheric centres will be more powerful from the very start of the physical existence. By the time the fourteenth year is reached, the quality and the nature of the incarnated soul and its approximate age or experience are determined, the physical, astral and mental elementals are under control, and the soul, the indwelling spiritual man, already determines the life tendencies and choices.   (17-463/4)

(e) SOUL CYCLES

1. I seek to elaborate somewhat the cyclic experience of a soul in incarnation, indicating the apparent ebb and flow of its unfoldment.

The outstanding cycle for every soul is that of its forthgoing into incarnation and its return or flowing back into the centre from whence it came. According to the point of view will be the understanding of this ebb and flow. Souls might esoterically be regarded as those "seeking the light of experience", and therefore turned towards physical expression, and those "seeking the light of understanding", and therefore retreating from the realm of human understanding to forge their way inward into the soul consciousness, and so become "dwellers in the light eternal". Without appreciating the significance of the terms, the psychologists have sensed these cycles and call certain types extroverts, and others, introverts. These mark an ebb and flow in individual experience and are the tiny life correspondences to the great soul cycles. This passing into, and passing out of the web of incarnated existence, are the major cycles of any individual soul. (4-243)

2. The occult sciences lay the emphasis upon cyclic law, and . . . the growing interest in the Science of Cyclic Manifestation. Death appears frequently to be so purposeless; that is because the intention of the soul is not known; past development, through the process of incarnation, remains a hidden matter; ancient heredities and environments are ignored, and recognition of the voice of the soul is not yet generally developed. These are matters, however, which are on the verge of recognition; revelation is on its way, and for that I am laying the foundation. . . . Seek to arrive at a new slant upon the subject and see law and purpose and the beauty of intention in what has hitherto been a terror and a major fear. (17-436)

(f) SOUL AGE

1. One of the first things that a disciple has to learn, is right judgment as to the relative soul age of his associates. He soon discovers that these vary. He learns then to recognise those whose wisdom and knowledge surpass his own, to co-operate with those who stand with him upon the Path, and to work for those whom he can help, but whose evolutionary status is not on an equality with his own. The ordered pattern of his life can then take on definite forms and he can begin to work with intelligence. (5-307)

2. The soul knows no age and can use its instrument if it makes itself into a suitable and available instrument. Are you too set and too pre-occupied with yourselves to achieve the detachment needed for world service? That is for you to find out and to prove to yourselves. (5-768)

(g) AWAKENING SOULS

The majority of the souls in the human family come into incarnation in obedience to the urge or the desire to experience, and the magnetic pull of the physical plane is the final determining factor. They are, as souls, oriented towards earth life. Increasingly, awakening souls, or those who are (occutly speaking) "coming to themselves", enter into physical life experience only dimly aware of another and higher "pull". They are, therefore, without as true an orientation to the physical plane as are the bulk of their fellow men. These awakening souls are the ones who can at times be influenced to retard or delay their entry into physical life, in order to effect a conditioning of the processes of civilisation. Or again, they can be prevailed upon to hasten their entrance into life so as to be available as agents for such a conditioning process. This process is not carried forward by them through any emphasised or intelligently appreciated activity, but it is naturally brought about by the simple effect of their living in the world and there pursuing their life objectives. They thus condition their surroundings by the beauty, the power, or the influence of their lives, and are themselves frequently quite unconscious of the effect that they are having. It will be apparent therefore, that the needed changes in our civilisation can be brought about rapidly or slowly, according to the number of those who are living as *souls in training.*

. . . These incoming souls have, through their highly developed understanding, and by means of their "self-willed power", frequently wrought havoc in various directions. However, if we could look on, as can Those on the other side, and if we were in a position to contrast the "light" of humanity as it is today with what it was two or three hundred years ago, we would recognise that enormous strides had been made. This is evidenced by the fact that the emergence of a band of "conditioning souls", under the name of the *New Group of World Servers*, has been possible since 1925. They can now come in because of the work already done by the group of souls who hastened their entrance into incarnation, under the impulse of the Hierarchy. The words "condition" or "conditioning" are here used quite frequently because of the aptness of the phrase to indicate function. These souls, because of their point in evolution, because of their stage in unfoldment, and because of their impressibility to the group idea and to the Plan, can come into incarnation and begin, more or less, to work out that Plan and evoke a response to it in their human consciousness. They are thus in a position to "prepare the way for the coming of the Lord". This latter is a symbolic phrase indicating a certain level of spiritual culture in humanity. They are sometimes dimly conscious of this stupendous task, but they are, in the majority of cases, quite unconscious of their "qualifying" destiny. As souls, under the guidance of the Hierarchy and prior to incarnation, they are conscious of the impulse to "go in and help the sorrowing planet and thus release the prisoners held in durance hard by low desire" (quoting from the *Old Commentary*), but once the garment of flesh has been assumed, that consciousness too dies out, and in the physical brain they are not aware of that which their souls have purposed. Only the urge for specific activities remains. The work nevertheless proceeds.

A few souls come into incarnation of their own free will and accord; they work with clear knowledge and proceed to the task of the day. They are the key people in any age, and the determining factors, psychologically, in any historical period. It is they who set the pace and do the pioneering work. They focus in themselves both the hatred and the love of the world; they work as the Builders or as the Destroyers, and they return eventually to their own place, carrying with them the spoils of victory in the shape of the freedom which they have won for themselves or for others. They bear the scars, psychologically speaking, which have been given to them by opposing workers, and they bear also the assurance that they have carried forward the task to which they have been assigned and which they have successfully undertaken.

This first category of people in incarnation has been greatly augmented during the past century, and it is for this reason that we can look for the rapid development of the characteristics of the incoming Aquarian Age. (15-260/3)

23. CHARACTERISTICS OF THE SOUL

1. 1. Only the soul has a direct and clear understanding of the creative purpose and of the Plan.

2. Only the soul, whose nature is intelligent love, can be trusted with the knowledge, the symbols, and the formulas which are necessary to the correct conditioning of the magical work.

3. Only the soul has power to work in all three worlds at once, and yet remain detached, and therefore karmically free from the results of such work.

4. Only the soul is truly group-conscious and actuated by pure unselfish purpose.

5. Only the soul, with the open eye of vision, can see the end from the beginning, and can hold in steadiness the true picture of the ultimate consummation. (4-126)

2. A potent personality may function in any field of human expression and his work will warrant the word "spiritual" just in so far as it is based on high idealism, the greatest good of the largest number, and self-sacri-

ficing endeavour. These three—idealism, group service and sacrifice—are characteristics of those personalities who are becoming increasingly sensitive to the soul aspect, the qualities of that soul being knowledge, love and sacrifice. . . .

The outstanding characteristics of those personalities who are not as yet soul-centered or controlled, are dominance, ambition, pride, and lack of love to the whole, though they frequently possess love for those who are necessary to them or to their comfort.   (4-395/6)

3. The steely, brittle, determined, dynamic will of the devoted aspirant must change into the steadfast, powerful, calm pupose of the soul, working through the disciple. The soul is fluid in adjustment but undeviating in aim. Likewise, the brilliant fanatical devotion to this, that or the other person or ideal, must give place to the gentle, unchanging love of the soul—the love of your soul for the soul of others. . . . In conformity to soul impulse mould your life and shift out of the realm of high desire and aspiration into that of settled purpose and an undeviating attachment to reality.   (5-243)

(a) INCLUSIVENESS

Inclusiveness is the outstanding characteristic of the soul, or self, whether it is the soul of man, the sensitive nature of the cosmic Christ, or the *anima mundi*, the soul of the world. This inclusiveness tends to synthesis. It can already be seen functioning at a definite point of fulfilment in man, because man includes in his nature all the gains of past evolutionary cycles (in other kingdoms in nature and in previous human cycles), plus the potentiality of a greater future inclusiveness. Man is the macrocosm of the microcosm; the gains and peculiar properties of the other kingdoms in nature are his, having been resolved into capacities of consciousness. He is, however, enveloped in and part of a still greater macrocosm, and of this greater Whole he must become increasingly aware. Let this word *"Inclusiveness"* govern your thinking.   (15-556/7)

(b) LOVE

1. The nature of the soul is love and the will-to-good.   (5-19)

2. Love in the personality gradually develops through the stage of love of self, pure and simple and entirely selfish, to love of family and friends, to love of men and women, until it arrives at the stage of love of humanity or group love consciousness, which is the predominant characteristic of

the Ego. A Master of Compassion loves, suffers with, and remains with His kind and with His kin. Love in the Ego gradually develops from love of humanity into love universal—a love that expresses not only love of humanity, but also love of the deva evolutions in their totality, and of all forms of divine manifestation. Love in the Personality is love in the three worlds; love in the Ego is love in the solar system, and all that it contains; whilst love in the Monad demonstrates a measure of cosmic love, and embraces much that is outside the solar system altogether. . . .

The Law of Love is in reality but the law of the system in demonstration on all the planes. Love was the impelling motive for manifestation, and love it is that keeps all in ordered sequence; love bears all on the path of return to the Father's bosom, and love eventually perfects all that is. It is love that builds the forms that cradle temporarily the inner hidden life, and love is the cause of the disruption of those forms, and their utter shattering, so that the life may further progress. Love manifests on each plane as the urge that drives the evolving Monad onwards on its goal, and love is the key to the deva kingdom, and the reason of the blending of the two kingdoms eventually into the divine Hermaphrodite. Love works through the concrete rays in the building of the system, and in the rearing of the structure that shelters the Spirit, and love works through the abstract rays for the full and potent development of that inherent divinity. Love demonstrates, through the concrete rays, the aspects of divinity, forming the persona that hides the one Self; love demonstrates through the abstract rays in developing the attributes of divinity, in evolving to fullest measure the kingdom of God within. Love in the concrete rays leads to the path of occultism; love in the abstract rays leads to that of the mystic. Love forms the sheath and inspires the life; love causes the logic vibration to surge forward, carrying all on its way, and bringing all to perfected manifestation. (3-593/4)

3. Knowledge you have. More love you need. When I say "love", I refer to soul love and not to affection, emotion or sentiment. I refer to that detached, deep love which can pour through the personality, releasing it from limited expression and at the same time streams out into the environment.

How release the love aspect of your soul? . . . By meditation, and by certain practical measures. . . . Self-pity must give place to compassionate interest in others—those in your own home, in your business relations, and in all whom you meet, and life and fate throws in your way. Isolation must give place to co-operation; not an enforced co-operation, but a spontaneous longing to be with and to share with others *the processes of living, loving, occult duty*. Ponder much upon this last phrase.   (5-494)

4. There is no light or dark to the soul, but only existence and love. . . . There is no separation but only identification with the heart of all love; the more you love the more love can reach out through you to others. The chains of love unite the world of men and the world of forms, and they constitute the great chain of the Hierarchy. The spiritual effort you are asked to make is that of developing yourself into a vibrant and powerful centre of that fundamental, universal *Love*.   (6-30)

5. "May that soul of mine, whose nature is love and wisdom, direct events, impel to action, and guide my every word and deed."   (6-479)

6. "Let the love of the soul attract and the light of the soul direct all whom I seek to help. Thus will humanity be saved by me and all affiliated with the Hierarchy."   (6-479)

7. Right attachment releases the love of the soul, and only love, consciously, intelligently, and deliberately applied, can make for successful work.   (6-506)

8. "Naught can dim the love which flows between my soul and me, the little self. Naught can come between my brothers and my self. Naught can stop the flow of strength between me and my soul, between my brothers and my soul, between the Master of my life and me, His pledged disciple."   (6-647)

9. The race has reached a point wherein the men of good intention, of some real understanding, and owning a measure of freedom from the love of gold (symbolic way of speaking of the glamour of materiality) are turning their desire to their duty, their responsibilities, their effects upon others, and to their sentimental understanding of the nature of love. Love, for many people, for the majority indeed, is not really love, but a mixture of the desire to love and the desire to be loved, plus a willingness to do anything to show and evoke this sentiment, and consequently to be more comfortable in one's own interior life. The selfishness of the people who are desirous of being unselfish, is great. So many contributing sentiments gather around the sentiment or desire to show those amiable and pleasant characteristics which will evoke a corresponding reciprocation towards the would-be lover or server who is still completely surrounded by the glamour of sentiment.

It is this pseudo-love, based primarily on a theory of love and service, which characterises so many human relationships, such as those existing, for instance, between husband and wife, parents and their children. Glamoured by their sentiment for them and knowing little of the love of the soul, which is free itself and leaves others free also, they wander in a dense fog, often dragging with them the ones they desire to serve, in order to draw forth a responsive affection. Study the word "affection", my brother, and see its true meaning. Affection is not love. It is that desire which we express through an exertion of the astral body and this activity affects our contacts; it is not the spontaneous desirelessness of the soul which asks nothing for the separated self. This glamour of sentiment imprisons and bewilders all the nice people in the world, imposing upon them obligations which do not exist, and producing a glamour which must eventually be dissipated by the pouring in of true and selfless love. (10-76/7)

10. It is this energy (of Love) which constitutes the cohering, unifying force, which holds the manifested universe or planetary form together, and is responsible for all relationships; it is this energy which is the soul of all things or of all forms, beginning with the *anima mundi,* and reaching its highest point of expression in the human soul, which is the constituent factor in the fifth kingdom in nature, the Kingdom of God or of Souls. An understanding of this human potency comes as a man makes contact with his own soul, and sets up a stable relationship with that soul; then he becomes a soul-infused personality. (11-130)

11. Love, true spiritual love as the soul knows it, can ever be trusted with power and opportunity and will never betray that trust. (13-279)

(c) Joy and Happiness

1. Cultivate happiness, knowing that depression, an over-morbid investigation of motive, and undue sensitiveness to the criticism of others leads to a condition wherein a disciple is almost useless. Happiness is based on confidence in the God within, a just appreciation of time, and a forgetfulness of self. Take all the glad things which may come as trusts to be used to spread joy, and rebel not at happiness and pleasure in service, thinking it an indication that all is not well. Suffering comes as the lower self rebels. Control that lower self, eliminate desire, and all is joy. (1-76)

2. To those who wrestle, strive, and hold on, the joy is doubled when the materialisation comes. The joy of contrast will be yours, for knowing the past of darkness you will revel in the light of fruition; the joy of

tried and tested companionship will be yours, for years will have proved to you who are your chosen associates, and in community of suffering will come the strengthened link; the joy of peace after victory will be yours, for to the tired warrior the fruits of achievement and rest are doubly sweet; the joy of participation in the Masters' plan will be yours, and all is well that associates you closely with Them; the joy of having helped to solace a needy world, of having brought light to darkened souls, of having healed in some measure the open sore of the world's distress, will be yours, and in the consciousness of days well spent, and in the gratitude of salvaged souls, comes the deepest joy of all—the joy a Master knows when He is instrumental in lifting a brother up a little higher on the ladder. This is the joy that is set before you all—and not so very far ahead it lies. So work, not *for* joy but *towards* it; not for reward, but from the inner need to help; not for gratitude, but from the urge that comes from having seen the vision and realisation of the part you have to play in bringing that vision down to earth.

It is helpful to differentiate between happiness, joy and bliss:

First, *happiness,* which has its seat in the emotions, and is a personality reaction.

Second, *joy,* which is a quality of the soul and is realised in the mind, when alignment takes place.

Third, *bliss,* which is the nature of the Spirit and about which speculation is fruitless until the soul realises its oneness with the Father. This realisation follows upon an earlier stage wherein the personal self is at-oned with the soul. Therefore speculation and analysis as to the nature of bliss is profitless to the average man whose metaphors and terminologies must perforce be personal and related to the world of the senses. Does the aspirant refer to his happiness or joy? If he refers to the latter, it must come as the effect of group consciousness, of group solidarity, of oneness with all beings, and may not be interpreted in terms of happiness after all. Happiness comes when the personality is meeting with those conditions which satisfy it in one part or other of its lower nature; it comes when there is a sense of physical well being, of contentment with one's environment or surrounding personalities, or of satisfaction with one's mental opportunitites and contacts. Happiness is the goal of the separated self.

When, however, we seek to live as souls, the contentment of the lower man is discounted and we find joy in our group relationships and in bringing about those conditions which lead to the better expression of the souls of those we contact. This bringing of joy to others in order to produce conditions in which they may better express themselves, may have a physical effect as we seek to better their material conditions, or an emotional effect as our presence brings to them peace and uplift, or an intellectual result as we stimulate them to clarity of thought and understanding. But the effect upon ourselves is joy, for our action has been selfless and non-acquisitive, and not dependent upon the aspirant's circumstance or worldly state. . . .

It is a platitude as well as an occult paradox to say that in the midst of profound personality distress and unhappiness, the joy of the soul may be known and felt. Such however is the case, and it is for this that the student must aim.   (4-368/70)

3. You can train yourself to build in that quality of joy which is the characteristic of a personality which is consciously anchored in the soul realm.   (5-398)

4. Aim at demonstrating happiness. Be joyous in your work and service. Be not so intense, but go happily along the lighted Way.   (5-408)

5. (Cultivate) a spirit of happiness and of joy, which is based on an inner assurance as to the Plan and your future work in relation to it.   (5-420)

6. Be joyful, for joy lets in the light, and where there is joy there is little room for glamour and misunderstanding.   (5-461)

7. Be happy. Learn to feel joy—a joy which is based on the knowledge that humanity has always triumphed and passed onward and forward in spite of apparent failures, and the destruction of past civilisations; a joy, which is founded upon the unshakable belief that all men are souls, and that "points of crisis" are factors which are of proven usefulness in calling in the power of that soul, both in the individual man, in a race, or in humanity as a whole; a joy which is related to the bliss which characterises the soul on its own level whereon the form aspects do not dominate. Ponder on these thoughts and remember you are grounded in the centre of your Being and can, therefore, see the world truly and with no limited vision; you can stand unperturbed, knowing the end from the beginning and realising that love will triumph.   (5-471)

8. Cultivate the joy that brings strength. This is not the time for gloom, despair or depression. If you give way to these, you become negative and destructive focal points in your environment. If you truly believe that the spiritual life is fundamental in the world today, if you do believe that

divinity guides the world, if you truly grasp the fact that all men are your brothers, and that we are all the children of the One Father, and if you are convinced that the heart of humanity is sound—are these not adequately potent ideas to hold us joyously steady in the midst of a changing world?   (13-82)

(d) SHARING

1. The Principle of Sharing which must govern economic relations in the future, is a soul quality or energy.   (5-40)

2. Ashramic sharing is one of the great compensations of discipleship. By means of it added light can be "occultly endured". I would like to have you ponder on that phrase. Great united strength can be brought to the service of the Plan, and the occult significance of the words : "My strength is as the strength of ten, because my heart is pure" can be grasped. The perfected strength of the Ashram (symbolised by the number 10) becomes available to the disciple whose purity of heart has enabled him to penetrate into the Ashram; his knowledge becomes more rapidly transmuted into wisdom as his mind is subjected to the play of the higher understanding of Those with Whom he is associated; gradually he begins to contribute his own quota of light and of understanding to those just entering and to those who are his equals.   (6-330)

(e) LONELINESS

1. Be prepared for loneliness. It is the law. As a man dissociates himself from all that concerns his physical, astral and mental bodies, and centres himself in the Ego, it produces a temporary separation. This must be endured and passed, leading to a closer link at a later period with all associated with the disciple through the karma of past lives, through group work, and through the activity of the disciple (carried on almost unconsciously at first) in gathering together those through whom later he will work.   (1-76)

2. Loneliness . . . is one of the first things that indicates to a disciple that he is being prepared for initiation. It will be apparent, therefore, that the loneliness to which I refer is not that which is incident to those weaknesses of character which repel one's fellow men, to an aloof or disagreeable nature, or to any form of self-interest which is so emphasised that it antagonises other people. There is much loneliness in a disciple's life which is entirely his own fault and which is subject to cure if he employs the

right measure of self-discipline. With these he must deal himself, for they concern the personality, and with your personalities I have no affair. I refer to the loneliness which comes when the accepting disciple becomes the pledged disciple and steps out of a life of physical plane concentration, and of identification with the forms of existence in the three worlds, and finds himself in the midway place, between the world of outer affairs and the inner world of meaning. His first reaction then is that he is alone; he has broken with the past; he is hopeful but not sure of the future; the tangible world to which he is accustomed must, he knows, be superseded by the intangible world of values and new responsibilities. This world he believes exists, and he steps forward bravely and theoretically, but it remains for a while wholly intangible; he finds few who think and feel as he does, and the mechanism of sure contact only exists within him in embryo. He is breaking loose from the mass consciousness with which he has been merged hitherto, but has not yet found his group, into which he will eventually be consciously absorbed. Therefore, he is lonely and feels deserted and bereft. Some of you feel this loneliness; few of you have, for instance, reached the point where you feel yourselves to be a definite integral part of the group; . . . your attitude is largely one of hope, coupled with the idea that it is your physical limitations which prevent your realising all that truly *is*, in connection with your inner affiliations. But, my brothers, such a sense of loneliness is only another form of self-consciousness, of undue self-interest, and (as you make progress upon the Path) you will find it disappearing. If you therefore feel lonely, you must learn to look upon it as a glamour or illusion, and as a limitation which must be overcome. You must begin to act as if it were not. If only more disciples would learn the value of acting *"as if"*. There is no time for any of you to be lonely these days, for there is no time for you to think about yourselves.   (6-45/6)

3. Be not afraid of loneliness. The soul that cannot stand alone has naught to give.   (6-755)

4. The revelation of a certain type of spiritual loneliness is one through which all disciples have to pass; it is a test of that occult detachment which every disciple has to master.   (6-762)

5. In this solitude there is no morbidness, there is no harsh withdrawing, and there is no aspect of separateness. There is only the "place where the disciple stands, detached and unafraid, and in that place of utter quiet the Master comes and solitude is not".   (6-764)

(f) SPIRITUAL INDIFFERENCE

1. What is indifference? . . . It means in reality the achieving of a neutral attitude towards that which is regarded as the Not-self; it involves a repudiation of similarity; it marks the recognition of a basic distinction; it signifies refusal to be identified with anything save the spiritual reality as far as that is sensed and known at any given point in time and space. It is, therefore, a much stronger and vital thing than what is usually meant when the word is used. It is active repudiation without any concentration upon that which is repudiated.   (10-262)

2. (Cultivate) indifference—that spiritual indifference which pays no undue attention to the physical body, or to moods and feelings, or to mental illusions. The body exists and must receive due care; the feelings and moods are potent and exhausting, and from them . . . come much of your physical discomfort. Deal with them not by struggling, but by substitution of other interests, ignoring them, and treating them with indifference, till they die of lack of attention and of slow attrition.   (5-494)

3. When will disciples learn that the attitude which involves a certain "don't care" reaction and a form of indifference, is one of the quickest ways by which to release the Self from personality claims? This is not the "don't care" spirit which will affect the disciples' attitude to other people. It is the attitude of the integrated thinking personality of the disciple towards the astral or emotional body. It leads him to assume the position that not one single thing which produces any reaction of pain or distress in the emotional body, matters in the very least. These reactions are simply recognised, lived through, tolerated and not permitted to produce any limitation. All disciples would do well to ponder what I have just said. The whole process is based on a deep-seated belief in the persistence of the immortal Being within the forms of soul and personality. (5-57)

(g) IMPERSONALITY

When man is beginning to live as a soul, and when his consciousness has shifted away from the world of illusion, then he can be useful. The first lesson he has to learn is a sense of values in time and space, and to know that we work with souls, and do not nurse the personality.

Seems this too hard a saying to you? If it is indeed so to you, it means that you are as yet somewhat self-centered and in love with your own individual soul, having not yet duly contacted it, and having but perhaps sensed its vibration and no more. You have not yet that true picture of the world's need which will release you from your own ambition and set you free to work as we (on the subjective side) work, with no thought of self or of spiritual happiness, and with no desire for any self-appointed task; with no longing for glittering promises of future success, and with no demanding ache for the tender touch and contact with those greater in consciousness than ourselves. If this lies still beyond your realisation, recognise the fact, and understand that there is no blame attached. It only indicates to you the ground whereon you stand, and that the illusion of the astral plane still holds you in its thrall and still leads you to place personality reactions before group realisation. As long as you walk on that plane and function on that level of consciousness, it is not possible to draw you consciously into the Masters' groups on mental levels. You are still too destructive and personal; you would be apt to hurt the group and cause trouble; you would see things (through the group stimulation) with a clarity for which you are not yet ready, and would be shattered thereby. You have need to learn the lessons of accepting guidance from your own soul, and of learning to work with harmony and impersonality on the physical plane with the group or groups to which your destiny impels you. When you have learnt the lesson of self-forgetfulness, when you seek nothing for the separated self, when you stand firmly on your own feet and look for aid within yourself, and when the trend of your life is towards co-operation, then you may pass from the stage of Observer to that of Communicator. This will happen because you can be trusted to communicate only that which is impersonal and truly constructive, and which will not feed the emotional nature and satisfy the desire-self. (14-116/7)

(h) DETACHMENT

1. You need to acquire that inner, divine detachment, which sees life in its true perspective. A man is thus left free and untouched by aught that may occur. The ideal attitude for you is that of the Onlooker who is in no way identified with aught that may happen on the physical and emotional planes, and whose mind is a limpid reflector of truth. This truth is intuitively perceived because there are no violent mental reactions or emotional states of response; the vehicles of perception are quiet and therefore there is nothing to offset correct attitude. When this state of consciousness is achieved, you will be able to teach with power and at the same time possess that also which must be taught. (5-146)

2. You are learning to detach yourself from people and from the clinging hands of those demanding presences who are to be found clamouring for your attention in their lives. This freedom must increase as you endeavour to meet perfectly the need of those around you, yet at the same time you must go on with increasing power detaching yourself from their inner hold upon you. They must fail to reach you in the inner fortress of your soul. There you must learn to stand, detached and unafraid. (5-393)

3. One of the problems which all sincere disciples have to solve, is to learn to live *as if* the physical body did not exist. By that I mean that its limitations and the hindrances which it imposes upon the expression of the free, spiritual consciousness are negated by an inner attitude of mind. It is the cultivation of a detached attitude to life and to circumstances. (5-433)

4. One of the first lessons every chela has to learn, is the growth of that inner detachment which will enable him to merge himself in the consciousness of his brother and so know and ascertain the best way to help him and stimulate him to renewed *self-effort*. He needs also to cultivate that true humility which will force him to give all he has in selfless service, and then to forget that he has thus given of himself. He must have no thought of himself as a factor in the case. Only when detachment and humility are present, can a disciple really serve. Cultivate, therefore, these qualities and continue the giving of yourself in service. (5-416/7)

5. Live always *above* your physical body, ignoring how you feel and seeking to dwell as far as is possible, with your waking consciousness blended and fused with that of the soul. Even if you *feel* it not, then *know* that it is there.

I wonder, my brother, if it is possible for me to indicate to you the life of *spiritual insulation* which is in no way the life of *personal isolation?* In this state of "insulated being" lies, for you, the solution of many of your problems. This insulation is brought about by emotional indifference to your environment and to people, but it is a spiritual indifference, founded on spiritual detachment and dispassion. When it is present, there comes the fulfilment of obligation and the performance of duty, but no identification with people or circumstance. The soul stands free, unattached, unafraid, and is not controlled by that which exists in the three worlds. This is the true spiritual indifference. (5-429)

6. Be attached to souls, my brother, but detached from personalities. Souls heal and aid each other's personalities. Personality relationships drain and devitalise. (5-455)

7. *The failure to be detached.* You tie yourself to those you love, and oft the clinging hands of love can hinder progress—not only our own, but also that of those we love. . . . As you live and love those in your immediate environment, do you ever ask yourself the question: Am I strengthening them as souls to handle life and serve? . . . It is your love, your clinging possessive love for those you have gathered close around you in the karmic process of life, that hinders your loving them in the strong, true way. . . . I ask you to love more truly.   (5-516/7)

8. Preserve ever the attitude of the Onlooker in the head. Thus the detachment of the soul will grow, whilst the attachment of the soul to souls will grow and increase.   (5-623)

9. The disciple learns eventually to know himself to be, above everything else (whilst in incarnation), the director of forces: these he directs from the altitude of the divine Observer and through the attainment of detachment. These are things which I have oft told you before. These truths are, for you, only the platitudes of occultism, and yet, if you could but grasp the full significance of detachment, and stand serene as the observing Director, there would be no more waste motion, no more mistaken moves, and no more false interpretations, no wandering down the by-paths of daily living, no seeing others through distorted and prejudiced vision, and —above all—no more misuse of force.   (10-243)

(i) FREEDOM

1. So feel free, my brother, but be quite sure that it is not a freedom demanded because group affiliation irks you. The more your soul grips your personality, the less you will be concerned with the problems of isolation and of freedom. Feel free, but be sure that it is not a freedom demanded because the steady discipline of occult training frets a temperament still essentially mystic. The more your soul grips you, the more your mind will awaken, and feeling (in the personal sense) fade out. Feel free, but be sure that it is not a freedom demanded because the sense of failure to organise your time and reduce your personality to rhythmic living hurts your pride. The more your soul grips you, the more assuredly you will learn to use time as a responsibility.   (5-289)

2. Time and again, along the Road, (the disciple) will revolt from control and will fall back into the glamour of his supposed freedom. There *is* freedom from the control of the personality. There *is* freedom from the control of personalities. But there is never any freedom from the Law of

Service, and from the constant interplay between man and man, and soul and soul. To stand really free is to stand in the clear unimpeded light of the soul, which is basically and intrinsically group consciousness. (10-48)

(j) SERENITY

I have pointed out to you before this, how difficult is the process of absorbing a new disciple into an Ashram; he has to be taught to advance gradually from the periphery of the group consciousness towards the centre. Each step forward necessitates care on the part of the Master in order to see that the Ashram is preserved from all disruptive activity. It is only when the chela has achieved *"occult serenity"* that he can be permitted to focus himself permanently within the group aura. This happens when he becomes conscious of the peculiar and specific vibration of the Master's aura. Hence, as you can well see, the need for serenity.

I would point out that serenity and peace are not identical. Peace must ever be temporary and refers to the world of feeling and to conditions susceptible of disturbance. It is essential to progress and an inevitable happening, that every step forward is marked by disturbances, by points of crisis and chaos, replaced later (when successfully handled) by periods of peace. But this peace is not serenity, and a chela is only permitted to dwell within the Master's aura when *serenity has been substituted for peace.* Serenity signifies that deep calm, devoid of emotional disturbance, which distinguishes the disciple who is focussed in a "mind held steady in the light". The surface of his life may be (from the worldly angle) in a state of violent flux. All that he cherishes and holds dear in the three worlds may be crashing around him. But in spite of all he stands firm, poised in soul consciousness, and the depths of his life remain undisturbed. This is not insensitivity or a forced auto-suggestion, neither is it a capacity to exteriorise the consciousness in such a manner that individual events and happenings are ignored. *It is intensity of feeling transmuted into focussed understanding.* When this has been attained, the chela has the right to live within the aura of the Master. There is nothing now in him which will require the Master to sidetrack His attention from vital efforts to the unimportant task of helping a disciple. (5-750)

(k) INNER CALM

1. Have patience. Endurance is one of the characteristics of the Ego. The Ego *persists,* knowing itself immortal. The personality becomes discouraged, knowing that time is short.

To the disciple naught occurs but what is in the Plan, and where the motive and sole aspiration of the heart are towards the carrying out of the Master's will and the serving of the race, that which eventuates has in it the seeds of the next enterprise, and embodies the environment of the next step forward. Herein lies much of clarification, and herein may be found that on which the disciple may rest when the vision is clouded, the vibration lower than perhaps it should be, and the judgment fogged by the miasmas arising from circumstances on the physical plane. With many, much arises in the astral body that is based on old vibration and has no foundation in fact, and the battleground is so to control the astral situation that out of present anxieties and worries may grow confidence and peace, and out of violent action and interaction there may be elaborated tranquility.

It is possible to reach a point where naught that occurs can ruffle the inner calm; where the peace that passeth understanding is known and experienced, because the consciousness is centred in the Ego, who is peace itself, being the circle of the buddhic life; where poise itself is known and felt, and equilibrium reigns because the centre of the life is in the Ego, who is—in essence—balance; where calm rules unruffled and unshaken, because the divine Knower holds the reins of government, and permits no disturbance from the lower self; where bliss itself is reached that is based, not on circumstances in the three worlds, but on that inner realisation of existence apart from the not-self, an existence that persists when time and space, and all that is contained therein, are not; that is known when all the illusions of the lower planes are experienced, passed through, transmuted and transcended; that endures when the little world of human endeavour has dissipated and gone, being seen as naught; and that is based on the knowledge that I AM THAT.

Such an attitude and experience is for all those who persist in their high endeavour, who count all things but naught if they may but achieve the goal, and who steer a steady course through circumstances, keeping the eyes fixed upon the vision ahead, the ears attentive to the Voice of the God within, that sounds in the silence of the heart; the feet firmly placed on the path that leads to the Portal of Initiation; the hands held out in assistance to the world, and the whole life subordinated to the call of service. Then all that comes is for the best—sickness, opportunity, success, and disappointment, the gibes and machinations of enemies, the lack of comprehension on the part of those we love—all is but to be used, and all exists but to be transmuted. Continuity of vision, of aspiration, and of the inner touch, is seen to be of more importance than them all. That continuity is the thing to be aimed at, in spite of, and not because of circumstances.

As the aspirant progresses he not only balances the pairs of opposites, but is having the secret of his brother's heart revealed to him. He becomes an acknowledged force in the world, and is recognised as one who can be depended upon to serve. Men turn to him for assistance and help along his recognised line, and he begins to sound forth his note so as to be heard in deva and human ranks. This he does—at this stage—through the pen in literature, through the spoken word in lecturing or teaching, through music, painting and art. He reaches the hearts of men in some way or another, and becomes a helper and server of his race. (1-76/8)

2. *Perfect Poise* indicates complete control of the astral body, so that emotional upheavals are overcome, or at least are greatly minimised in the life of the disciple. It indicates also, on the higher turn of the spiral, an ability to function freely on the buddhic levels, owing to complete liberation (and consequent poise) from all the influences and impulses which are motivated from the three worlds. This type or quality of poise connotes—if you will think deeply—an abstract state of mind; nothing which is regarded as non-perfection can create disturbance. You can realise surely that, if you were entirely free from all emotional reactions, your clarity of mind and your ability to think clearly, would be enormously increased, with all that that involves.

Naturally, the perfect poise of an initiated disciple and that of the initiated Master are different, for one concerns the effect of the three worlds or their non-effect, and the other concerns adaptability to the rhythm of the Spiritual Triad; nevertheless, the earlier type of poise must precede the later achievement, hence my consideration of the subject. This perfect poise (which is a possible achievement for you who read) is arrived at by ruling out the pulls, the urges, impulses and attractions of the astral or emotional nature, and also by the practice of what I have earlier mentioned: *Divine Indifference.* (17-672/3)

(l) RESPONSIBILITY

From the angle of the esoteric science, the sense of responsibility is *the first* and the outstanding characteristic of the soul. In so far, therefore, as a disciple is in contact with the soul and is becoming a soul-infused personality, and is consequently under soul direction, so far will he undertake the task presented to him. (6-390)

(m) WISDOM

Wisdom is the product of the Hall of Wisdom. It has to do with the development of the life within the form, with the progress of the spirit through those ever-changing vehicles, and with the expansions of consciousness that succeed each other from life to life. It deals with the life side of evolution. Since it deals with the essence of things, and not with the things themselves, it is the intuitive apprehension of truth apart from the reasoning faculty, and the innate perception that can distinguish between the false and the true, between the real and the unreal. It is more than that, for it is also the growing capacity of the Thinker to enter increasingly into the mind of the Logos, to realise the true inwardness of the great pageant of the universe, to vision the objective, and to harmonise more and more with the higher measure. For our present purpose (which is to study somewhat the Path of Holiness and its various stages) it may be described as the realisation of the "Kingdom of God within", and the apprehension of the "Kingdom of God without" in the solar system. Perhaps it might be expressed as the gradual blending of the paths of the mystic and the occultist—the rearing of the temple of wisdom upon the foundation of knowledge.

Wisdom is the science of the spirit, just as knowledge is the science of matter. Knowledge is separative and objective, whilst wisdom is synthetic and subjective. Knowledge divides; wisdom unites. Knowledge differentiates, whilst wisdom blends. What then is meant by understanding?

The *understanding* may be defined as the faculty of the Thinker in Time to appropriate knowledge as the foundation for wisdom, that which enables him to adapt the things of form to the life of the spirit, and to take the flashes of inspiration that come to him from the Hall of Wisdom and link them to the facts of the Hall of Learning. Perhaps the whole idea might be expressed in this way :

Wisdom concerns the one Self, knowledge deals with the not-self, whilst the understanding is the point of view of the Ego, or Thinker, or his relation between them.

In the Hall of Ignorance the form controls, and the material side of things has the predominance. Man is there polarised in the personality or lower self. In the Hall of Learning the higher self, or Ego, strives to dominate that form until gradually a point of equilibrium is reached where the man is controlled entirely by neither. Later the Ego controls more and more, until in the Hall of Wisdom it dominates in the three lower worlds, and in increasing degree the inherent divinity assumes the mastery. (1-11/2)

(n) INTUITION

1. *Intuition is the synthetic understanding which is the prerogative of the soul, and it only becomes possible when the soul, on its own level, is reaching in two directions*: towards the Monad, and towards the integrated and, perhaps (even if only temporarily) co-ordinated and at-oned personality. It is the first indication of a deeply subjective unification which will find its consummation at the third initiation.

Intuition is a comprehensive grip of the principle of universality, and when it is functioning there is, momentarily at least, a complete loss of the sense of separateness. At its highest point it is known as that Universal Love which has no relation to sentiment or to the affectional reaction but is predominantly in the nature of an identification with all beings. Then is true compassion known; then does criticism become impossible; then only is the divine germ seen as latent in all forms.

Intuition is light itself, and when it is functioning, the world is seen as light, and the light bodies of all forms become gradually apparent. This brings with it the ability to contact the light centre in all forms, and thus again an essential relationship is established and the sense of superiority and separateness recedes into the background.

Intuition, therefore, brings with its appearance three qualities:

(a) *Illumination.* By illumination I do not mean the light in the head. That is incidental and phenomenal, and many truly intuitive people are entirely unaware of this light. The light to which I refer is that which irradiates the Way. It is "the light of the intellect", which really means that which illumines the mind and which can reflect itself in that mental apparatus which is held "steady in the light". This is the "Light of the World", a Reality which is eternally existent, but which can be discovered only when the individual interior light is recognised as such. This is the "Light of the Ages", which shineth ever more until the Day be with us. The intuition is therefore the recognition in oneself, not theoretically, but as a fact in one's experience, of one's complete identification with the Universal Mind, of one's constituting a part of the great World Life, and of one's participation in the eternal persisting Existence.

(b) *Understanding.* . . . To have understanding involves an increased ability to love all beings and yet, at the same time, to preserve personality detachment. This detachment can be so easily founded on an inability to love, in a selfish concern for one's own comfort—physical, mental or spiritual, and above all, emotional. First ray people dread emotion, and despise it, but sometimes they have to swing into an emotional condition before they can use emotional sensitivity in the right manner.

Understanding involves contact with life as an integrated personality, plus egoic reaction to the group purposes and plans. It connotes personality-soul unification, wide experience, and a rapid activity of the indwelling Christ principle. Intuitional understanding is always spontaneous. Where the reasoning *to* an understanding enters, it is not the activity of the intuition.

(c) *Love.* As earlier said, this is not affectionate sentiment, or the possession of a loving disposition; these two latter aspects are incidental and sequential. When the intuition is developed, both affection and the possession of a spirit of loving outgo will necessarily, in their pure form, be demonstrated, but that which produces these is something much more deep and comprehensive. It is that synthetic, inclusive grasp of the life and needs of all beings (I have chosen these two words with intent!) which it is the high prerogative of a divine Son of God to operate. It negates all that builds barriers, makes criticism, and produces separation. It sees no distinction, even when it appreciates *need,* and it produces in one who loves as a soul immediate identification with that which is loved. (10-2/5)

2. Those who have . . . trained the mind in the art of clear thinking, the focussing of the attention, and consequent receptivity to truth, have always been with us, but hitherto have been few and far between. They are the outstanding minds of the ages. But now they are many and increasingly found. The minds of the race are in process of training and many are hovering on the borders of a new knowledge. The intuition which guides all advanced thinkers into the newer fields of learning, is but the forerunner of that omniscience which characterises the soul. The truth about all things exists, and we call it omniscience, infallibility, the "correct knowledge" of the Hindu philosophy. When man grasps a fragment of it and absorbs it into the racial consciousness, we call it the formulation of a law, a discovery of one or other of nature's processes. Hitherto this has been a slow and piecemeal undertaking. Later, and before so very long, light will pour in, truth will be revealed and the race will enter upon its heritage—the heritage of the soul. (4-15/6)

3. *Right Action:*

What is the criterion whereby a man may know which out of several lines of activity is the right line to take? Is there, in other words, a re-

92 THE SOUL

vealing something which will enable a man unerringly to choose the right action and go the right way? The question has no reference to a choice existing between the path of spiritual endeavour and the way of the man of the world. It refers to right action when faced with a choice. . . .

(The aspirant) can wait, resting back upon an inner sense of direction, knowing that in due time he will ascertain, through the closing of all doors but one, which is the way he should go. For there is only one open door through which such a man can go. Intuition is needed for its recognition. . . . In (this) case, mistakes are impossible and only right action can be taken.

. . . All resolves itself into an understanding of one's place upon the ladder of evolution. Only the highly advanced man can know the times and seasons and can adequately discern the subtle distinction between a psychic inclination and the intuition. . . . Let not the man who should use his common sense and take a line of action based upon the use of the concrete mind, practise the higher method of waiting for a door to open. He is expecting too much in the place where he is. He has to learn through right decision and right use of the mind to solve his problems. Through this method he will grow, for the roots of intuitive knowledge are laid deep within the soul, and the soul, therefore, must be contacted before the intuition can work. One hint only can here be given: The intuition ever concerns itself with group activity and not with petty personal affairs. If you are still a man centered in the personality, recognise it, and with the equipment available, govern your actions. If you know yourself to be functioning as a soul and are lost in the interest of others, untrammelled by selfish desire, then your just obligation will be met, your responsibilities shouldered, your group work carried forward, and the way will unfold before you, whilst you do the next thing and fulfil the next duty. Out of the duty, perfectly performed, will emerge those larger duties which we call world work; out of the carrying of family responsibilities will come that strengthening of our shoulders which will enable us to carry those of the larger group. What then is the criterion?

For the high grade aspirant, let me repeat, the choice of action depends upon a sound use of the lower mind, the employment of a sane common-sense, and the forgetfulness of selfish comfort and personal ambition. This leads to the fulfilment of duty. For the disciple there will be the automatic and necessary carrying forward of all the above, plus the use of the intuition which will reveal the moment when wider group responsibilities can be justly shouldered and carried simultaneously with those of the smaller group. Ponder on this. The intuition reveals not the way ambition can be fed, nor the manner in which desire for selfish advancement can be gratified.   (4-67/70)

4. When the use of the subjective instrument becomes *voluntary* and a man knows how it should be employed, when he is using it, and can discontinue its use to resume it at will, then his whole status changes and his usefulness increases. Through the use of the mind humanity has become aware of the purposes and employment of the physical apparatus. Now through the use of a still higher faculty, which is characteristic of the soul, he enters into voluntary and intelligent control of his instrument, and learns to understand the purposes for which it exists. This higher faculty is the *intuition.*   (4-167)

5. I urge upon each and all who read these Instructions the necessity for renewed effort to fit themselves for service by a conscious and deliberate effort to develop the intuition and to achieve illumination. Every human being who reaches the goal of light and wisdom, automatically has a field of influence which extends both up and down, and which reaches both inwards to the source of light and outwards into the "fields of darkness". When he has thus attained he will become a conscious centre of life giving force, and will be so without effort. He will stimulate, energise and vivify to fresh efforts all lives that he contacts, be they his fellow aspirants, or an animal, or a flower. He will act as a transmitter of light in the darkness. He will dispel the glamour around him and let in the radiance of reality.

When large numbers of the sons of men can so act, then the human family will enter upon its destined work of planetary service. Its mission is to act as a bridge between the world of spirit and the world of material forms. All grades of matter meet in man, and all the states of consciousness are possible to him. Mankind can work in all directions and lift the subhuman kingdoms into heaven and bring heaven down to earth. (4-537/8)

6. The power of the intuition, which is the goal of much of the work which disciples must do, requires the unfoldment of another faculty in man. The intuition is a function of the mind also, and when rightly used, it enables man to grasp reality with clarity and to see that reality free from glamour and the illusions of the three worlds. When the intuition functions in any human being, he is enabled to take direct and correct action, for he is in touch with the Plan, with pure and unadulterated fact and undistorted ideas—free from illusion and coming direct from the

divine or universal mind. The unfoldment of this faculty will bring about
a world recognition of the Plan and this is the greatest achievement of
the intuition in this present world cycle. When that Plan is sensed, there
comes the realisation of the unity of all beings, of the synthesis of
world evolution, and of the unity of the divine objective. All life and all
forms are seen then in their true perspective; a right sense of values and
of time then eventuates. When the Plan is truly intuited and at first hand,
then constructive effort becomes inevitable and there is no lost motion.
It is the partial realisation of the Plan and its interpretation at second or
third hand by the ignorant, which is responsible for the wasted effort
and the foolish impulses which characterise the present occult and world
organisations.   (5-25)

7. *Glamour and the Intuition*: The objective before the Hierarchy at this
time is to break and dissipate the world glamour. This has to happen on
a world scale, just as it happens in the life of every disciple. Just as a man
shifts his focus of consciousness (when on the Path of Discipleship) on
to the mental plane, and learns to smash the glamour which has hitherto
held him on the astral plane, so the problem before the Hierarchy today
is to bring about a similar happening in the life of humanity as a whole,
for humanity is at the cross roads, and its consciousness is being rapidly
focussed on the mental plane. A death blow must be struck at the world
illusion for it holds the sons of men in thrall. By learning to break
through the glamour in their own lives and to live in the light of the intuition, disciples can strengthen the hands of Those Whose task it is to
awaken the intuition in man.   (5-26)

8. The manifestation of intuitive perception upon the physical plane is
greatly aided by the effort to read, to understand and then to express
that understanding in words. This is never an easy task for a natural
intuitive . . ., but it is one that will bring high reward.   (5-329)

9. The intuition is a growth, primarily, in sensitivity and in an inner
response to the soul. This must be cultivated with care, and no attention
should be paid to the factor of time.   (5-595)

10. *Spiritual instinct* is the capacity of the soul to register contact with
the Hierarchy of which the soul is inherently a part, just as in the body a
man's mechanical, instinctual responses, reactions and reflexes are an integral part of the material mechanism. In the case of the spiritual instincts, it is the intuition which interprets and illumines the mind
(5-697/8)

11. Initiation is never taken unless the intuition is becoming active. Spiritual instinct, the lowest aspect of the intuition, indicates readiness for the first initiation; an illumined mind and spiritual intelligence are the definite sign that a man can take the second initiation, whilst spiritual perception or intuitive instinct signifies preparedness for the Transfiguration, the third initiation. (6-267)

12. (The disciple) learns finally to substitute the intuition—with its swiftness and its infallibility—for the slow and laborious work of the mind, with its deviousness, its illusions, its errors, its dogmatisms and its separative thinking and cultures. (6-415)

13. That which is the opposite pole of illusion is, as you well know, the intuition. The intuition is that recognition of reality which becomes possible as glamour and illusion disappear. An intuitive reaction to truth will take place when—along a particular line of approach to truth—the disciple has succeeded in quieting the thought-form-making propensities of the mind, so that light can flow directly, and without any deviation, from the higher spiritual worlds. The intuition can begin to make its presence felt when glamour no longer grips the lower man, and a man's low or high desires, interpreted emotionally or self-centredly, can no longer come between his brain consciousness and the soul. Fleeting moments of this high freedom come to all true aspirants at times during their life struggle. They have then an intuitive flash of understanding. The outline of the future and the nature of truth sweeps momentarily through their consciousness, and life is never again exactly the same thing. They have had their guarantee that all struggle is warranted and will evoke its adequate reward. (10-67)

14. The intuition is a higher power than is the mind, and is a faculty latent in the Spiritual Triad; it is the power of pure reason, an expression of the buddhic principle, and lies beyond the world of the ego and of form. Only when a man is an initiate can the exercise of the true intuition become normally possible. By that I mean that the intuition will then be easily operative as is the mind principle in the case of an actively intelligent person. The intuition, however, will make its presence felt much earlier in extremity, or on urgent demand. (10-81/2)

15. The intuition is the source or the bestower of revelation. Through the intuition, progressive understanding of the ways of God in the world and on behalf of humanity are revealed. (10-135/6)

16. Even the neophyte upon the way of the intuition can begin to develop in himself the power to recognise that which the lower mind cannot give him. Some thought of revealing potency, to be used for the helping of the many, may drop into his mind; some new light upon an old, old truth may penetrate, releasing the truth from the trammels of orthodoxy, thus illumining his consciousness. This he must use for all and not for himself alone. Little by little, he learns the way into the world of the intuition; day by day, and year by year, he becomes more sensitive to divine Ideas, and more apt in appropriating them wisely for the use of his fellow men.

The hope of the world and the dispelling of illusion lies in the development of intuitives and their conscious training. There are many natural intuitives whose work is a blend of the higher psychism, with flashes of true intuition. There must be the training of the exact intuitive. Paralleling their intuitive response and their effort to precipitate their intuition into the world of human thought, there must also be the steady development of the human mind, so that it can grasp and apprehend what is projected, and in this too lies the hope of the race.   (10-184)

17. The intuition is concerned with nothing whatsoever in the three worlds of human experience, but only with the perceptions of the Spiritual Triad and with the world of ideas. *The intuition is to the world of meaning what the mind is to the three worlds of experience.* It produces understanding, just as the light of soul produces knowledge through the medium of that experience. Knowledge is not a purely mental reaction, but is something which is found on all levels, and is instinctual in some form in all kingdoms. This is axiomatic. The five senses bring physical plane knowledge; psychic sensitivity brings a knowledge of the astral plane; the mind brings intellectual perception, but all three are aspects of the light of knowledge (coming from the soul) as it informs its vehicles of expression in the vast threefold environment in which it chooses to imprison itself for purposes of development.

On a higher turn of the spiral, the intuition is the expression of the threefold Spiritual Triad, placing it in relation to the higher levels of divine expression; it is a result of the life of the Monad—an energy which carries revelation of divine purpose. It is in the world of this divine revelation that the disciple learns eventually to work, and in which the initiate consciously functions. Of this higher experience, the active life of the three worlds is a distorted expression, but constitutes also the training ground in which capacity to live the *initiate life of intuitional perception* and to serve the Plan, is slowly developed. . . . Disciples will reach a point in their development where they will show whether they are reacting to the light of the soul or to the intuitional perception of the Triad. (10-194/5)

18. *Future Intuitional Civilisation*: The intuition is the infallibly sensitive agent, latent in every human being; it is based, as you know, upon the direct knowledge, unimpeded by any instrument normally functioning in the three worlds. Of this intuitional future age, Christ is the *Seed Man*, for "He knew what was in man". Today, a group or a unit of groups can be the nurturers of the seed of the intuition; the cultivation of sensitivity to telepathic impression is one of the most potent agencies in developing the coming use of the intuitive faculty. (11-35)

19. An intuition is an idea clothed in etheric substance, and the moment a man becomes responsive to those ideas, he can begin to master the techniques of etheric control. . . . An idea which comes from the intuitive levels of the divine consciousness, is a true idea. It is noted or apprehended by the man who has within his equipment substance of the same quality—for it is the magnetic relation between the man and the idea which has made its apprehension possible. (11-189)

24. LIGHT

1. The object for which life takes form and the purpose of manifested being, is the unfoldment of consciousness, or the revelation of the soul. This might be called the *Theory of the Evolution of Light*. When it is realised that even the modern scientist is saying that light and matter are synonymous terms, thus echoing the teaching of the East, it becomes apparent that through the interplay of the poles, and through the friction of the pairs of opposites, light flashes forth. The goal of evolution is found to be a gradual series of light demonstrations. Veiled and hidden by every form, lies light. As evolution proceeds, matter becomes increasingly a better conductor of the light, thus demonstrating the accuracy of the statement of the Christ "I am the Light of the World". (4-9/10)

2. When a man literally walks in the light of his soul and the clear light of the sun pours through him—revealing the Path—it reveals at the same time the Plan. Simultaneously, however, he becomes aware of the fact that the Plan is very far as yet from consummation. The dark becomes

more truly apparent; the chaos and the misery and failure of the world groups stand revealed; the filth and dust of the warring forces are noted, and the whole sorrow of the world bears down upon the astounded yet illuminated aspirant. Can he stand this pressure? Can he become indeed acquainted with grief and yet rejoice forever in the divine consciousness? Has he the ability to face what the light reveals and still go his way with serenity, sure of the ultimate triumph of good? Will he be overwhelmed by the surface evil and forget the heart of Love which beats behind all outer seeming? This situation should ever be remembered by the disciple, or he will be shattered by that which he has discovered.

But with the advent of the light, he becomes aware of a new (for him) form of energy. He learns to work in a new field of opportunity. The realm of the mind opens up before him, and he discovers that he can differentiate between the emotional nature and the mental. He discovers also that the mind can be made to assume the position of the controller, and that the sentient forces respond with obedience to mental energies. "The light of reason" brings this about—light that is always present in man but which only becomes significant and potent when seen and known, either phenomenally or intuitionally.   (4-355)

3. In the light of the Whole, the light of the little self fades out, just as the light that is inherent in every atom of the body is gathered together and obliterated in the light of the soul when that blazes forth in all its glory.

When this stage of selflessness, of service, of subordination to the One Self, and of sacrifice to the group becomes the objective, a man has reached the point where he can be received into that group of world mystics and knowers and group workers which is the physical plane reflection of the planetary Hierarchy.   (4-397/8)

4. "I am a messenger of Light. I am a pilgrim on the way of love. I do not walk alone but know myself as one with all great souls, and one with them in service. Their strength is mine. This strength I claim. My strength is theirs, and this I freely give. A soul, I walk on earth. I represent the ONE".   (5-140)

5. Be not discouraged. By our failures and our reactions to glamour, we learn to tread with confidence the Way of Light. . . . Learn from the past but refuse to be held by that past. Do not let the words or the influence of anyone lead you. May the light of your own soul lead you from strength to strength, and reveal to you a purity of motive which will flood your life with love.   (5-240)

6. The whole theme of revelation is the revelation of light, and that implies many different interpretations of the word "light"; it concerns the discovery of the lighted areas of being which otherwise remain unknown, and therefore hidden. We create light; we employ light; we discover greater lights which serve to reveal to us the Unknown God. It is the guiding light within us which eventually reveals those brighter lights which usher in the process of revelation. I am, my brother, speaking symbolically as you can well understand.   (6-436)

7. It might be stated that this process of bringing light into dark places falls naturally into three stages:

1. The stage wherein the beginner and the aspirant endeavour to eradicate glamour out of their own life by the use of the light of the mind. The *light of knowledge* is a major dispelling agent in the earlier phases of the task and effectively eliminates the various glamours which veil the truth from the aspirant.

2. The stage wherein the aspirant and disciple work with the light of the soul. This is the *light of wisdom* which is the interpreted result of long experience, and this streams forth, blending with the light of knowledge.

3. The stage wherein the disciple and the initiate work with the *light of the intuition.* It is through the blended medium of the light of knowledge (personality light) and the light of wisdom (soul light) that the Light is seen, known and appropriated. This light puts out the lesser lights through the pure radiance of its power.

You have therefore the light of knowledge, the light of wisdom, and the light of the intuition, and these are three definite stages or aspects of the One Light.   (10-191/2)

8. The Science of the Antahkarana, technically speaking, and for group purpose, is especially the science of light manifestation, with its results of revelation and consequent changes. It should be remembered that:

(a) Light is substantial, and from the angle of the spirit is a sublimation or higher form of material matter.

(b) Light is also the quality or major characteristic of the soul in its own realm, and of the etheric body (a reflection of the soul eventually) in the three worlds of human evolution.

(c) The object of the science with which we are dealing, is to fuse the lower and the upper lights, so that one light shines forth in physical manifestation, and a synthesis of light is consequently brought about.

(d) Technically speaking, two light bodies exist—the vital or etheric body and the soul vehicle. One is the result of aeons of incarnating life, and becomes in time a powerful repository of energies gathered out of a wide range of contacts, though conditioned by the ray type in its three aspects. The etheric body exists and is today functioning powerfully. The soul body is in process of being slowly constructed, and is that "house not made with hands, eternal in the heavens" to which the New Testament refers (II Cor. 5: 1). It is interesting to note that the Old Testament refers to the etheric body (Ecc. 12: 6-7) and its construction, and the New Testament deals with the building of the spiritual body.   (12-143/4)

9. Light, or radiation (is) the effect of the interplay between the life and the environment.

. . . The soul is that factor in matter (or rather that which emerges out of the contact between spirit and matter) which produces sentient response and what we call consciousness in its various forms; it is also that latent or subjective essential quality which makes itself felt as light or luminous radiation. It is the "self-shining from within" which is characteristic of all forms. Matter, *per se*, and in its undifferentiated state, prior to being swept into activity through the creative process, is *not* possessed of soul and does not therefore possess the qualities of response and of radiation. Only when—in the creative and evolutionary process—these two are brought into conjunction and fusion, does the soul appear and give to these two aspects of divinity the opportunity to manifest as a trinity, and the chance to demonstrate sentient activity and magnetic radiatory light. . . . It might be stated that only when the soul aspect is dominant is the response apparatus (the form nature of man) fulfilling its complete destiny, and only then does true magnetic radiation and the pure shining forth of light become possible. Symbolically, in the early stages of human evolution, man is, from the angle of consciousness, relatively unresponsive and unconscious, as is matter in its early stages in the formative process. The achievement of full awareness is of course the goal of the evolutionary process. Again symbolically speaking, the unevolved man emits or manifests no light. The light in the head is invisible, though the clairvoyant investigators would see the dim glow of the light within the elements which constitute the body, and the light hidden in the atoms which constitute the form nature.

As evolution proceeds, these dim points of "dark light" intensify their glow; the light within the head flickers at intervals during the life of the average man, and becomes a shining light as he enters upon the path of discipleship. When he becomes an initiate, the light of the atoms is so bright, and the light in the head so intense (with a paralleling stimulation of the centres of force in the body), that the light body appears. Eventually this body of light becomes externalised and of greater prominence than the dense tangible physical body. This is the body of light in which the true son of God consciously dwells. After the third initiation, the dual light becomes accentuated and takes on a still greater brilliancy through the blending with it of the energy of spirit. This is not really the admission or the re-combining of a third light, but the fanning of the light matter and the light of the soul into greater glory through the *Breath* of the spirit. . . . In the understanding of these aspects of light comes a truer perspective as to the nature of the fires in the human expression of divinity. (14-130/1)

10. You are in process of incarnation; you are following your choosen way. Is the house you are building yet lit? Is it a lighted house? Or is it a dark prison? If it is a lighted house, you will attract to its light and warmth all who are around you and the magnetic pull of your soul, whose nature is light and love, will save many. If you are still an isolated soul, you will have to pass through the horrors of a more complete isolation and loneliness, treading alone the dark way of the soul. Yet this isolation, this loneliness and this separation in the dark night, are all part of the Great Illusion. It is, however, an illusion into which the whole of humanity is now precipitated in preparation for unity, freedom and release. Some are lost in the illusion and know not what is reality and truth. Others walk free in the world of illusion for the purposes of saving and lifting their brothers, and if you cannot do this, you will have to learn so to walk. (16-343)

(a) THE LIGHT OF THE SOUL

1. The attention of a Master is attracted to a man by the brilliance of the indwelling light. When that light has reached a certain intensity, when the bodies are composed of a certain grade of matter, when the aura has attained a certain hue, and when the vibration has reached a specific rate and measure, and when a man's life commences to *sound occultly* in the three worlds (which sound is to be heard through the life of service), some one particular Master begins to test him out by the application of some higher vibration, and by the study of his reaction to that vibration. The choice of a pupil by a Master is governed by past karma and by old as-

sociation, by the ray on which they both may be found, and by the need of the hour.   (2-274)

2. Through the medium of the light of the soul, the soul can be known. Therefore seek the light of your own soul, and know that soul as your director. When soul contact is established, your own soul will, if I may so express it, introduce you to your Master.   (4-594)

3. Above all I would say: Seek to recover the fervour of your earlier, spiritual aspiration and self-discipline. If you have never lost it (though many disciples have) seek to force that energy of inspiration to work out in an effective display of definite action upon the physical plane. How, you ask, my brothers? By increasing the radiance of your light in the world, through love and meditation, so that others may turn to you as to a beacon light in the dark night of life which seems in this century to have descended upon humanity; seek to love more than you have ever believed possible, so that others—frozen and chilled by life circumstance and the present horror of human existence—may turn to you for warmth and comforting. What I and all who are affiliated with the Hierarchy seek to do at this time of desperate crisis is to find those who are dependable points of living energy, and through them pour out the love, the strength and the light which the world needs and must have if this storm is to be weathered. I ask you to render this service to me and to humanity. I ask nothing spectacular; it will, however, require a strenuous effort of your souls if you are to respond adequately; I ask nothing impossible; I would remind you that the apathy of the physical body and brain, the inertia of the feeling nature, and the sense of futility of the mind when confronted with large issues, will seem to hinder you.   (5-99/100)

4. My word for you is: Work more in the light and see all people as in that light with you. All that any disciple or aspirant has to do in relation to his fellow men, is to stimulate the light that is in them, leaving them free to walk in their own light and way upon the Path.   (5-417)

5. Let the light of your soul direct and the love of your soul determine attitudes, guide policies, and release into your field of service the power which will bring the desired results.   (5-489)

6. For you there must be the steady growth of the light of your own soul, fostered by meditation, expressed in selfless service, and increasing in radiance through the intensification of your soul's life. Live, therefore, as a soul and forget the personality. Give not so much time to the considera-

tion of the faults and mistakes of the past. Self-depreciation is not necessarily a sign of spiritual growth. It is often the first result of a soul contact, and means the revelation of personality limitations covering many years. That has a temporary value, provided you again turn your eyes to the soul. Forgetting the things that lie behind, let the light of your soul lead you where it will. (5-599)

7. "I am one with the light which shines through my soul, my brothers and my Master". (6-647)

8. "From darkness lead us to light. I tread the way of life and light because I am a soul. With me there walk my brothers and my Master. Therefore, within, without, and every side, there is light and love and strength". (6-648)

9. Let the light and radiance of the soul illumine your service and let your intellect not prove to be the dominating factor. Let spontaneous love and not a cultivated kindness condition your relations with your fellow men. (6-656)

10. The quality and the major characteristic of the soul is light. Therefore, if that light is to be used and that quality expressed by the disciple and the worker, he must first of all achieve a recognised contact with the soul through meditation. (10-140)

11. It might be said that the inner light is like a searchlight, swinging out into the world of glamour and of human struggle from what one Master has called "the pedestal of the soul and the spiritual tower or beacon". . . . Power to use this light as a dissipating agent only comes when these symbols are dropped and the server begins to regard *himself* as the light and as the irradiating centre. Herein lies the reason for some of the technicalities of the occult science. The esotericist knows that in every atom of his body is to be found a point of light. He knows that the nature of the soul is light. For aeons he walks by means of the light engendered within his vehicles, by the light within the atomic substance of his body and is, therefore, guided by the light of matter. Later, he discovers the light of the soul. Later still, he learns to fuse and blend soul light and material light. Then he shines forth as a Light bearer, the purified light of matter and the light of the soul being blended and focussed. The use of this focussed light, as it dispels individual glamour, teaches the disciples the early stages of the technique which will dispel group glamour and eventually world glamour. (10-196/7)

12. The soul must be seen by the probationer as the sun of the life. All lesser lights must be put out by the light of the central luminary; all little fires must be obliterated by solar fire. The solar Angel controls the personality life and its forces. This, in the New Age, is the goal of the probationary path and of the applicant for discipleship. Hitherto it has been the goal of all the teaching given anent the Path of Discipleship, but the higher rate of intelligence of the modern applicant warrants a change, and as time goes on, the present requirements for disciples, up to and including the second initiation, will be the requirements for the Probationary Path.   (18-114)

(b) THE SEARCH FOR LIGHT

1. The human being—simply because he is himself fragmentary and incomplete—has always this urge within himself to seek other and greater than himself. It is this that drives him back to the centre of his being, and it is this that forces him to take the path of return to the All-Self. Ever, throughout the aeons, does the Prodigal Son arise and go to his Father, and always latent within him is the memory of the Father's home and the glory there to be found. But the human mind is so constituted that the search for light and for the ideal is necessarily long and difficult. "Now we see through a glass darkly, but then face to face"; now we catch glimpses through the occasional windows we pass in our ascension of the ladder, of other and greater Beings than ourselves; They hold out to us helping hands, and call to us in clarion tones to struggle bravely on if we hope to stand where They are now standing.

We sense beauties and glories surrounding us that as yet we cannot revel in; they flit into our vision, and we touch the glory at a lofty moment, only again to lose the contact and to sink back again into the murky gloom that envelops. But we *know* that outside and further on is something to be desired; we learn also the mystery that that external wonder can only be contacted by withdrawing within, till the centre of consciousness is found that vibrates in tune with those dimly realised wonders, and with those radiant Souls Who call Themselves our Elder Brothers. Only by trampling on the external sheaths that veil and hide the inner centre, do we achieve the goal, and find the Ones we seek. Only by the domination of all forms, and the bringing of those forms under the rule of the God within, can we find the God in all, for it is only the sheaths in which we move upon the plane of being that hide from us our inner God, and that shut us off from Those in Whom the God transcends all outer forms.

The great Initiate, Who voiced the words I quote, added still other words of radiant truth: "Then shall we know even as we are known". The future holds for each and all who strive, who unselfishly serve and occultly meditate, the promise of knowing Those Who already have full knowledge of the struggler. Therein lies the hope for the student of meditation; as he struggles, as he fails, as he perseveres, and as he laboriously reiterates from day to day the arduous task of concentration and of mind control, there stand on the inner side Those Who know him, and Who watch with eager sympathy the progress that he makes.

Forget not the earlier part of the Initiate's remarks where he points out the way whereby the darkness is dispelled, and knowledge of the Great Ones is reached. He emphasises that only by *love* is the path of light and knowledge trodden. Why this emphasis upon love? Because the goal for all is love, and therein lies the merging. . . .

This is the path to be trodden by one and all, and the method is meditation. The goal is perfect love and wisdom; the steps are the surmounting of sub-plane after sub-plane on all the three planes; the method is that of occult meditation; the reward is the continuous expansion of consciousness that puts a man eventually en rapport with his own Ego, with other selves, with the waiting eager Master to Whom he is assigned, with fellow disciples and more advanced Initiates whom he may contact in that Master's aura, till he finally contacts the One Initiator, is admitted into the Secret Place, and knows the mystery that underlies consciousness itself. (2-257/9)

2. Grant me the light that I may shine. Let me throughout the world of time and space radiate light, create a light, transmit the Light, and treading thus the Lighted Way (which is my Lighted Self), enter the light, and so return the light to those who need, to Those likewise from whence it came. (6-561)

(c) THE LIGHT IN THE HEAD

Unless there is indication that the man is what is termed esoterically "a lighted lamp" it is useless for the Master to waste His time. The light in the head, when present, is indicative of:

(a) The functioning to a greater or less extent of the pineal gland, which is (as is well known) the seat of the soul and the organ of spiritual perception. It is in this gland that the first physiological changes take place incident upon soul contact, and this contact is brought about

through definite work along meditation lines, mind control, and the inflow of spiritual force.

(b) The aligning of the man on the physical plane, with his ego, soul
or higher self on the mental plane, and the subordination of the physical
plane life and nature to the impress and control of the soul. . . .

(c) The downflow of force via the sutratma, magnetic cord, or thread
from the soul to the brain via the mind body. The whole secret of spiritual vision, correct perception, and right contact, lies in the proper
appreciation of the above statement. . . . The light of illumination
streams down into the brain cavity and throws into objectivity three
fields of knowledge. This is often forgotten and hence the undue distress
and premature interpretations of the partially illuminated disciple or
probationer.

The light first throws into relief and brings into the foreground of consciousness those thought-forms and entities which depict the lower life,
and which (in their aggregate) form the Dweller on the Threshold.

Thus the first thing of which the aspirant becomes aware, is that which
he knows to be undesirable, and the revelation of his own unworthiness
and limitations, as the undesirable constituents of his own aura burst on
his vision. The darkness which is in him is intensified by the light which
glimmers faintly from the centre of his being, and frequently he despairs
of himself and descends into the depths of depression. All mystics bear
witness to this and it is a period which must be lived through until the
pure light of day drives all shadows and darkness away, and little by
little the life is brightened and lightened until the sun in the head is shining in all its glory.

(d) Finally, the light in the head is indicative of the finding of the
Path and there remains then for the man to study and understand the
technique whereby the light is centralised, intensified, entered and eventually becomes that magnetic line (like unto a spider's thread) which
can be followed back until the source of the lower manifestation is
reached and the soul consciousness is entered. The above language is
symbolic and yet vitally accurate, but is expressed thus in order to convey information to those who know, and protect those who as yet know
not.

"The path of the just is as a shining Light" and yet at the same time a
man has to become that path himself. He enters the light and becomes the

light and functions then as a lamp set in a dark place, carrying illumination to others and lighting the way before them.   (4-183/5)

(d)   THE PATH OF LIGHT

1. From this hour and henceforth upon the *Way,* I seek to *Be.* I seek no more to know, because this life has taught me how to know, and with this knowledge gained, I now can serve by *Being.*

Before me streams the Path of Light. I see the Way. Behind me lies the mountain path, with stones and cobbles on the way. Around me are the thorns. My feet are tired. But straight ahead stretches the Lighted Way and on that Way I walk.   (6-648)

2. The Path of Evolution is in fact the path of recognitions, leading to revelation. The whole process of evolution is initiatory in character, leading from one expansion of consciousness to another, until the worlds of the formless and of form stand revealed in the light which the initiate generates and in which he walks. These lights are varied and variously revealing; there is:

1. The light of matter itself, found in every atom of substance.

2. The light of the vital or etheric vehicle—a light which is the reflection of the One Light because it unifies the three types of light within the three worlds.

3. The light of the instinct.

4. The light of the intellect or the light of knowledge.

5. The light of the soul.

6. The light of the intuition.

From light to light we pass, from revelation to revelation, until we pass out of the realm of light into the realm of life, which is as yet to us pure darkness.

It will be obvious to you that this increasing light brings with it a constantly developing series of revelations which, like all else in the world of human experience, unfolds before the eyes first of all the world of forms, then the world of ideals, then the nature of the soul, of ideas, and of divinity. I am choosing but a few of the words which embody the revelation and are symbolic of its character. But all these revelations constitute one great unified revelation which is slowly unfolding before the eyes of humanity. The light of the personal lower self reveals to man the world of form, of matter, of instinct, of desire and of mind; the light of the soul reveals the nature of the relation of these forms of life to the world of the formless and of the conflict between the real and the unreal. The light of the intuition unfolds before the vision of the *soul within the personality,* the nature of God, and the unity of the Whole. The restlessness of material desire, seeking its satisfaction in the three worlds, eventually gives place to aspiration towards soul contact and soul life. This in its turn is recognised as a step towards those great fundamental experiences to which we give the names of the five major initiations. These reveal to man the hitherto unrealised fact of his non-separateness and of the relation of his individual will to the divine will.   (10-205/6)

3. The new culture will emerge and come into being, as all of those who have a consciousness of light, and the goal of pure service (which such a consciousness inevitably entails) proceed with their appointed task—a self-appointed task in every case—of living and teaching the truth about light, as opportunity offers.   (12-142)

(e) ILLUMINATION

1. It is illumination that the majority of aspirants . . . must seek; and they must cultivate the power to use the mind as a reflector of soul light, turning it upon the levels of glamour, and therefore dissipating it. The difficulty, my brothers, is to do so when in the midst of the agonies and deceptions of glamour. It requires a quiet withdrawing in mind and thought and desire from the world in which the personality habitually works, and the centering of the consciousness in the world of the soul, there silently and patiently to await developments, knowing that the light will shine forth, and illumination eventually take place.   (10-82)

2. I will . . . briefly define illumination, asking you to bear in mind that we are not here dealing with the illumination which reveals Reality, or the nature of the soul, or which makes clear to your vision the kingdom of the soul, but with that form of illumination which is thrown down by the soul into the world of the astral plane. This involves the conscious use of light and its employment, first of all, as a searchlight, scanning the astral horizon and localising the glamour which is causing the trouble, and secondly, as a focussed distribution of light, turned with intention upon that area of the astral plane wherein it is proposed that some effort be made to dissipate the fog and mist which are there concentrated.   (10-140)

3. In defining illumination as the antithesis of glamour, it is obvious that my remarks must necessarily be limited to certain aspects of illumination, and will only concern those directed forms of work and those presentations of the problem which will concern the use of light upon the astral plane. . . . There are many other definitions possible, for the light of the soul is like an immense searchlight, the beams of which can be turned in many directions and focused on many levels. We are, however, only concerned here with its specialised use.

Illumination and the light of knowledge can be regarded as synonymous terms and many glamours can be dissipated and dispersed when subjected to the potency of the informative mind, for the mind is essentially the subduer of emotion through the presentation of fact. The problem is to induce the individual or the race or nation, which is acting under the influence of glamour, to call in the mental power of assessing the situation, and subject it to a calm, cold scrutiny. Glamour and emotion play into each other's hands, and feeling runs so strong usually in relation to glamour, that it is impossible to bring in the light of knowledge with ease and effectiveness.

Illumination and perception of truth are also synonymous terms, but it should be remembered that the truth in this case is not truth on the abstract planes, but concrete and knowable truth—truth which can be formulated and expressed in concrete form and terms. Where the light of truth is called in, glamour automatically disappears, even if only for a temporary period. But, again, difficulty arises, because few people care to face the actual truth, for it involves eventually the abandonment of the beloved glamour, and the ability to recognise error and to admit mistakes, and this the false pride of the mind will not permit. Again I would assure you that humility is one of the most potent factors in releasing the illuminating power of the mind, as it reflects and transmits the light of the soul. The determined facing of the factual life, and the stern recognition of truth—coldly, calmly, and dispassionately—will greatly facilitate the calling in of the flood of illumination which will suffice to dispel glamour. (10-144/5)

4. There is no life activity, no vocational calling, no mental occupation and no condition, which cannot provide the key to the unlocking of the door into the desired wider world, or serve to lead a man to the mountain top from which the wider horizon can be seen, and the larger vision grasped. A man must learn to recognise that his chosen school of thought, his peculiar vocation, his particular calling in life, and his personal trend,

are only part of a greater whole, and his problem is to integrate *consciously* his small life activity into the world activity.

It is this we call *illumination* for lack of a better word. All knowledge is a form of light, for it throws light into areas of awareness of which we have hitherto been unconscious. All wisdom is a form of light, for it reveals to us the world of meaning which lies behind the outer form. All understanding is an evocation of light, for it causes us to become aware of, or conscious of, the causes which are producing the outer forms which surround us (including our own) and which condition the world of meaning of which they are the expression. But when this fact is first seen, grasped, and when the initial revelation has come, when the place of the part in relation to the whole is sensed, and when the world which includes our little world is first contacted, there is always a moment of crisis and a period of danger. Then, as familiarity grows and our feet have wandered in and out of the door we have opened, and we have accustomed ourselves to the light which the unshuttered window has released into our little world of daily living, other psychological dangers eventuate. We are in danger of thinking that what we have seen is all there is to see, and thus —on a higher turn of the spiral and in a larger sense—we repeat the dangers (earlier considered) of undue emphasis, of wrong focus, of narrow minded belief, and *ideé fixe*. We become obsessed with the idea of the soul; we forget its need of a vehicle of expression; we begin to live in an abstracted, detached world of being and of feeling, and we fail to keep in contact with the factual life of physical plane expression. We thus repeat—again on a higher turn of the spiral—the condition we considered in which the soul or ego was not present, reversing the condition so that there is no form of life really present in the focused consciousness of the man. There is only the world of souls and a desire for creative activity. The handling of daily living on the physical plane drops below the threshold of physical consciousness, and the man becomes a vague, impractical, visionary mystic. These states of mind are dangerous if they are permitted to exist.   (15-466/8)

25. CONSCIOUSNESS

1. Consciousness might be defined as the faculty of apprehension, and concerns primarily the relation of the Self to the not-self, of the Knower to the Known, and of the Thinker to that which is thought about. All these definitions involve the acceptance of the idea of duality, of that which is objective and of that which lies back of objectivity.

Consciousness expresses that which might be regarded as the middle point in manifestation. It does not involve entirely the pole of Spirit. It is produced by the union of the two poles, and the process of interplay and of adaptation that necessarily ensures . . .

The whole aim of progressive development is to bring the Son of the Father and the Mother, to a point of full realisation, of complete self-consciousness, and to full and active knowledge.   (3-243/4)

2. Each point of life within a centre has its own sphere of radiation, or its own extending field of influence; this field is necessarily dependent upon the type and the nature of the indwelling Consciousness. It is this magnetic interplay between the many vast centres of energy in space which is the basis of all astronomical relationships—between universes, solar systems, and planets. Bear in mind, however, that it is the CONSCIOUSNESS aspect which renders the form magnetic, receptive, repudiating, and transmitting; this consciousness differs according to the nature of the entity which informs or works through a centre, great or small. Bear in mind also that the life which pours through all centres and which animates the whole of space, is *the life of an Entity;* it is therefore, the same life in all forms, limited in time and space by the intention, the wish, the form and the quality of the indwelling consciousness; the types of consciousness are many and diverse, yet life remains ever the same and indivisible, for it is the ONE LIFE.   (11-180)

3. All forms are composed of many forms, and all forms—aggregated or single in nature—are the expression of an indwelling or ensouling life. The fusion of life with living substance, produces another aspect of expression : that of *consciousness.* This consciousness varies according to the natural receptivity of the form, according to its point in evolution, and to its position also in the great chain of Hierarchy.   (11-182)

(a) EXPANSION OF CONSCIOUSNESS

1. Each unit of the human race is a part of the divine consciousness, and is that which is conscious of, or is aware of something without itself—

111

something which knows itself to be differentiated from the vehicle which encloses it or the forms which environ it.

At this particular stage in evolution the average man is simply conscious of differentiation, or of being separated off from all other members of the human family, thus forming in himself a unit among other units. He acknowledges this and acknowledges the right of all other separated units so to consider themselves. He adds to this a recognition that somewhere in the universe there exists a supreme Consciousness, Whom he theoretically calls God, or Nature. Between this purely *selfish* point of view (I use the term "selfish" in the scientific sense and not as a belittling adjective) and the nebulous theory of God immanent, there are to be found numerous stages, at each of which occurs an expansion of consciousness, or an enlargement of the point of view, that leads that self-recognising unit, step by step, from self-recognition to the recognition of superior selves, to the fitting of himself to be likewise recognised as a superior self, and eventually to the occult recognition of his own superior Self. He comes to recognise his Higher Self or Ego as his true Self, and from that stage passes on into that of the group consciousness. Here he realises first his egoic group, and then other egoic groups.

This stage is succeeded by the recognition of the universal principle of Brotherhood; it involves not just a theoretical recognition, but a merging of the consciousness into that of the human consciousness in its entirety; this is really that development of consciousness which enables a man to realise not only his egoic group affiliations but his place in the human hierarchy on its own plane. He knows himself in fact as a part of one of the great Heavenly Men. This expands later into an almost inconceivably vast point of view—that of his place in the Grand Heavenly Man, as represented by the Logos Himself.

... It is necessary first to grasp that the place where the expansion takes place, and the realisation has to be felt, has to be finally in the *thinking, waking consciousness.* The Ego on its own plane may be well aware of the unity of its consciousness with all other consciousnesses, and be realising his group as one with himself, but until the man (in physical plane consciousness) has raised himself to that same plane, and is likewise aware of his group consciousness, and likewise regards himself as the Higher Self within the egoic group and not as a separated unit, it is of no more use than a recognised theory is of use when not carried out in experience.

The man has to experience these stages in his physical consciousness and to know experimentally and not just theoretically that whereof I speak, before he is deemed ready to pass on into the succeeding stages. The whole matter resolves itself into the expansion of the mind until it dominates the lower, and into the faculty of abstract conception which results eventually in physical plane manifestation. It means making your highest theories and ideals demonstrable facts, and it is that blending of the higher and the lower and the equipping of that lower until it provides a fitting expression for the higher. It is here that the practice of meditation plays its part. The true scientific meditation provides graded forms whereby the consciousness is raised and the mind expanded until it embraces:

1. Its family and friends.

2. Its environing associates.

3. Its affiliated groups.

4. Its egoic group.

5. Other egoic groups.

6. That Man of the Heavens of which the egoic groups form a centre.

7. The Grand Heavenly Man.

. . . Each man who enters upon occult development and who aspires towards the higher, has passed the stage of the average man—the man who regards himself from the purely isolated standpoint and who works for what is good for himself. The aspirant is aiming at something different; he seeks to merge himself with his higher Self and with all that is entailed when we use that term. The stages beyond that, in all their intricacies, are the secrets of Initiation and with them we have naught to do.

Aspiration towards the Ego and the bringing in of that higher consciousness with the subsequent development of group consciousness, very directly concern all who will read these letters. It is the next step ahead for those upon the Probationary Path. It is not achieved by simply giving thirty minutes a day to certain set forms of meditation. It involves an hour by hour attempt, all day long and every day, to keep the consciousness as near to the high pitch attained in the morning meditation as possible. It presumes a determination to consider oneself at all times as the Ego, and not as a differential Personality. Later, as the Ego comes more and more into control, it will involve also the ability to look upon oneself as part of a group, with no interests and desires, no aims or wishes apart from the good of that group. It necessitates a constant watchfulness every hour of the day to prevent the falling back into the lower vibration. It entails a constant battle with the lower self that drags down; it is a ceaseless fight to preserve the higher vibration. And—which is the point I am aiming to impress upon you—the aim should be the development of the habit of meditation all the day long, and the living in the higher consciousness till that consciousness is so stable that the lower mind, desire and the physical elementals, become so atrophied and starved through lack of nourishment, that the threefold lower nature becomes simply the means whereby the Ego contacts the world for purposes of helping the race. (2-141/5)

2. Graded expansions of consciousness . . . are the result of imparted training; these lead a man on from step to step till he contacts his higher Self, his Master, his egoic group, the First Initiator, the One Paramount Initiator, until he has contacted the Lord of his Ray and has entered into the bosom of his "Father Which is in Heaven". (2-304)

3. No man who strives for mastery, who struggles to attain, and who aims at expansion of consciousness, but is having some effect—in ever widening spirals—upon all whom he contacts, devas, men, and animals. That he knows it not, and that he may be totally unaware of the subtle stimulating emanation which proceeds from him may be true, but nevertheless the law works. (3-465)

4. Much work is being accomplished by man for men, and through the agency of scientific, religious and educational endeavour, the human consciousness is steadily expanding, until one by one the Sons of God are breaking through their limitations into the world of souls. In the retrospect of history, the picture of the emerging prisoner, Man, can be seen in clear delineation. Little by little he has mastered the planetary boundaries; little by little he has grown from the stage of cave man to that of a Shakespeare, a Newton, a Leonardo da Vinci, an Einstein, a St. Francis of Assisi, to a Christ and a Buddha. The capacity of man to achieve in any field of human expression, seems practically unlimited, and if the past few thousand years have seen such a tremendous growth, what shall we see in the next five thousand years? If prehistoric man, little more than an animal, has grown into the genius, what unfoldment is not possible as more and more of innate divinity makes its presence felt? The superman is with us. What will the world manifest when *all* mankind is tending towards a concrete manifestation of superman powers?

Man's consciousness is being released in varying directions and dimensions. It is expanding into the world of spiritual realities, and beginning to embrace the fifth or spiritual kingdom, the kingdom of souls. It is inter-penetrating, through scientific research, the world of superhuman endea-vour, and investigating the many aspects of the Form of God, and of the forms that constitute the Form.   (4-536/7)

5. A consciousness, an awareness, and a sensitivity to an ever-widening and more inclusive contact, is gradually being developed, and this is the consciousness of God, the awareness of the solar Logos, and the sensitivity of the cosmic Son of God.

The form through which that Life expresses Itself, the sensitive res-ponse apparatus through which that Consciousness works, are of secon-dary importance, and are in the nature of an automatic mechanism. It is the mechanism, nevertheless, with which we have hitherto identified our-selves, and we have forgotten that that mechanism is but an expression of an aspect of consciousness, and that it indicates, at any particular time, the point of evolution of the informing entity. Let me reiterate : The two factors which are of major importance during manifestation, are the evolving consciousness and the manifesting life. When this is borne in mind, it will be noted how each stage upon the way can be seen whole as a kingdom in nature. Each of these kingdoms carries the consciousness aspect forward to a greater stage of perfection, and demonstrates a greater sensitivity and responsiveness to outer and inner environing conditions than does the preceding kingdom. Each manifests a fuller revelation of the inner hidden glory. When, however, a unit of life is immersed in form, and when the consciousness is identified (in time and space) with any particular form, it is not possible for it to realise its divinity, or to express it consciously. Its psychology is that of the partial and the particular, and not that of the universal and the whole. The greater and closer the identifi-cation with the form aspect, the greater is the lower unity and synthesis, but at the same time, the greater the darkness and, speaking symbolically, the denser is the prison. Such is the consciousness in the lower or sub-human kingdoms in nature. The more the unit of life is identified with "the one who is conscious", the greater again is the higher, yet different, unity and synthesis. Such also is the consciousness of the three higher king-doms, the superhuman. The tragedy, the problem and the glory of man, is that he can identify himself with both aspects—the form and the life; and his psychological state is such that during the period wherein he forms part of the human kingdom, his kingdom, his consciousness fluctuates between these pairs of opposites. He can identify himself with the sub-human forms, and this he invariably does in the early stages. He can identify himself with the life aspect, and this he does in the final stages. In the midway stage of the average man, he is torn violently between both, and is himself the battle ground.

. . . I want you to get a picture of the synthesis of the unfoldment from the inchoate to the sentient, from the sentient to the mentally realised, and from the mentally realised to the "divinely appreciated", as it is occultly termed. I give you pictures, but they are pictures of a whole. Endeavour to think in wholes, and try not to fit every point of detail into the whole, but remember that what may appear to be a contradiction may be but a fragment of temporary detail for which you—as yet—see no place or explanation.   (14-248/50)

6. All that concerns humanity at this time is the necessity for a steadily unfolding conscious response to the evolutionary revelation, and a gradual apprehension of the Plan, which will enable man to:

(a) Work consciously and intelligently.

(b) Realise the relation of form and quality to life.

(c) Produce that inner transmutation which will bring into manifestation the fifth kingdom in nature, the Kingdom of Souls.

All this has to be accomplished in the realm of conscious awareness or response, through the medium of steadily improving vehicles or response mechanisms, and with the aid of spiritual understanding and interpretation.   (15-6/7)

(b)   EGOIC CONSCIOUSNESS

1. The attainment of a certain amount of causal consciousness . . . is indicative of the pupils having developed (mayhap in small degree, yet definitely realised) the power to enter somewhat into Their (the hierarchical) world. The faculty of abstract thought and contemplation, the power to transcend the limitations of time and space, are powers of the body egoic, and as all egoic groups are—as aforesaid—controlled by some one Master, the development of egoic consciousness (when consciously recognised) is indicative of contact and access. Many (individuals) unconsciously contact their Ego, and temporarily have flashes of egoic consciousness, but when the pupil can consciously raise himself, when he with deliberation identifies his vibration, and transfers his polarisation into the body egoic, even if for a brief moment, then he can know that he is for that brief moment vibrating to the key of the Master of his group.

He has made contact. He may not remember in his physical brain at first the details of that contact, he may not realise the appearance of the Master, or the words that passed His lips, but having consciously conformed to rule, and entered within the silence of the high places, the law ever works, and he *has* made his contact. Some disciples know their Master intimately on the inner planes, and work under His direction, but many lives may elapse before they comprehend the law and with deliberation can make the channel of access, through power developed in meditation.

As time elapses this ability to contact increases, until the point is reached, when the pupil can at any time find out what is the will of the Master and have access to His heart.   (2-292/3)

2. In the training to be given during the next few decades, the unfoldment of astral vision and hearing will be entirely ruled out, or (if it exists) will eventually have to be overcome. The true disciple has endeavoured to centre himself on the mental plane, with the object in view of transferring his consciousness higher still, into the wider and inclusive awareness of the soul.

His aim is to include the higher, and there is no need for him, at this stage, to regain that astral facility which was the possession, as you well know, of the little evolved races of the earth, and of many of the higher animals. Later on, when adeptship has been reached, he can function on the astral plane should he so choose, but it should be remembered, that the Master works with the soul aspect of humanity (and of all forms) and does not work with their astral bodies. This has been oft forgotten by teachers both in the East and West.

In working with souls, the true technique of evolution is carried forward, for it is the soul within the forms in every kingdom in nature which is responsible for the developing work of, and within, the form. May I say therefore to students that their main objective is to become aware of the soul, to cultivate soul consciousness, and to learn to live and work as souls. Until such time as their use of their apparatus becomes voluntary, they would be well advised to train their minds, study the laws governing manifestation, and learn to include all that which we now cover by the word "higher"—a misnomer, but it must suffice.   (4-166/7)

3. Many are as yet in the initial stage of registering an awareness of a field of expression which they know exists—the field of soul awareness—but which is not yet for them their normal field of expression. Many know a great deal about it, theoretically, but the practical effects of applied

knowledge are not yet theirs. Many are conscious of consciousness, and are aware of the kingdom of the soul and of an occasional reaction to impression from that kingdom, but they are not yet consciousness itself, nor so identified with the soul that consciousness of all else drops away. To achieve that is their main objective.   (14-12/3)

4. The soul itself is a major centre of experience in the life of the Monad; the lower bodies are centres of expression in the life of the soul. As the consciousness of the man shifts continuously into the higher bodies through which expression can become possible, the soul gradually becomes the paramount centre of experience *in consciousness,* and the lesser centres of experience (the lower bodies) assume less and less importance. The soul experiences less through them, but uses them increasingly in service.

This same thought must be carried into our concept of the soul as a centre of consciousness. The soul uses the bodies in the earlier stages of evolution as centres of *conscious* experience, and upon them and upon the experience is the emphasis laid. But as time progresses, the man becomes more soul-conscious and the consciousness which he experiences (as a soul in the three bodies) is of decreasing importance, until finally the bodies become simply instruments of contact through which the soul comes into understanding relationship with the world of the physical plane, of the feeling, sentient levels, and with the world of thought. (15-314)

(c) SELF REALISATION

The various energies which play upon the human being and produce his unfoldment, constitute his field of experience. Those two words— *unfoldment* and *experience*—should ever be linked, for each produces the other. As one is subjected to experience in the form world, a paralleling unfoldment of consciousness is carried forward. As that unfoldment produces constant changes in realisation and a consequent constant reorientation to a new state of awareness, it necessarily leads to new experience— experience of fresh phenomena, of new states of being, and of dimensional conditions hitherto unknown. Hence the frequent reaction of the disciple to the fact that for him, as yet, there is no point of peace. Peace was the objective of the Atlantean aspirant. Realisation is that of the Aryan disciple. He can never be static; he can never rest; he is constantly adjusting himself to new conditions; constantly learning to function therein, and then subsequently finding them pass away to give place, in their turn, to new. This goes on until the consciousness is established in the Self, in the

One. Then the initiate knows himself to be the onlooking Unity, watching the phenomenal phantasmagoria of life in form.

He passes from one sense of unity to a sense of duality, and from thence again into a higher unity. First, the Self identifies itself with the form aspect to such an extent that all duality disappears in the illusion that the Self is the form. We have then the form constituting apparently all that there is. This is followed by the stage wherein the indwelling Self begins to be aware of Itself as well as of the form, and we talk then in terms of the higher and the lower self; we speak of the Self and its sheaths, and of the Self and the not-self. This dualistic stage is that of the aspirant and of the disciple, up to the time of his training for the third initiation. He begins with a knowledge that he is a spiritual entity confined in a form. His consciousness for a long period of time remains predominantly that of the form. Gradually this changes—so gradually that the aspirant learns the lesson of endurance (even to the point of enduring the not-self!) until there comes a life of balance, wherein neither preponderates. This produces in the man a state of apparent negativity and inertia which may last for one life or two, and he seems to accomplish little in either direction. This is, for workers, a valuable hint in their dealings with people. Then the point of balance changes, and the soul appears to dominate from the standpoint of influence, and the entire consciousness aspect begins to shift into the higher of the two aspects. Duality however, still persists, for the man is sometimes identified with his soul and sometimes with his form nature; this is the stage wherein so many most earnest disciples are at this time to be found. Little by little however he becomes "absorbed" in the soul, and thus comes en rapport with all aspects of the soul in all forms, until the day dawns when he realises that there is nothing but soul and then the higher state of unity supervenes. (4-374/5)

26. RELATIONSHIPS OF THE SOUL

Three things may be imparted, which—when wisely meditated upon—may lead to illumination:

1. The Ego on its own plane, realises *consciously* its relationship to the Master, and seeks to transmit that consciousness to the Personality.

2. The Higher Self on its own plane, is not trammelled by time and space, and (knowing the future as well as that which is past) seeks to bring the desired end nearer and make it more rapidly a fact.

3. The Higher Self or Ego on its own plane has direct relationship with other egos on the same ray, and on a corresponding concrete or abstract ray, and—realising that progress is made in group formation —works on that plane at the helping of his kind. (2-33/4)

(a) THE SOUL AND THE PERSONALITY

1. The soul is very little aware of the personality nature, its disposition and ideas. The soul can be conscious of the limitations within the personality and of the barriers opposed to the inflow of soul energy, but the details are of no interest to the soul. The soul is occupied with *recognising* hierachical planning, with *registering* world need, and with *responding* (faintly, very faintly at first) to the developing monadic inflow. These attitudes and reactions of the soul (upon its own plane of being) affect profoundly and fundamentally the personality life and produce those basic changes which evoke the vocation of the disciple. (6-67)

2. All of you need to become so sensitive to the quality of my Ashram, and so preoccupied with the opportunity to serve which confronts every disciple these days, that your own personal development, your unique problem (so regarded by you) and your reactions should be forgotten. You need to remember that you are not as interesting to your soul as you may think.

From the angle of the Master, it is the ability of the soul to control its instrument, the personality, and to work through it, that is of interest; it is for these types of ability that He looks, and not at the reaction of the personality. This is hard, if not humiliating, for the disciple to remember. The more engrossed he is with his personal responsiveness and capacities, the more impenetrable the barriers he is setting up between himself (upon the physical plane) and his soul; as a result of this, barriers are then being set up between the disciple and the life of the Ashram of which he is intended to form a part. Have this in mind and be, therefore, so occupied with the life of the soul that you have no time for personality introspection. (6-69)

3. The results of soul contacts on human beings, and the effect to be seen in the personality life, might be stated to be as follows:

1. *Conflict,* turmoil, opposed loyalties, inner warfare and a collision of divergent views.

2. *A sensitivity to ideas.* This amounts in the earlier stages to a flexibility of response, amounting almost to instability, and producing constant change of viewpoint. This leads to a sensitivity to the intuition, which will enable an individual to distinguish promptly between the unreal and the real.

3. *A process of detachment.* This is the difficult and painful process of laying down the lines of demarcation between the soul and the personality. This inevitably produces at first separation and divided interests, leading later to a submergence of personality interests in those of the Plan, and the absorption of personal desire in the aspects of the soul.

4. *A period of creativity,* due to the third aspect of the soul, which is the creator aspect. This development will produce definite habit changes in the physical plane life of the aspirant. It will lead to the consecration of the disciple to certain types of endeavour summed up in the words "artistic career".

These four effects of soul activity, . . . are in reality only the pouring in of soul force, through the channel of contact which the man has opened. (15-706)

(b) THE EGO AND THE MASTERS

1. As we have been told, there are *sixty thousand million units of consciousness* or spirits (Monads) in the evolving human hierarchy. These are found on causal levels, though the numbers are slightly less now, owing to the attainment of the fourth Initiation by individuals from time to time. These egos, at different stages of development, are all linked with their Monad, Spirit or Father in Heaven, in much the same way (only in finer matter) as the Ego is linked with the Personality.

All the Monads are, as you know, under the control, or rather form part of the consciousness of one of the Planetary Spirits. On egoic levels, the egos are in a similar condition. An Adept of their ray supervises their general evolution, dealing with them *in groups*. These groups are formed under three conditions:

(a) As to sub-ray of the egoic ray.

(b) As to period of individualisation or of entrance into the human kingdom.

(c) As to point of attainment.

The Adept of their ray handles the general supervision, but under Him work the Masters, each on His own ray, and with Their own individual groups, who are affiliated with Them through period, through karma, and through point of vibration. Under the Masters work the disciples who have the consciousness of the Higher Self, and are therefore able to work on causal levels and aid in the development of those egos whose causal bodies are less developed than their own.

All is beautifully subject to law, and as the work of developing the egoic body is dependent upon the progress made in the threefold personality, the Ego is consequently aided on lower levels by two different disciples, one working on emotional levels and reporting to another disciple who works upon the mental vehicle. He in his turn reports to the disciple with causal consciousness, who reports again to the Master. All this is done with the co-operation of the indwelling consciousness in the causal body. This, as you see, entails five factors concerning themselves with the aiding of the Ego in his evolutionary development:

1. The Adept of his Ray.

2. The Master of his group.

3. A disciple with causal consciousness.

4. A disciple on the mental plane.

5. A helper on the emotional plane.   (2-34/5)

2. Certain factors, governing the Master's relation to the disciple, are gradually recognised, and begin increasingly to govern the disciple's life:

(a) He recognises that his points of contact with his Master are governed by group emergency and need, and deal with his group service. It gradually dawns on him that his Master is only interested in him insofar as his Ego can be used in service, through the personality on the physical plane. He begins to realise that his Master works with his soul and that it is his Ego, therefore, which is *en rapport* with the Master and not the personal self. His problem, therefore, becomes increasingly clear, and this is the problem of all disciples. It is to keep the channel of communication open between the soul and the brain, via the mind, so that when the Master seeks to communicate, He can do so at once and easily. Sometimes a Master has to wait weeks before He can get His disciple's ear, for the channel upward is closed and the soul is not en rapport with the brain. This is especially true of the early stages of discipleship.

(b) He finds that it is *he* who shuts the door in the majority of cases, through lower psychism, physical disability, and lack of mind control, and he therefore discovers that he has to work constantly and ceaselessly with his lower self.

(c) He finds that one of the first things he has to do is to learn to discriminate between :

His own soul's vibration.
The vibration of the group of disciples with whom he is associated.
The vibration of the Master.

All three are different, and it is easy to confuse them, especially at first. It is a safe rule for aspirants to assume when they contact a high vibration and stimulus, that it is their own soul contacting them, the Master in the Heart, and not run off with the idea (so flattering to their pride and personality) that the Master is endeavouring to   reach them. (4-170/1)

3. The life of a disciple is a gradual but steady moving in towards the centre, and accepted disciples are definitely a part of the Hierarchy. The Hierarchy is a place of fusion of all the souls upon the higher levels of the mental plane. Just in so far as a person comes under soul impression, then soul control and final identification with the soul, just so far does he move towards the centre of fusion. As your love for humanity increases and your interest in yourself decreases, so will you move towards that centre of light and love where the Masters stand in spiritual being.   (5-682)

4. The Masters have no personalities as you understand personality. Their conditioning factors are the three aspects of the Spiritual Triad, and these aspects, being creative, build the phenomenal apparatus or mechanism by means of which a Master makes contact with the three worlds.   (6-761)

5. The Master's influence as He seeks to aid His disciple, always produces transitory turmoil—transitory from the angle of the soul, but frequently appalling from the angle of the personality. (18-32)

6. The Masters have each and all renounced that which is material; They have been lifted out of the three worlds by Their own effort; They have detached themselves from all hindrances; They have left hell behind and the term "spirits that are in prison" no longer applies to Them. This They have done for no selfish purpose. In the early days of the Probationary Path, selfish aspiration is foremost in the consciousness of the aspirant; however, as he treads the Path, and likewise the Path of Discipleship, he leaves all such motives behind . . . and his one aim, in seeking liberation and freedom from the three worlds, is to aid and help humanity. This dedication to service is the mark of the Hierarchy. (18-702/3)

(c) THE SOUL AND THE MASTER'S ASHRAM

1. There is a great difference between a Master's group and His Ashram. This is seldom realised. Many people can be found in a Master's group, but the personnel of His Ashram is picked out of that of the group. In a group, the Master is in touch with and aware of the aspiring disciple and he has had a definite contact with Him, but this has involved a personality as well as a soul relation. But in an Ashram only that is to be found within the sphere of influence of an Ashram which is of the soul. Nothing of the personality is allowed to enter in—personality reactions, disabilities, limitations, personality thoughts, and all that is material and connected with the lower nature, never reaches the Ashram at all. In the early stages, therefore, of a disciple's work, it is possible that there is little or nothing that the disciple will be able to contribute of any kind for a long time. Only those positively sensed intuitions, and those definite soul impressions and impulses which the disciple may succeed in evoking (through meditation and growing purity of intention) can contribute anything to the life of the Ashram. There is consequently a law which protects the Ashram from your limitations. I have been using the word "Ashram" quite definitely in my effort to lead you to discriminate between a group and an Ashram. An Ashram is basically formed of those who through their knowledge, devotion and service, have worked their way out of a group into an inner centre where the Master's energy, wisdom and effort is more easily available. In order to work their way from the group into the Ashram, disciples will need most carefully to discriminate

between their high grade personality inclinations, their responses to truth and ideals, and their true soul reactions, spiritual wisdom and intuitive perception.   (5-694/5)

2. An Ashram is a subjective fusion of individuals and not of personalities, gathered together for service purposes. It is a blending of individual activity into one whole—a whole which is united on objective and vision, but which may (and frequently does) have differing methods and techniques. The work of the Ashram is essentially the presentation to the world of those service purposes which are carried forward as seems best to the individual disciple, under the "impression of the Master" and with the co-operation of His group. A group of disciples is not pledged to do the same type of work in the same way and at the same time. They are pledged to work under the inspiration of their soul, as their souls may direct and dictate, strengthened by contact with the Master and with each other. They are related to each other through identity of vision and of vibration, plus mutual respect and complete freedom—particularly the latter.   (5-702)

3. An Ashram is not confined to a few who may know each other and who may even meet together as Ashram members. An Ashram is an international group; it is composed of souls in incarnation and out of incarnation; it is a synthesis of initiates of various degrees and of accepted disciples.   (5-728)

4. The disciple . . . is faced with the proposition of making his life of such a nature that it furthers the group purpose, enhances the group strength, eliminates all that might hinder group usefulness, and brings closer the objective for which the group was formed—the carrying out of the Master's plans. It was the disciple's innate, instinctual and individual response to this ray objective, and his effort to subordinate his personality to the dimly sensed soul dedication, which led the Master in the first instance to recognise him and incorporate him into His Ashram. The moment that happened, the disciple came not only under an increased impact of egoic force and egoic impulsive intention (using those words in their occult sense), but the group radiation began its beneficent work upon him. The magnetic "pulling" power which had hitherto led him forward, is now superseded by a radiating stimulating potency; it effects great changes in him, and produces both eliminating and substituting results. The effect of the life of the Ashram, as far as the group which forms it is concerned, and apart from the Master's own potency, can be described as follows:

1. The life of the personality is steadily weakened, and its grip upon the soul is definitely loosened. The soul begins to dominate in a very real sense.

2. The necessity of incarnation becomes appreciably less, and finally life in the three worlds of human manifestation becomes needless. All the lessons have been learnt and the soul objective has been attained.

3. The Will of the Monad begins to be sensed; the will aspect blends with the love aspect and makes the intelligence aspect fruitful and effective for the carrying out of divine purpose, focused for the disciple through the Ashram.

4. The purposes of time and space, of events and extension, of matter and consciousness, have been achieved and are eventually superseded by something for which we have as yet no term and of which we have no conception. It is that which begins to express itself after the third initiation, when the Father aspect "comes into view"—I know not how else to word it.

5. The whole is seen to be of more vital importance than the part, and this not as a dream, a vision, a theory, a process of wishful thinking, an hypothesis or an urge. It is realised as an innate necessity and as inevitable. It connotes death, but death as beauty, as joy, as spirit in action, as the consummation of all good.

. . . Life is approached from the angle of the Observer and not from that of a participator in actual experiment and experience in the three worlds. This Observer is different to the Observer on the probationary Path. Most of the experiment and experience has been left behind, and a new orientation to a world of values, higher than even the world of meaning, has set in. This attitude might well be described as the mode of approach of all who form a part of an Ashram. Those who form the Ashram are living in the three worlds of experience if they are accepted disciples, but the focus of their attention is not there. If they are initiated disciples, they are increasingly unaware of the activities and reactions of their personalities, because certain aspects of the lower nature are now so controlled and purified, that they have dropped below the threshold of consciousness and have entered the world of instinct; therefore there is no more awareness of them than a man asleep is conscious of the rhythmic functioning of his sleeping physical vehicle. This is a deep and largely unrealised truth.   (18-98/100)

(d)   THE SOUL AND THE HIERARCHY

1. The Hierarchy is simply the world of souls; it is consciously aware of the Plan, sensitive to the Purpose, and creatively and constantly impressing humanity, with the aim in view of expanding the human consciousness. Of this your soul—in its pure nature—is a part.   (6-137)

2. There are, it should be pointed out, three types of hierarchical workers:

1. *Souls;* i.e., those initiates who have taken the fourth Initiation of Renunciation and in whom the soul body, the causal body, has been destroyed. They are the Custodians of the Plan.

2. *Soul-infused personalities;* these are the disciples and the initiates of the first three initiations, through whom the "souls" work in the carrying out of the Plan.

3. *Intelligent aspirants,* who are not yet soul-infused personalities but who recognise the necessity of the Plan, and who seek the welfare of their fellow men.

The highest group formulates the Plan; the second group "modifies, qualifies, and adapts" the Plan to contemporary human requirements and thus ensures the gradual and steady continuity of the Plan; the third group are the agents who carry this Plan to mankind and seek to make it workable, guided by spritual compromise—the compromise evidenced by the second group.   (6-391/2)

3. The work of the Hierarchy in connection with mankind falls into two parts: —the work with individual human beings, in order to awaken them to soul consciousness, and then the work with them, as souls, so that (functioning then on soul levels and as conscious units in the kingdom of God) they can begin to vision the objective of God Himself.   (15-240)

(e)   THE SOUL AND DIVINE WILL

When the lure of substance is overcome and desire dies, then the attractive power of the soul becomes dominant, and the emphasis (so long laid upon individual form and individual living and activity) gives place to group form and group purpose. Then the attractive power of the Hierarchy and of the Masters' groups of disciples supersedes the lower attractions and the lesser focal points of interest. When these then assume their rightful place in consciousness, then the dynamic pull of the Will Aspect of divinity can be felt—entirely unrelated to form or forms, or to groups or a group.   (8-71/2)

(f) THE SOUL AND THE RAYS

1. Every human being is swept into manifestation on the impulse of some ray, and is coloured by that particular ray quality, which determines the form aspect, indicates the way he should go, and enables him (by the time the third initiation is reached) to have sensed and then to have co-operated with his ray purpose. . . .

The human soul is a synthesis of material energy, qualified by intelligent consciousness, plus the spiritual energy which is, in turn, qualified by one of the seven ray types   (14-61)

2. *The Ray of the Ego.* In starting our study of the ray of the Ego or Soul, certain major premises might be briefly stated and incorporated into a series of propositions, fourteen in number. They are as follows:

1. The egos of all human beings are to be found upon one or another of the seven rays.

2. All egos found upon the fourth, the fifth, the sixth and the seventh rays must eventually, after the third initiation, blend with the three major rays, or monadic rays.

3. The monadic ray of every ego is one of the three rays of aspect, and the sons of men are either monads of power, monads of love, or monads of intelligence.

4. For our specific purposes, we shall confine our attention to the seven groups of souls found upon one or other of the seven rays or streams of divine energy.

5. For the major part of our racial and life experience we are governed sequentially, and later simultaneously by:

(a) The physical body, which is dominated by the ray governing the sum total of the atoms of that body.

(b) The emotional desire nature, which is to be found influenced and controlled by the ray which colours the totality of astral atoms.

(c) The mind body or mental nature, and the calibre and quality of the ray determining its atomic value.

(d) Later, on the physical plane, the soul ray begins to work in and with the sum total of the three bodies, which constitute—when aligned and functioning in unison—the personality. The effect of that general integration is actively to produce an incarnation, and incarnations wherein the personality ray emerges clearly, and the three bodies or selves constitute the three aspects or rays of the lower personal self.

6. When the personality ray becomes pronounced and dominant, and the three body rays are subordinated to it, then the great fight takes place between the egoic ray or soul, and the personality ray. The differentiation becomes clearly marked, and the sense of duality becomes more definitely established. . . .

7. Eventually, the soul ray or influence becomes the dominating factor, and the rays of the lower bodies become the sub-rays of this controlling ray. This last sentence is of basic importance, for it indicates the true relation of the personality to the ego or soul. The disciple who understands this relation and conforms to it, is ready to tread the path of initiation.

8. Each of the seven groups of souls is responsive to one of the seven types of force, and all of them are responsive to the ray of the planetary Logos of our planet, which is the third Ray of Active Intelligence. All are therefore upon a sub-ray of this ray, but it must never be forgotten that the planetary Logos is also upon a ray, which is a sub-ray of the Second Ray of Love-Wisdom. . . . (14-401/3)

3. The egoic ray of the individual, plus the egoic ray of the fourth kingdom, gradually negate the rays governing the personality as the man nears the path of probation and discipleship.

Man therefore is an aggregate of forces which dominate him serially and together; these colour his nature, produce his quality, and determine his "appearance", using this word in its occult sense of *exteriorisation.* For ages he is wielded by one or other of these forces, and is simply what they make him. As he arrives at a clearer understanding, and can begin to discriminate, he definitely chooses which of them shall dominate, until he eventually becomes controlled by the Soul ray, with all the other rays subordinated to that ray, and used by him at will.   (14-405)

(g) THE SOUL AND ESOTERIC STUDIES

Esoteric study, when coupled with esoteric living, reveals in time the world of meaning, and leads eventually to the world of significances. The esotericist starts by endeavouring to discover the reason *why;* he wrestles with the problem of happenings, events, crises and circumstances, in order to arrive at the meaning they should hold for him; when he has ascertained the meaning of any specific problem, he uses it as an invitation to penetrate more deeply into the newly revealed world of meaning; he then learns to incorporate his little personal problems into the problem of the larger Whole, thus losing sight of the little self and discovering the larger Self. The true esoteric viewpoint is always that of the larger Whole. He finds the world of meaning spread like an intricate network over all activity and every aspect of the phenomenal world.

Esotericism is not, however, concerned with the centres as such, and esotericism is not an effort scientifically to awaken the centres, as many students think. Esotericism really is training in the ability to function freely in the world of meaning; it is *not* occupied with any aspect of the mechanical form; *it is occupied entirely with the soul aspect*—the aspect of Saviour, Redeemer and Interpreter—and with the mediating principle between life and substance. This mediating principle is the soul of the individual aspirant or disciple (if one may use such misleading wording); it is also the *anima mundi* in the world as a whole.

Esotericism therefore involves a life lived in tune with the inner subjective realities; it is only possible when the student is intelligently polarised and mentally focused; it is only useful when the student can move among these inner realities with skill and understanding. Esotericism involves also comprehension of the relation between forces and energies, and the power to use energy for the strengthening, and then for the creative use of the forces contacted; hence their redemption. . . . Esotericism is the art of "bringing down to earth" those energies which emanate from the highest sources, and there "grounding them" or anchoring them. . . .

All true esoteric activity produces light and illumination; it results in the inherited light of substance being intensified and qualified by the higher light of the soul—in the case of humanity consciously functioning. . . .

I would challenge all esotericists to attempt the practical approach which I have here outlined. I would ask them to live redemptive lives, to unfold their innate mental sensitivity, and to work continuously with the meaning which is to be found behind all individual, community, national and world affairs. If this is done, then the light will suddenly and increasingly shine upon your ways. You can become light-bearers, knowing then that "in that light you will see the Light"—and so will your fellow men.   (12-66/8)

(h)   THE SOUL AND OTHER EGOS

1. *The factor of activity.* This is largely a matter of ray, and affects closely the relationship between egos. Those on similar rays coalesce and vibrate more readily to each other than those on different rays, and it is only as the second or wisdom aspect is developed, that synthesis becomes possible.   (2-38)

2. Nothing matters but the soul. Nothing counts in the long run but service. Take your mind away from all your personality problems and the problems of those with whom you have chosen to walk in this incarnation the path of life. Trust their souls. Make and keep contact with them via their souls, refusing to be glamoured by their personalities. . . .

Know you not that as you add your soul force to theirs (ignoring the form aspect) that you can galvanise those souls into increased spiritual activity? But, my brother, as you note these happenings, be not tempted to aid. Leave the personalities to their own wise, pure and loving souls. (5-505/6)

3. The usefulness of disciples to those who are linked karmically to them and for whom they feel—rightly or wrongly—a sense of responsibility, shifts from stage to stage with growth. One's physical care for one's loved ones may and must persist in some measure, though a mother's care for her child cannot persist into adult years. There may be a responsibility which one chooses to shoulder (again rightly or wrongly), but it must not offset or undermine any responsibility which it should be theirs to shoulder. One's mental assistance should be always available, but it should not be given when one's mind is bewildered by the fogs of questioning and doubt, or when there is a spirit of criticism. One's *spiritual responsibility* is, curiously enough, usually the last to be recognised; and action taken on that recognition is equally slow. Yet, in the last analysis, it is by far the most important, for one's spiritual influence can be lasting and can carry with it releasing power to those we love, whereas the other responsibilities—being those of personality relationships—always carry with them glamour and that which is not of the kingdom of spirit. (5-518/9)

4. You have no responsibility for your children and never have had since they reached maturity and the right to live their own lives. You have earned the right to your own soul's freedom and expression. (5-324)

(i) THE EGO AND THE ENVIRONMENT

1. Correct response to one's environment will result in correct rapport between the soul aspect, hidden in every form, and will produce right relations between the various parts of the inner nervous structure to be found in every kingdom of nature, subhuman and superhuman. This is as yet practically unknown but is rapidly coming into recognition, and when it is proven and realised, it will be discovered that therein lies the basis of brotherhood and of unity. As the liver, the heart, the lungs, the stomach, and other organs in the body are separate in existence and in function, and yet are unified and brought into relation through the medium of the nervous system throughout the body, so will it be found that in the world such organisms as the kingdoms in nature have their separate life and functions, yet are correlated and co-ordinated by a vast intricate sensory system which is sometimes called the soul of all things, the *anima mundi,* the underlying consciousness.   (4-21)

2. *Solitude:* One of the primary conditions that a disciple has to culti-vate, in order to sense the Plan and be used by the Master, is solitude. In solitude the rose of the soul flourishes; in solitude the divine self can speak; in solitude the faculties and the graces of the higher self can take root and blossom in the personality. In solitude also the Master can ap-proach and impress upon the quiescent soul the knowledge that He seeks to impart, the lesson that must be learnt, the method and plan for work that the disciple must grasp. In solitude the sound is heard. The Great Ones have to work through human instruments, and the Plan and the vision are much handicapped by failure on the part of these instruments. (4-132)

(j) THE SOUL AND HEALTH

1. Only when the pupil has an intelligent appreciation of the trouble or troubles affecting him, only when he has the ability to conscientiously follow the imparted formulas, and only when his object is unselfish, will he be trusted with these forms. When his object is to equip himself for service, when he aims only at the acquirement of healthy vehicles for the better carrying out of the Plan of the Great Ones, and when he desires not to escape disease for his own personal benefit, only then will the for-mulas work in connection with the egoic consciousness. The downflow of life from the God within results in sound vehicles, so that it is only as the Personality becomes merged in the Ego, and the polarisation shifts

from the lower to the higher, that the work becomes possible. That time is nearing now for many.   (2-161)

2. The personalities of the "weary pilgrims on the Way" are indeed tired and worn. Humanity today is very weary. The vehicles have been used for many cycles, and their potency (in a positive sense) is wearing out, which is the approaching goal. For long cycles, the soul has been negative in its effect upon the personality, and the personal equipment has been the positive expression of the spiritual man. Then that lower aggregation of forces begins to wear down; its vibration weakens, and because much of the consciousness is still identified with the body nature, the disciple is conscious of fatigue, pain, distress and a deep weariness. It has been the "personality fatigue" of the human race which partially was responsible for the excessive misery complex, the sense of inferiority, and the pining-for-release psychology of the Christian presentation of truth.

As still further progress is made, the joy of the soul begins to pour through the worn and weary vehicles, and gradually the positive nature of the soul takes hold. When this is strong enough and the man is sufficiently decentralised, it is the soul quality which will persist in spite of physical limitations, and the inner sense of weariness will then be carefully negated and consciously and intelligently transmuted. There will be the recognition of personality distress, but also a planned effort to transcend it. This process of "divine imposition" gradually brings in the healing force, and thus perfect health in some life is the reward of the initiate's effort to live as a soul and not to feel as a personality. It is this divine pouring in of the soul's quality of life which is the true key to self-induced healing.   (5-557)

3. The over-emphasis which people put on disease is bewildering to the soul, for it places the transient, constantly changing form-nature in a position of undue prominence, whereas—from the angle of the soul—the vicissitudes of the body are only of importance just in so far as they contribute to the enrichment of soul experience.   (17-296)

4. Disease is an effect of the basic centralisation of a man's life energy. . . . Where the consciousness of the man is focused, there the life energy will gather its forces. . . .

Where the consciousness is stabilised in that of the soul, there will be little disease present, and the difficulties of the highly developed patient will then be associated with the impact of the soul energy upon an unready physical vehicle; at that stage only certain of the major diseases will affect him. He will not be susceptible to the little complaints and the constant small infections which render the life of the average man or of the undeveloped man so trying and difficult. (17-559/60)

(k) THE SOUL AND HEALING

1. *Law I:* All disease is the result of inhibited soul life, and that is true of all forms in all kingdoms. The art of the healer consists in releasing the soul, so that its life can flow through the aggregate of organisms which constitute any particular form. (17-5)

2. All disease (and this is a platitude) is caused by lack of harmony—a disharmony to be found existing between the form aspect and the life. That which brings together form and life, or rather, that which is the result of this intended union, we call the soul, the self where humanity is concerned. Disease appears where there is a lack of alignment between these various factors, the soul and the form, the life and its expression, the subjective and the objective realities. Consequently, spirit and matter are *not* freely related to each other. This is one mode of interpreting Law I. (17-12)

3. When human thought reverses the usual ideas as to disease, and accepts disease as a fact in nature, man will begin to work with the law of liberation, with right thought, leading to non-resistance. At present, by the power of his directed thought and his intense antagonism to disease, he only tends to energise the difficulty. When he reorients his thought to truth and the soul, physical plane ills will begin to disappear. This will become apparent as we study later the method of eradication. Disease exists. Forms in all kingdoms are full of inharmony and out of alignment with the indwelling life. Disease and corruption and the tendency towards dissolution are found everywhere. I am choosing my words with care. (17-13)

4. The highest and the newest method (of healing) is that of calling into positive activity a man's own soul. The true and the future healing is brought about when the life of the soul can flow without any impediment and hindrance throughout every aspect of the form nature. It can then vitalise it with its potency, and can also eliminate those congestions and obstructions which are such a fruitful source of disease. (17-17)

5. (Two words) sum up the healer's story: *Magnetism and Radiation.* . . .

> *Rule One:* The healer must seek to link his soul, his heart, his brain and his hands. Thus can he pour the vital healing force upon the

patient. This is *magnetic work.* It cures disease, or may increase the so-called evil state, according to the knowledge of the healer.

The healer must seek to link his soul, his brain, his heart, and auric emanation. Thus can his presence feed the soul life of the patient. This is the *work of radiation.* The hands are needed not. The soul displays its power. The patient's soul responds through the response of his aura to the radiation of the healer's aura, flooded with soul energy. (17-17/8)

6. *Split Personality:* . . . The conditions which are undesirable are regarded as the result of lack of soul contact and of soul control. The patient (if I might so call him) is taught to take his eyes, and consequently his attention, away from himself, his feelings, his complexes and his fixed ideas and undesirable thoughts, and to focus them upon the soul, the divine Reality within the form, and the Christ consciousness. This could well be called the process of scientific substitution of a fresh dynamic interest for that which has hitherto held the stage; it brings into functioning activity a co-operative factor whose energy sweeps through the lower life of the personality and carries away wrong psychological tendencies, undesirable complexes, leading to erroneous approaches to life. This eventually regenerates the mental or thought life, so that the man is conditioned by right thinking under the impulse or the illumination of the soul. This produces the "dynamic expulsive power of a new affection"; the old *ideés fixes,* the old depressions and miseries, the hindering and handicapping ancient desires—these all disappear, and the man stands free as a soul and master of his life processes.   (17-119)

7. All energy is from the soul in the secondary instance, but in the primary sense all energy is simply life, functioning under direction of some kind.

As to the part love has to play in the healing process: *Love* is the life expression of God Himself; love is the coherent force which makes all things whole (I would have you ponder upon this phrase), and love is all that *is.* The main characteristic of the distinction between soul energy and personality force, as applied to healing, lies in the region of the application and the expression of love. Personality force is emotional, full of feeling, and—when in use—the personality is ever conscious of itself as the healer, and is the dramatic centre of the stage upon which are two players, the healer and the one to be healed. Soul energy functions unconsciously and is wielded by those who are in contact with their souls and who are consequently decentralised; they are "off the stage" themselves, if I might use that expression, and they are completely occupied with group love, group activity, and group purpose. (17-356/7)

(l)   THE EGO AND THE DARK FORCES

The Dark Brothers are—remember this always—*brothers,* erring and misguided, yet still sons of the One Father though straying far, very far, into the land of distances. The way back for them will be long, but the mercy of evolution inevitably forces them back along the path of return in cycles far ahead. Anyone who over-exalts the concrete mind and permits it continuously to shut out the higher, is in danger of straying on the lefthand path. Many so stray . . . but come back, and then in the future avoid like errors in the same way as a child once burnt avoids the fire. It is the man who persists in spite of warning and of pain, who eventually becomes a brother of darkness. Mightily fights the Ego at first to prevent the Personality so developing, but the deficiencies of the causal body (for forget not that our vices are but our virtues misused) result in a lopsided causal body, over-developed in some direction and full of great gulfs and gaps where virtue should be.

The dark brother recognises no unity with his species, only seeing in them people to be exploited for the furtherance of his own ends. This then, on a small scale, is the mark of those who are being used by them wittingly or unwittingly. They respect no person, they regard all men as fair prey, they use everyone to get their own way enforced, and by fair means or foul they seek to break down all opposition and for the personal self acquire that which they desire.

The dark brother considers not what suffering he may cause; he cares not what agony of mind he brings upon an opponent; he persists in his intention and desists not from the hurt of any man, woman or child, provided that in the process his own ends are furthered. Expect absolutely no mercy from those opposing the Brotherhood of Light. . . .

Oft too the Dark Brother masquerades as an agent of the Light, oft he poses as a messenger of the gods, but for your assurance I would say that he who acts under the guidance of the Ego, will have clear vision, and will escape deception. (2-134/6)

(m)   THE SOUL AND SERVICE

1. You will ask what your service is to be? That, my brother, will grow out of your meditation. It is not for me to tell you what activity your personality must follow; it is your own soul which must do so. (5-574)

2. Many are still too preoccupied with what *they* are attempting to do, with their own development and with their own capacity or non-capacity to help; but at the same time they are inadequately handling the problem of self-effacement and complete dedication to their fellow men. "What can I *do*"? is of less importance to them than "What am I learning, and is the Master satisfied with me"? I shall be satisfied with you when you have forgotten both yourself and me in your strenuous service for mankind.

Service . . . is a scientific process, calling forth all the soul powers into full expression on the physical plane. It is service which causes a divine manifestation or what you call a divine incarnation. If a man is truly serving, he will perforce draw upon all the resources of spiritual strength and light, and all the wisdom and directing power of his soul, because the task to be done is always too big for the personality. Some of the world's greatest servers are men and women who are very close to the spiritual Hierarchy, and working under its direction, inspiration and impression, but who know naught of esotericism so-called, do not recognise the Hierarchy, and (in their brain consciousness) remain unaware of its Personnel, the Masters of the Wisdom.   (6-24/5)

3. Regard all that has happened to you as special training, what might be called "basic training", in order that your future initiate service may be carried out according to plan. That service is the choice of your soul. It is not imposed upon you . . . by any other factor save your soul.   (6-665)

4. *The Science of Service.* . . . As the linking up of soul and personality proceeds, and as the knowledge of the Plan and the light of the soul pour out into the brain consciousness, the normal result is the subordination of the lower to the higher. Identification with group purposes and plans is the natural attribute of the soul. As this identification is carried forward on mental and soul levels, it produces a corresponding activity in the personal life, and this activity we call service. Service is the true science of creation and is a scientific method of establishing continuity. (12-97)

5. The definition of *"Service"* is not easy. There has been too much attempt to define it from the angle of personality knowledge. Service can be briefly defined as the spontaneous effect of soul contact. This contact is so definite and fixed that the life of the soul can pour through into the instrument which the soul must perforce use upon the physical plane. It is the manner whereby the nature of that soul can demonstrate in the world of human affairs. Service is not a quality or a performance; it is

not an activity towards which people must strenuously strive, nor is it a method of world salvage. This distinction must be clearly grasped, or else our whole attitude to this momentous demonstration of the success of the evolutionary process in humanity will be at fault. Service is a life demonstration. It is a soul urge, and as much an evolutionary impetus of the soul as the urge to self-preservation or to the reproduction of species is a demonstration of the animal soul. This is a statement of importance. It is a soul instinct, if we may use such an inadequate expression and is, therefore, innate and peculiar to soul unfoldment. It is the outstanding characteristic of the soul, just as *desire* is the outstanding characteristic of the lower nature. It is group desire, just as in the lower nature it is personality desire. It is the urge to group good. It cannot, therefore, be taught or imposed upon a person as a desirable evidence of aspiration, functioning from without and based upon a theory of service. It is simply the first real effect, evidenced upon the physical plane, of the fact that the soul is beginning to express itself in outer manifestation. Neither theory nor aspiration will or can make a man a real server. (15-124/5)

6. All these laws of the Soul (and the Law of Service is no exception) manifest inevitably in two ways.

First, there is their effect upon the individual. This occurs when the soul has been definitely contacted and the mechanism of the soul begins to respond. Evidence of this should work out now among the esoteric students, scattered over the world, for they have reached a point where the true server can emerge from their ranks, and give evidence of an established soul contact.

Secondly, these soul laws are beginning to have a group effect in humanity itself, and to influence the race of men as a whole. This effect is somewhat in the nature of a reflection in the lower nature of a higher consciousness, and therefore today we have much running after service, and much philanthropic effort. All of it is, however, deeply coloured by personality, and it often produces much harm, for people seek to impose their ideas of service and their personal techniques upon other aspirants. They may have become sensitive to impression, but they ofttime misinterpret the truth and are biased by personality ends. They must learn to lay the emphasis upon soul contact and upon an active familiarity with the egoic life, and not upon the form side of service. May I beg those of you who respond to these ideas and are sensitive to soul impression (ofttimes misinterpreting the truth, being biased by personality ends) to lay the emphasis upon soul contact, and not upon the form side of service. Activity of the form side lays stress upon personality ambition, veiling them with the glamour of service. If care over the essential of service—soul contact—is taken, then the service rendered will flow with spontaneity along the right lines and bear much fruit. Of this, the selfless service and the deep flow of spiritual life, which have been demonstrated in the world work of late, is a hopeful indication.   (15-126)

7. When the personal lower self is subordinated to the higher rhythms and obedient to the new Law of Service, then the life of the soul will begin to flow through the man to others, and the effect in a man's immediate family and group will be to demonstrate a real understanding and a true helpfulness. As the flow of life becomes stronger through use, the effect will spread out from the small surrounding family group to the neighbourhood. A wider range of contacts becomes possible, until eventually (if several lives have been thus spent under the influence of the Law of Service) the effect of the outpouring life may become nationwide and worldwide. But it will not be planned, nor will it be fought for, as an end in itself. It will be a natural expression of the soul's life, taking form and direction according to a man's ray and past life expression; it will be coloured and ordered by environing conditions—by time, by period, by race and age. It will be a living flow, and a spontaneous giving forth, and the life, power and love demonstrated, being sent forth from soul levels, will have a potent, attractive force upon the group units with which the disciple may come in contact in the three worlds of soul expression. There are no other worlds wherein the soul may at this time thus express itself. Nothing can stop or arrest the potency of this life of natural, loving service, except in those cases wherein the personality gets in the way. Then service, as the Teachers on the inner side of life understand it, gets distorted and altered into busy-ness. It becomes changed into ambition, into an effort to make others serve as we think service should be rendered, and into a love of power which hinders true service, instead of into love of our fellow men. There is a point of danger in every life when the theory of service is grasped, and the higher law is recognised; then the imitative quality of the personality, its monkey nature, and the eagerness of a high grade aspiration can easily mistake theory for reality, and the outer gestures of a life of service for the natural, spontaneous flow of soul life through its mechanism of expression.   (15-128/9)

8. When, in the terms of the occult science, we are told to serve and obey, we are not interested. Yet service is the mode, *par excellence,* for awaken-

ing the heart centre, and obedience is equally potent in evoking the response of the two head centres to the impact of soul force, and unifying
them into one field of soul recognition. So little do men understand the
potency of their urges! *If the urge to satisfy desire is the basic urge of
the form life of man, the urge to serve is an equally basic urge of the
soul in man.* This is one of the most important statements in this section.
It is as yet seldom satisfied. Indications of its presence are ever to be found,
nevertheless, even in the most undesirable types of human beings; it is
evoked in moments of high destiny, or immediate urgency, and of
supreme difficulty. The heart of man is sound, but oft asleep.

Serve and obey (the soul!). These are the watchwords of the disciple's
life. They have been distorted into terms of fanatical propaganda, and
have thus produced the formulas of philosophy and of religious theology;
but these formulas do, at the same time, veil a truth. They have been
presented to the consideration of man in terms of personality devotions
and of obedience to Masters and leaders, instead of service of, and
obedience to, the soul in all. The truth is, however, steadily emerging,
and must eventually triumph. Once the aspirant upon the Probationary
Path has a vision of this (no matter how slight it may be), then the law
of desire, which has governed him for ages, will slowly and surely give
place to the Law of Repulse, which will, in time, free him from the thraldom of not-self. It will lead him to those discriminations and that dis-
passionate attitude which is the hallmark of the man who is on his way
to liberation. Let us remember, however, that a discrimination which is
based upon a determination to be free, and a dispassion which is the indication of a hard heart, will land the aspirant in the prison of a crystal-
lised shell, which is far harder to break than the normal prison of the life
of the average selfish man. This selfish spiritual desire is oft the major
sin of so-called esotericists, and must be carefully avoided. Therefore, he
who is wise will apply himself to serve and obey. (15-158/9)

(n) THE SOUL AND ADVANCED YEARS

If you stand steady, with an open heart, a seeing eye, and a ready response to all who come your way, the door to renewed service will open
and much can be done by you. . . . Do not distrust yourself, but go ahead.
Your field of service lies all around you.

The problem that has to be faced by all who have passed through the
fires of Renunciation, who are walking the way of humility whilst conscious of the grandeur of the soul, and who are, at the same time, far

from young in years, is that of facing the last decade or so of life with understanding, and with no fear of physical limitations. So many in the final years of life, live, think and act in such a manner that the soul withdraws its attention. Thus only the personality remains. To all of you who have passed the half century I would say: Face the future with the same joy as in youth, yet with an added usefulness, knowing that the wisdom of experience is yours, the power to understand is yours, and that no physical limitation can prevent a soul from useful expression and service. I would remind you of something which is oft forgotten: It is far easier for the soul to express itself through an older experienced body, than through one that is young and inexperienced, provided that there is no pride and no desired selfishness, but only longing to love and serve. (5-465/6)

(o) THE SOUL AND THE USE OF WORDS OF POWER

1. Words of Power (and this is true also of the O.M.) are all of second ray origin. This is the ray of the manifestation of consciousness. They are, therefore, intended for *soul use* because the soul is the expression of the second aspect of divinity, and only the soul can really employ these Words and sounds and thus produce the desired results which are always in line with the divine Plan. It is frequently forgotten that they must be used by the soul in a dynamic manner, involving the serious recognition of the *will aspect*. The Great Invocation, the O.M. and all such Words of Power must go forth from the soul (whose nature is love and whose purpose is solely group good), backed by or "occultly propelled forth" (to use a translation of an almost untranslatable occult idea) by the dynamic will aspect, and carried outwards as an integrated thoughtform upon a stream of living, illumined mental substance. This process therefore brings into activity the will, the love and the intelligence of the man who is using these words and formulas. Frequently, however, an hiatus occurs even when a man has integrated these three controlling factors within himself as far as he is able to do so at his particular point in evolution. All that he has succeeded in doing is the retaining of the created thoughtform upon the mental plane; he fails to make its presence felt upon the physical plane and to achieve the desired results because his brain (the lower receiving and distributing centre within the head) is incapable of the needed dual activity—retaining awareness of the intent, meaning and purpose of the formula being used and, at the same time, carrying on the task of sending forth the potency, hidden yet conveyed by the Words

or sounds. These two activities must be carried on simultaneously by the soul on its own plane through the medium of the mind and the brain. Here again is one of the objectives of all meditation work, but one which is not emphasised as it is a sequential happening and not an objective. Effectiveness is, therefore, dependent upon a grasp of the above facts, and a developed and trained integration between soul, mind, desire, brain and the spoken Word or sound.

What I am telling you refers not only to the use of the Great Invocation, but also to the daily and constant use of the Sacred Word by occult students and aspirants in their daily meditation. They could change their lives, reorient their life purpose, and focus and achieve spiritual unfoldment and expansion if they could use the O.M. as it should be used. (13-145/6)

2. Only those can use the formulas effectively who live, work, think and feel as souls, which means ever in group terms.

Today, however, there are those in every land who are rapidly becoming aware of the soul as a controlling factor in consciousness, who respond to world affairs and conditions increasingly as souls, and who can, therefore, be trained to work upon the physical plane. When this is so, it becomes possible to impart certain of these Words of Power and mantrams, and to institute that new and potent activity which will bring the Hierarchy and Humanity into conscious and direct co-operation, as well as Shamballa and certain great Forces which are interplanetary or solar, and also great cosmic Energies. . . .

The objective of these processes of invocation is (amongst others) . . . to invoke the soul of humanity, and so bring about its freer expression upon the physical plane. This can be brought about in two ways:

(a) The stimulation of the souls of men everywhere by the increased inflow of the Christ principle of love, which will express itself in world understanding, goodwill, co-operation, and peace.

(b) The setting up of a vibration within humanity itself of such potency that it will magnetically attract a response from the waiting, watching Hierarchy, and bring about a much closer and likewise *conscious* rapport between the two planetary centres, the Hierarchy and Humanity. (13-149/50)

3. Our duty is to learn rightly to contact the Hierarchy, via our own souls; rightly to use the Great Invocation as souls, and rightly to render ourselves responsive to and sensitive to the resultant effects. (13-161)

27. THE FORM-BUILDING PRINCIPLE

The (following are) certain basic premises of the Ageless Wisdom:

1. The soul is the form-building principle, producing attraction and cohesion.

2. This soul is an aspect or type of energy, distinguished from that of matter itself.

3. The atom has been recognised as an energy unit, but as yet the energy which sweeps atoms into aggregates, which we call organisms and forms, has not been isolated. This the mystics in the scientific world will sense and work to demonstrate during the next generation. It is this type of energy, the energy of the form-building aspect of manifestation, which is the source of all magical work; and it is this energy in the various kingdoms of nature that produces form, shape, species, kind, type and the differentiations which mark and distinguish the myriad forms through which life itself manifests. It is the quality of the energy which produces the quantity of forms; it is the light which causes the emergence into consciousness of the race of heterogeneous shapes which aggregates of atoms can assume.

4. This type of energy which produces the shapes and forms and coherent organisms in all the kingdoms of nature, is not the life principle. The life principle will remain undiscovered and unrecognised until such time as the soul or qualifying principle, the builder of the forms, is studied, recognised, and in its turn investigated.

5. This is only possible as man steps forth into a fuller conscious possession of his divine heritage, and working as a soul and in control of his mechanism (physical, emotional, and mental), can work consciously en rapport with the soul in all forms.

This will be possible only as the race grasps the above hypothesis, and recognises it as a possibility and seeks to demonstrate the fact of the soul factor lying back of its structure or body of manifestation, or equally, seeks to disprove it. All great scientists and workers in the realm of objective nature have worked as souls, and all the most amazing of the developments in the realm of physics and chemistry, as in other departments of human knowledge, have been made when the worker in any particular field has launched forth with faith in some hypothesis he has formed, and has investigated and progressed his work forward, stage by stage, until he has contacted an aspect of the truth hitherto unformulated by man. Then, having through the use of his intuition entered into a new realm of thought, he takes the knowledge there discovered and formulates it in such a way by theory, principle, experiment and mechanical contrivance, that it becomes the possession of the group, and in due time is understood and utilised by the world. But in its genesis it has been mystical work and based on a mystical intuition.   (4-332/3)

28.   EGOIC LIFE PURPOSE

1. The Ego on his own plane and on a tiny scale, repeats the action of the Logos. For certain ends he builds a certain form; he gathers certain material, and aims at a definite consummation that shall be the result of that gathered material vibrating to a certain measure, governed in one specific life by certain rules and aiming at some one particular object— *not all possible objects.*

Each personality is to the Ego what the solar system is to the Logos. It is his field of manifestation and the method whereby he attained a demonstrable object. That aim may be the acquirement of virtue by paying the price of vice; it may be the attainment of business acumen by the struggle to provide the necessities of life; it may be the development of sensitiveness by the revealing cruelties of nature; it may be the building in of unselfish devotion by the appeal of needy dependents; or it may be the transmutation of desire by the method of meditation on the Path. It is for each soul to find out. What I want to impress upon you is the fact that there is a certain danger incident to this very factor. If, for instance, in the acquirement of the mental capacity to meditate, the student misses the very thing he came into the physical body to acquire, the result is not so much a gain, as an unequal development and a temporary loss of time. . . . (If) he does not fulfil the desire of the Ego, but misses opportunity, he suffers much, and in the next life is necessitated a similar staging and a stronger urge, and a closer ring-pass-not until he complies with the will of the Ego.   (2-108/9)

2. The soul has no individual destiny, but is submerged into the One. Its destiny is the destiny of the group, and of the Whole; its desire is the working out of the great Plan, and its will is the glorification of the incarnated Logos.   (4-296)

3. Human beings are apt to be primarily concerned with their higher group relations, with their return to the Father's home, and with the trend which we call "upwards" and away from the phenomenal world. They are principally occupied with the finding of the centre within the form aspect, that which we call the soul, and, having found it, with the work then of acquainting themselves with that soul and thus finding peace. This is right and in line with divine intention, but it is *not* all of the plan for man, and when this remains the prime objective, a man is dangerously near falling into the snare of *spiritual selfishness* and separateness. (4-529)

4. The uses of *pain* are many, and they lead the human soul out of darkness into light, out of bondage into liberation, out of agony into peace. That peace, that light and that liberation, with the ordered harmony of the cosmos, are for all the sons of men. (4-533)

5. And so they stand—Humanity and the Hierarchy. And so you stand, my brother, personality and soul, with freedom to go forward into the light if you so determine, or to remain static and unprogressive, learning nothing and getting nowhere; you are equally free to return to identification with the Dweller, negating thus the influence of the Angel, refusing imminent opportunity and postponing—until a much later cycle—your determining choice. This is true of you and of Humanity as a whole. Will humanity's third ray materialistic personality dominate the present situation, or will its soul of love prove the most powerful factor, taking hold of the personality and its little issues, leading it to discriminate rightly and to recognise the true values and thus bring in the age of soul or hierarchical control? Time alone will show. (10-160)

6. Man reads his destiny in the heavens and writes out that destiny in his life upon the earth; he reduces, knowingly or unknowingly, the idea of his soul to due and proper form, so that each life adds, subtracts and multiplies, until the sum of each soul's experiencing is complete. (12-16)

7. Steadily the unfolding purpose of our own souls (those "angels of persistent and undying love") should gain fuller and deeper control over each of us, and this, at any personal cost and sacrifice, should be our steadfast aim. For this, in truth and sincerity, we should strive. (15-18)

29. MYSTICAL PERCEPTION

Civilisations, cultures, races and nations appear and disappear, but the same *individualities* come and go with them, garnering the fruits of experience, and progressively marching on to fuller *Self*-government and group organisation and synthesis.

I would remind you also that there is a peculiar quality in every human being—an innate, inherent characteristic which is inevitably present—to which one might give the name of "mystical perception". I use this term in a far wider sense than is usually the case, and would have you regard this quality of mystical perception as inclusive of:

1. The mystical vision of the soul, of God and the universe.

2. The power to contact and appreciate the world of meaning, the subjective world of the emerging reality.

3. The power to love and to go out to that which is other than the self.

4. The power to grasp and to intuit ideas.

5. The ability to sense the unknown, the desirable and the desired. The consequent determination and persistence which enable man to seek, search for and demand that unknown reality. It is the mystical tendency which has produced the great mystics of world renown, the large number of explorers, discoverers and inventors.

6. The power to sense, register and record the good, the beautiful and the true. It is this that has produced the writer, the poet, the artist and the architect.

7. The urge to discover and to penetrate to the secrets of God and of nature. It is this which produced the scientist and the religious man.

From a study of these definitions you will see how inclusive the term "mystical perception" is. It is no more and no less than the power, innate in man, to reach out and to grasp that which is greater and better than himself, and which has driven him on, through progressively developing cultures and civilisations, until today he stands on the verge of a new kingdom in nature. It is the power to appreciate and to strive after the apparently unattainable good. Let this broad and general thesis therefore be in your minds as we study man's developing power of self-expression, self-determination, and self-government.   (12-113/4)

30. THE MYSTIC AND THE OCCULTIST

1. The mystic eliminates or endeavours to transcend *mind* in his process of finding the Self. The occultist, through his intelligent interest in the forms which veil the Self and by the employment of the *principle of mind* on both its levels, arrives at the same point. He recognises the sheaths that veil. He applies himself to the study of the laws that govern the manifested solar system. He concentrates on the objective, and in his earlier years may at times overlook the value of the subjective. He arrives eventually at the central life by the elimination, through conscious knowledge and control, of sheath after sheath. He meditates upon form until the form is lost sight of, and the creator of the form becomes all in all. (2-151)

2. The value to the public thought of a true explanation of the evolution of the Ego, and its gradually developing power on earth, is very great. There are two ways in which man may view this matter, both of which provide food for meditation, and well merit serious consideration. . . . By sheer devotion and strenuous application, and by a severe disciplining of the physical body, *the mystic* effects his entrance into the heart centre of his little system, and his life becomes irradiated by the beams of his own central sun—the egoic light divine. The problem may again be regarded as one in which the effort of the man is concentrated in an attempt to bring down into the physical brain consciousness, and thus on the physical plane, the life and power and energy of the inner centre, the Ego. This involves necessarily a scientific apprehension of the laws of being, and a recognition of the dual nature of the Self. It involves a devotion to the work of bringing about a domination of the lunar lords through the radiant control of the solar Lord. This is the *occult method.* It is the method of studying the constitution of those entities who form the fourfold lower nature, the personality, and a close investigation of those divine Essences Who build the body of the Ego or Higher Self. To this must be added a severe application of the laws of nature to the individual problem.   (3-815/6)

3. The mystic is ever conscious of duality. He is the seeker in search of light, of the soul, of the beloved, of that higher something which he senses as existing and as that which can be found. He strives after recognition of and by the divine; he is the follower of the vision, a disciple of the Christ, and this conditions his thinking and his aspiration. He is a de-

votee and one who loves the apparently unattainable—the Other than himself.

Only when he becomes the occultist does the mystic learn that all the time the magnet which attracted him, and the dualism which coloured his life and thoughts and which gave motive to all he sought to do, was his true self, the one Reality. He recognises then that assimilation into and identification with that one reality enables duality to be transmuted into unity, and the sense of search to be transformed into the effort to become what he essentially is—a Son of God, one with all Sons of God. Having accomplished that, he finds himself one with the ONE in Whom we live and move and have our being.   (17-116/7)

31. "LOST SOULS"

If (man) neglects his spiritual development (from life to life), and concentrates on intellectual effort turned to the manipulation of matter for selfish ends, if he continues this in spite of the promptings of his inner Self, and in spite of the warnings that may reach him from Those Who watch, and if this is carried on for a long period, he may bring upon himself a destruction that is final for this manvantara or cycle. He may, by the uniting of the two fires of matter (kundalini and pranic) and the dual expression of mental fire, succeed in the complete destruction of the physical permanent atom, and thereby sever his connection with the higher self for aeons of time. H.P.B. has somewhat touched on this when speaking of "lost souls"; we must here emphasise the reality of this dire disaster and sound a warning note to those who approach this subject of the fires of matter with all its latent dangers. The blending of these fires must be the result of spiritualised knowledge, and must be directed solely by the Light of the Spirit, who works through love and is love, and who seeks this unification and this utter merging *not* from the point of view of sense or of material gratification, but because liberation and purification is desired in order that the higher union with the Logos may be effected; this union must be desired, not for selfish ends, but because *group perfection* is the goal and scope for greater service to the race must be achieved.   (3-127)

32. TRAINING OF THE VEHICLES FOR SOUL SERVICE

1. Always the calling forth of the response (of the Master) must be the work of the pupil, and the hour of that response depends upon the earnestness of his work, the consecration of his service and his karmic liabilities. When he merits certain response it will be demonstrated in his stars, and naught can hinder or delay. Equally, naught can really hasten, so the pupil need not waste time in doleful ponderings upon the lack of response. His is the part to obey the rules, to conform to the forms laid down, to ponder and wisely adhere to the prescribed instructions, and to definitely work and to ardently serve his fellow men. When he has done all this, when he has built the necessary vibrating material into his three lower bodies, when he has aligned them with the body egoic (even if only for a brief minute) suddenly he may see, suddenly he may hear, suddenly he may sense a vibration, and then forever he may say that faith is merged in sight, and aspiration has become recognition.   (2-295)

2. The need arises these days for tested instruments. When Those Who guide human evolution at this period cast Their eyes over the race in the search for such instruments, They see few as yet ready for the service required. But likewise They see some who, with a certain amount of training, will fill the need fairly adequately.

As evolution proceeds, the polarisation of the race changes. Men are polarised now principally in their emotional bodies—the feelings, desires, the concerns of the personality sway them. The emotional body is the focal point for the personality. It acts as the clearing house for all that concerns it, and as the junction of the lower and the higher. It is like a busy railroad terminus, that receives cargo from all directions and empties it into the great city of the personal physical plane life. Then, as progress is made, the scene shifts higher, and the mental body becomes the focal point. Later the causal body becomes the important unit, and later still comes the ultimate sacrifice of even that, until the man stands bereft of all that vibrates to the three worlds, and all is over as regards the personal life—naught remains but the life of the Spirit, and the voluntary giving of that life for the helping of the world.

In the speeding up of evolution, certain things have to be brought about before the man can be used as a reliable instrument, true as tempered steel, for the helping of his race. Forget not that, as a rule, a man (when tested and tried) forms the best tool, because he comprehends ut-

terly the race consciousness, and because he enters into the problems of
the day in a manner more thorough than an Ego from an earlier period.
Hence the Masters desire to use those of you who live now, to heal the
wounds of the present suffering generation. What then has to be done?
The matter I now give contains nothing very unusual, but it does hold
thought for consideration by any who may desire to help. . . . In preparing a soul for service the Guides of the race have to deal with each of
the bodies (the physical, the etheric, the emotional and the mental).
(2-333/4)

3. Once the magic of the soul is grasped by the personality, that soul
steadily dominates and can be trusted to carry forward the training of
the man to fruition, unhampered (as you necessarily are) by thoughts of
time and space, and by an ignorance of the past career of the soul concerned. It should always be borne in mind that, when dealing with individuals, the work required is twofold:

First. To teach them how to link up the personal lower self with the
overshadowing soul, so that in the physical brain there is an assured
consciousness as to the reality of that divine fact. This knowledge renders the hitherto assumed reality of the three worlds futile to attract
and hold, and is the first step out of the fourth, into the fifth kingdom.

Second. To give such practical instruction as will enable the aspirant
to:

(a) Understand his own nature. This involves some knowledge of the
teaching of the past as to the constitution of man and an appreciation
of the interpretations of modern Eastern and Western investigators.

(b) Control the forces of his own nature and learn something of
the forces with which he is surrounded.

(c) Enable him so to unfold his latent powers that he can deal with
his own specific problems, stand on his own feet, handle his own
life, solve his own difficulties, and become so strong and poised in
spirit that he forces recognition of his fitness, to be recognised as a
worker in the plan of evolution, as a white magician, and as one of
that band of consecrated disciples whom we call the "hierarchy of
our planet".   (4-55/6)

4. The apparatus of the human being, which is the mechanism whereby
the soul contacts the three worlds which would be otherwise (under the
present plan) sealed and hidden to the experience and experiment of the

soul, has been more acutely sensitised and developed during the past two thousand years than in any previous period of ten thousand years. The reason for this is that the mind of man has been consciously aiding in the process of co-ordinating the instincts and transmuting instinctual reaction, translating it into intelligent perception. In the case of the world disciples, this process has been carried forward into the next stage of unfoldment, to which we give the name of intuitional knowledge.   (9-115)

5. One of the first lessons that humanity will learn under the potent influence of the seventh ray, is that the soul controls its instrument, the personality, through ritual, or through the imposition of a regular rhythm, for rhythm is what really designates a ritual. When aspirants to discipleship impose a rhythm on their lives, they call it a discipline, and they feel happy about it. What groups do who are gathered together for the performance of any ritual or ceremony whatsoever (Church ritual, the Masonic work, the drill of the army or navy, business organisations, the proper functioning of a home, of a hospital, or of an entertainment, etc.) is of an analogous nature, for it imposes on the participants a simultaneous performance, an identical undertaking, or a ritual. No one on this earth can evade ritual or ceremonial, for the rising and setting of the sun imposes a ritual, the cyclic passing of the years, the potent movements of the great centres of population, the coming and the going of trains, of ocean liners and of mails, and the regular broadcasting of the radio organisations—all of these impose a rhythm upon humanity, whether this is recognised or not. Of these rhythms the present great experiments in national standardisation and regimentation, are also an expression, as they demonstrate through the masses in any nation.

There is no evading the process of ceremonial living. It is unconsciously recognised, blindly followed, and constitutes the great discipline of the rhythmic breathing of life itself.   (14-365)

(a) TRAINING THE PHYSICAL BODY

1. This involves certain definite requirements:

The building in of matter of the higher sub-planes, and the elimination of the lower and coarser matter. This is needed because it is impossible for those with coarse bodies to contact high vibration. It is impossible for the Ego to transmit the higher knowledge and guidance through a coarse physical body. It is impossible for the loftier currents of thought to impact the little evolved physical brain. Hence the refinement of the physical body is an essential. It is effected in various ways, all of them reasonable and utilitarian:

By pure food. . . .
By cleanliness. . . .
By sleep. . . .
By sunshine. . . .

When these four requirements are attended to adequately, a definite process of elimination proceeds, and in the course of a few years the whole physical body shifts its polarisation gradually up until ultimately you will have a body composed of atomic sub-plane matter. . . . This may take several incarnations, but it should be borne in mind that at each fresh incarnation a body is taken of the exact quality (if I may so put it) as the one previously discarded at death. Hence time is never lost in building. Eventually two other methods will be available by which more rapid refining may be effected:

The use of coloured lights. . . .
The stimulation of music. . . .

One more point I would like to give, and that is that in the manipulation of *electricity* lies hid much that concerns vivification of the bodies. (2-334/6)

2. (Another hindrance to occult study) is found in the physical body, which has been built up by the aid of meat and fermented foods and drinks, and nurtured in an environment in which fresh air and sunlight are not paramount factors. . . . When fresh fruit and vegetables, clear water, nuts and grains, cooked and uncooked, form the sole diet of the evolving sons of men, then will be built bodies fitted to be vehicles for highly evolved Egos. (4-84)

(b) TRAINING OF THE ETHERIC BODY

This coincides with that of the physical body. The method consists principally of living in the sunlight, in protection from cold, and in the assimilation of certain definite combinations of vitamins which before long will be given to the race. . . . The study of etheric diseases—congestion and atrophy—will ere long be a recognised study, and will lead to definite treatments and formulas. As before said, all that you can now do in sensitising the dual physical, is to attend to the above rules, and allow time to bring about the remainder of the work. (2-337)

(c) TRAINING OF THE EMOTIONAL BODY

1. The emotional body is simply a great reflector. It takes colour and movement from its surroundings. It receives the impress of every passing

desire. It contacts every whim and fancy in its environment; every current sets it in motion; every sound causes it to vibrate unless the aspirant inhibits such a state of affairs and trains it to receive and register only those impressions which come from the intuitional level via the Higher Self, and therefore via the atomic sub-plane. The aim of the aspirant should be to so train the emotional body that it will become still and clear as a mirror, so that it may reflect perfectly. His aim should be to make it reflect only the causal body, to take on colour only in line with the great Law, and to move under definite direction and not just as blow the winds of thought, or rise the tides of desire. What words should describe the emotional body?—the words: still, serene, unruffled, quiet, at rest, limpid and clear, of a quality mirrorlike, of surface even, a limpid reflector—one that accurately transmits the wishes, the desires, the aspirations of the Ego and not of the personality. How should this be accomplished? In several ways, some at the direction of the aspirant, and some at the direction of the Master:

(a) By the constant watching of all desires, motives and wishes that cross the horizon daily, and by the subsequent emphasising of all those that are of a higher order, and by inhibition of the lower.

(b) By a constant daily attempt to contact the Higher Self, and to reflect His wishes in the life. At first mistakes will be made, but little by little the building-in process proceeds, and the polarisation in the emotional body gradually shifts up each sub-plane until the atomic is reached.

(c) By definite periods daily directed to the stilling of the emotional body. So much emphasis is laid in meditation on the stilling of the mind, but it should be remembered that the stilling of the emotional nature is a step preliminary to the quieting of the mental; one succeeds the other, and it is wise to begin at the bottom of the ladder. Each aspirant must discover for himself wherein he yields most easily to violent vibrations, such as fear, worry, personality desire of any kind, personality love of anything or anyone, discouragement, over-sensitiveness to public opinion; then he must overcome that vibration, by imposing on it a new rhythm, definitely eliminating and constructing.

(d) By work done on the emotional body at night under the direction of more advanced Egos, working under the guidance of a Master. Stimulation of vibration or the deadening of vibration follows on the application of certain colours and sounds. . . .

Remember that the work is gradual, and as the polarisation shifts up, the moment of transition from one sub-plane to another is marked by certain tests applied at night, what one might term a series of small initiations that eventually will be consummated in the second great initiation, that marks the perfection of the control of the body of the emotions. (2-337/9)

2. If man only realised it, the devas of the astral plane at present very largely control what he does and says, and his goal of evolution (his immediate goal) is to liberate himself from their control in order that he, the real Ego or Thinker, may be the dominating influence. (3-662)

(d) TRAINING OF THE MENTAL BODY

1. Three things (are necessary) before the plane of the mental unit is achieved, and before the causal consciousness (the full consciousness of the Higher Self) is reached:

1. *Clear thinking,* not just on subjects wherein interest is aroused, but on all matters affecting the race. It involves the formulation of thought matter, and the capacity to define. It means the ability to make thought-forms out of thought matter, and to utilise those thought-forms for the helping of the public. He who does not think clearly, and who has an inchoate mental body, lives in a fog, and a man in a fog is but a blind leader of the blind.

2. *The ability to still the mental body* so that thoughts from abstract levels and from the intuitional planes can find a receptive sheet whereon they may inscribe themselves. This thought has been made clear in many books on concentration and meditation, and needs not my elucidation. It is the result of hard practice carried over many years.

3. *A definite process* brought about by the Master with the acquiescence of the disciple, which welds into a permanent shape the hard won efforts and results of many years. At each initiation, the electrical or magnetic force applied has a stabilising effect. It renders durable the results achieved by the disciple. Like as a potter moulds and shapes the clay and then applies the fire that solidifies, so the aspirant shapes and moulds and builds, and prepares for the solidifying fire. Initiation marks a permanent attainment and the beginning of a new cycle of endeavour.

Above all two things should be emphasised:

First. A steady, unshaken perseverence, that recks not of time nor hindrance, but goes on. This capacity to persevere explains why the non-spectacular man so frequently attains initiation before the genius, and before the man who attracts more notice. The capacity to plod is much to be desired.

Second. A progress that is made without undue self-analysis. Pull not yourselves up by the roots to see if there is growth. It takes precious time. Forget your own progress in conforming to the rules and in the helping of others. When this is so, sudden illumination may come, and the realisation break upon you that the point has been reached when the Hierophant can demand your presence and bestow initiation upon you. You have, by hard work and sheer endeavour to conform to the Law and to love all, built into your bodies the material that makes it possible for you to stand in His Presence. The great Law of Attraction draws you to Him and naught can withstand the Law. (2-340/1)

2. *Mental Laziness:* The training of the mental body has a value, and may evade such technicalities, hiding behind an emphasis upon the life side of truth, all due to an inherent mental laziness. This that you now receive is but the A.B.C. of esotericism. Waste not time however in too detailed deduction. All that is now possible is a broad general outline, patient reserve, a willingness to recognise physical brain limitations, and the accepting of an hypothesis. Believe these hypotheses possible unless your intuition revolts or they are contradicted by past teaching given by other of the Lodge's Messengers. I do not dogmatise to you. I only, in these instructions, give you certain information—the correctness of which I leave the future to demonstrate. I simply ask that you make record, and in the coming years much that may now seem peculiar or mayhap even contradictory will be elucidated, slowly unravelled, and more easily comprehended. A little knowledge leads to much confusion unless laid aside for future use when the years of instruction have increased the store. (4-363/4)

3. For man the Universal Mind can best be grasped as it expresses itself through what we call the concrete mind, the abstract mind, and the intuition or pure reason.

The concrete mind is the form building faculty. Thoughts are things. The abstract mind is the pattern building faculty, or the mind which works with the blue prints upon which the forms are modelled. The intuition or pure reason is the faculty which enables man to enter into contact with the Universal Mind and grasp the Plan synthetically, to seize upon divine Ideas or isolate some fundamental and pure truth.

The goal of all the work of an aspirant is to understand those aspects of the mind with which he has to learn to work. His work therefore might be summed up as follows:

1. He has to learn to think; to discover that he has an apparatus which is called the mind and to uncover its faculties and powers. . . .

2. He has to learn next to get back of his thought processes and form building propensities and discover the ideas which underlie the divine thought-form, the world process, and so to learn to work in collaboration with the Plan and subordinate his own thought-form building to these ideas. He has to learn to penetrate into the world of these divine ideas and to study the "pattern of things in the Heavens" as it is called in the Bible. He must begin to work with the blue prints upon which all that is, is modelled and moulded. He becomes then a student-symbolist, and from being an idolater he becomes a divine idealist. I use these words in their true sense and connotation.

3. From that developed idealism, he must progress even deeper still, until he enters the realm of pure intuition. He can then tap truth at its source. He enters into the mind of God Himself. He intuits as well as idealises and is sensitive to divine thoughts. They fertilise his mind. He calls these intuitions later, as he works them out, ideas or ideals, and bases all his work and conduct of affairs upon them.

4. Then follows the work of conscious thought-form building, based upon these divine ideas, emanating as intuitions from the Universal Mind. This goes forward through meditation.

Every true student knows that this involves *concentration* in order to focus or orient the lower mind to the higher. Temporarily the normal thought-form building tendencies are inhibited. Through *meditation,* which is the mind's power to hold itself in the light, and in that light become aware of the Plan, he learns to "bring through" the needed ideas. Through *contemplation* he finds himself able to enter into that silence which will enable him to tap the divine mind, wrest Gods' thought out of the divine consciousness and to *know.* This is the work before each aspirant and hence the necessity of his understanding the nature of his mental problem, the tools with which he must perforce work, and the use he must make of what he learns and gains through right use of the mental apparatus. (4-365/6)

. . . How is this to be done? How bring through and how build after-wards? . . . (For the answer see: 4-366/74)

4. *Mental polarisation:* Increasingly must your inner life be lived upon the mental plane. Steadily and without descent must the attitude of meditation be held—not for a few minutes each morning, or at specific moments throughout the day, but constantly, all day long. It infers a constant orientation to life and the handling of life from the angle of the soul. This does not refer to what is so often referred to as "turning ones back upon the world". The disciple faces the world but he faces it from the level of the soul, looking clear-eyed upon the world of human affairs. "In the world, yet not of the world" is the right attitude—expressed for us by the Christ. Increasingly must the normal and powerful life of the emotional, astral desire and glamorous nature, be controlled and rendered quiescent by the life of the soul, functioning through the mind. The emotions which are normally self-centred and personal, must be transmuted into the realisations of universality and impersonality; the astral body must become the organ through which the love of the soul can pour; desire must give place to aspiration and that, in its turn, must be merged in the group life and the group good; glamour must give place to reality, and the pure light of the mind must pour into all the dark places of the lower nature. These are the results of mental polarisation, and are brought about by definite meditation and the cultivation of the meditative attitude.   (5-50/1)

33.   THE EGO AND THE CENTRES

1. The centres are formed entirely of streams of force, pouring down from the Ego, who transmits it from the Monad. In this we have the secret of the gradual vibratory quickening of the centres as the Ego first comes into control or activity, and later (after initiation) the Monad, thus bringing about changes and increased vitality within these spheres of fire or of pure life force.

The centres, therefore, when functioning properly, form the "body of fire" which eventually is all that is left, first to man in the three worlds, and later to the Monad. This body of fire is "the body incorruptible" or indestructible, spoken of by St. Paul, and is the product of evolution, of the perfect blending of the three fires, which ultimately destroy the form. When the form is destroyed, there is left this intangible spiritual body of fire, one pure flame, distinguished by seven brilliant centres of intenser burning. This electric fire is the result of the bringing together of the two poles, and demonstrates at the moment of complete at-one-ment, the occult truth of the words "Our God is a consuming Fire".

Three of these centres are called major centres, as they embody the three aspects of the threefold Monad—Will, Love and Intelligence:

1. The Head Centre . . . The Monad. Will or Power.

2. The Heart Centre . . . The Ego. Love and Wisdom.

3. The Throat Centre . . . The Personality. Activity or Intelligence.

. . . We must disabuse our minds of the idea that these centres are *physical things*. They are whirlpools of force that swirl etheric, astral and mental matter into activity of some kind.   (3-166/7)

2. Usually among the ignorant, the centres are first studied objectively, psychic exercises are undertaken in order really to produce *feeling* in the centres, and so make the man conscious of their locality and quality. Later an effort is made through meditation to contact the soul.

This order is wrong. Man should become aware of the centres as a final stage, and this because his emphasis and identification is with the soul and not with the form aspect, of which the centres are a part. Be careful in all instruction that you may later give on these matters, to make this point adequately clear.   (6-575)

3. The soul anchors itself in two streams of energy at two points of contact: the life stream in the heart and the consciousness stream in the head. This consciousness aspect is itself dual, and that which we call self-consciousness is gradually unfolded and perfected until the ajna centre, or the centre between the eyebrows, is awakened. The latent group-consciousness, which brings realisation of the greater Whole, is quiescent for the greater part of the evolutionary cycle, until the integrative process has proceeded to such a point that the personality is functioning. Then the head centre begins to awaken, and the man becomes conscious in the larger sense. Head and Heart then link up, and the spiritual man appears in fuller expression.   (15-415)

4. The head centre is the seat of soul energy, or the centre through which the conscious, *spiritual* man functions. The heart centre is the seat of life, of the highest principle which expresses itself through man.   (15-435)

5. *The Heart Centre* corresponds to the "heart of the Sun" and therefore to the spiritual source of light and love.

It is brought into functioning activity after the second initiation. That initiation marks the completion of the process whereby the emotional nature (with its outstanding quality of desire) is brought under soul control, and the desire of the personal lower self has been transmuted into love. It is the organ for the distribution of hierarchical energy, poured out via the soul into the heart centre of all aspirants, disciples and initiates. (17-156/7)

6. Goodwill is already making its presence felt in the world today, indicating the coming into activity of the heart centre, and proving that the heart centre in the head is beginning to unfold as a result of the growing activity of the heart centre up the spine.

It is the organ of fusion, just as the head centre is the organ of synthesis. As the heart centre becomes active, the individual aspirant is slowly drawn into an increasingly closer relation to his soul, and then two expansions of consciousness take place, which are interpreted by him as events or happenings:

(a) He is drawn into the Ashram of one of the Masters, according to his soul ray, and becomes an accepted disciple in the technical sense. The Master is Himself the heart centre of the Ashram and He can now reach His disciple, via the soul, because that disciple, through alignment and contact, has put his heart into close rapport with the soul. He then becomes responsive to the heart of all things which, as far as humanity is at present concerned, is the Hierarchy.

(b) He is drawn into close service relationship with humanity. His growing sense of responsibility, due to heart activity, leads him to serve and work. Eventually he too becomes the heart of a group or of an organisation—small at first, but becoming worldwide as his spiritual power develops and he thinks in terms of the group and of humanity. These two relationships on his part are reciprocal. Thus the love aspect of divinity becomes active in the three worlds, and love is anchored on earth and takes the place of emotion, of desire and of the material aspects of feeling. Note that phrase. (17-160/1)

7. The centres are the major agency upon the physical plane through which the soul works, expresses life and quality, according to the point reached under the evolutionary process, and . . . the glandular system (the endocrine glands) is simply an effect—inevitable and unavoidable—of the centres through which the soul is working. The glands . . . express fully the point in evolution of the man, and according to that point are re-

sponsible for defects and limitations, or for assets and achieved perfections. The man's conduct and behaviour upon the physical plane is conditioned, controlled and determined by the nature of his glands, and these are conditioned, controlled and determined by the nature, the quality and the livingness of the centres; these, in their turn are conditioned, controlled and determined by the soul, in increasing effectiveness as evolution proceeds. Prior to soul control, they are conditioned, qualified and controlled by the astral body, and later by the mind. The goal of the evolutionary cycle is to bring about this control, this conditioning, and this determining process by the soul; human beings are today at every imaginable stage of development within this process.   (17-623/4)

34.   ALIGNMENT OF THE EGO WITH THE PERSONALITY

1. It is in the aligning of the three vehicles, the physical, the emotional, and the lower mind body, within the causal periphery, and their establishing there, by an effort of the will, that the real work of the Ego or Higher Self in any particular incarnation can be accomplished. The great thinkers of the race, the true exponents of lower mind, are fundamentally those whose three lower bodies are aligned; that is to say, those whose mental body holds the other two in circumspect alignment. The mental body then is in direct communication, unobstructed and free from interference, straight through to the physical brain.

When the alignment is fourfold, and when the three above-mentioned bodies are aligned with the body of the Higher Self, the causal or egoic body, and held steady within its circumference, then the great leaders of the race—those who emotionally and intellectually sway mankind—can be seen working; then the inspirational writers and dreamers can bring down their inspirations and dreams; and then the synthetic and abstract thinkers can transfer their conceptions to the world of form. It is, right through, a question of an unimpeded channel. Study, therefore, in this connection and when time permits, physical co-ordination; then to physical co-ordination add emotional stability, and you have the two vehicles functioning as one. When the co-ordination extends to the mental body, the threefold lower man is reaching his apotheosis, and has rung most of the changes in the world of form.

Later comes co-ordination perfected with the Higher Self, the channel of communication reaching in line direct—via an unimpeded funnel, if so I might express it—to the physical brain consciousness. Heretofore it has only been direct at rare intervals. The four lesser brain centres are functioning at high vibration in the man of a highly co-ordinated personality; when the Ego is nearing alignment with the lower bodies, the pineal gland and the pituitary body are in process of development; and when they are functioning with correlation (which eventuates by the time the third Initiation is taken), then the third, or alta major centre, intensifies its hitherto gentle vibration. When the fifth Initiation is taken, the interplay between the three centres is perfected, and the alignment of the bodies is geometrically rectified; you have then the perfected fivefold superman.

For the average man, then, this alignment occurs only at intervals—in moments of stress, in hours of needed humanitarian effort and in times of intensest aspiration. Abstraction of a more or less degree has to enter in before the Ego takes continued notice of the personality or lower self. When that abstraction involves the emotions, is based in the mentality and contacts the physical brain, then alignment is commencing.

Hence the work of meditation, for it tends to abstraction and seeks to awaken to abstract consciousness both the emotions and the mentality.

. . . Real abstract thought becomes possible only when the Personality has, by vibration reciprocal to that of the Ego, aligned itself sufficiently to form a fairly unimpeded channel. Then at intervals, rare at first but of increasing frequency, will abstract ideas begin to filter down, to be followed in due time by flashes of real illumination or intuition from the Spiritual Triad or the true threefold Ego itself.

The Chord of the Ego

When I use the term "reciprocal vibration", what do I mean? I mean the adaptation of the Personality or Lower Self, to the Ego or Higher Self, the dominating of the Personality ray by the ray of the Ego and the combining of their tones. I mean the blending of the primary colour of the Higher Self with the secondary hue of the Lower Self until beauty is obtained. At first, there is dissonance and discord, a clashing of the colours, and a fight between the Higher and the Lower. But as time progresses, and later with the aid of the Master, harmony of colour and tone is produced (a synonymous matter), until eventually you will have the basic note of matter, the major third of the aligned Personality, the dominant fifth of the Ego, followed by the full chord of the Monad or Spirit.   (2-1/4)

2. *Alignment with the Ego.* This . . . is only possible to the man who has reached the Probationary Path, or a certain very definite point in evolution. Through knowledge and practice, the power has been acquired of automatically and scientifically utilising the sutratma (or channel) as a means of contact. When to this ability is added that of utilising with equal ease the antahkarana (or bridge between the Triad and the personality), then we have a powerful agent of the Hierarchy on the earth. . . . In the early stages of alignment, it has to be concisely and carefully brought about through concentration and meditation. Later, when the right rhythm has been set up in the bodies, and the purification of the sheaths has been rigidly pursued, the dual activity will become practically instantaneous, and the student can then turn his attention to the work of *conscious* building and vitalisation; his point of concentration will not then be given to the attainment of alignment.

Accurate alignment entails :

Mental quiescence, or stable vibration.

Emotional stability, resulting in limpid reflection.

Etheric poise, producing a condition in the head centre which would permit of the direct application of force to the physical brain via the centre.   (3-959/60)

3. For a disciple direct alignment with the Ego via the centres and the physical brain, is the goal of his life of meditation and of discipline. This is in order that the Inner God may function in full consciousness, and wield full control on the physical plane. Thus will humanity be helped and group concerns furthered.   (3-1149)

4. Let us simplify matters if we can, by three clear statements; in them we will sum up the work the disciple accomplishes, as he struggles with and masters the energies of the mental world.

1. Work on the mental plane produces realisation of duality. The disciple seeks to blend and merge the soul with its vehicle and to do this consciously. He seeks to fuse them into a unity. He aims at the realisation that, here and now, they are ONE. The unification of the Self and of the not-self is his objective. The first step in this direction is taken when he begins to cease identifying himself with the form, and recognises (during this transitional period) that he is a duality.

2. The mind, rightly used, becomes therefore a recorder of two types of energy, or of two aspects of the manifestation of the One Life. It records and interprets the world of phenomena. It records and interprets the world of souls. It is sensitive to the three worlds of human evolution. It becomes equally sensitive to the kingdom of the soul. It is the great mediating principle in this interim of dual recognition.

3. Later, the soul and its instrument become so unified and at-one, that duality disappears, and the soul knows itself to be all that is, all that has been, and all that will be.   (4-385/6)

5. You have been apt to think of alignment in terms of the process whereby the personality is brought into relation with the soul. This is entirely accurate, yet alignment is a term which in reality covers four processes :

1. The alignment of soul and personality, resulting in a conscious relation to the Kingdom of God.

2. The alignment of soul and personality with the Ashram, resulting in a conscious relation with the Master of the Ashram.

3. The alignment of the initiate of higher degree with the Spiritual Triad and the consequent result of a recognition of monadic energy.

4. The alignment of all the centres in the etheric body of the disciple. This results in the ability of these centres to register and transfer energies which enter into the lower mechanism as a consequence of the three higher alignments—listed above.   (6-152/3)

6. When the personality has reached a point of purification, of dedication and of illumination, then the attractive power of the soul, whose nature is love and understanding, can function, and fusion of these two will take place.   (8-134)

7. Man is therefore (from the angle of force expression) a mass of conflicting energies and an active centre of moving forces, with a shift of emphasis constantly going on, and with the aggregation of the numerous streams of energy presenting a confusing kaleidoscope of active interrelations, interpenetration, internecine warfare, and interdependence until such time as the personality forces (symbolic of divine multiplicity) are subdued or "brought into line" by the dominant soul. That is what we really mean by the use of the word "alignment". This alignment results from :

1. The control of the personality by the soul.

2. The downpouring of soul energy, via the mental and the emotional bodies, into the brain, thus producing the subjugation of the lower nature, the awakening of the brain consciousness to soul awareness, and a new alignment of the bodies.

3. The right arrangement, according to ray type, of the energies which are motivating and dynamically arousing the centres into activity. This leads eventually to a direct alignment of the centres upon the spine, so that soul energy can pass up and down through the centres from the directing centre in the head. . . .

Eventually, the monadic ray takes control, absorbing into itself the rays of the personality and of the soul (at the third and fifth initiations) and thus duality is finally and definitely overcome and "only the *One Who Is*" remains.   (15-340/1)

35.   INTEGRATION

1. Just what do we mean by *Integration*? We are apt to bandy words about with unthinking lightness and inexactitude, but, dealing as we are with a development which is becoming increasingly prevalent in the human field, it might profit us for a moment to define it and seek to understand one or two of its major implications. It has to be regarded as an essential step, prior to passing (in full and waking consciousness) into the fifth, or spiritual kingdom.

We regard the physical body as a functioning aggregate of physical organs, each with its own duties and purposes. These, when combined and acting in unison, we regard as constituting a living organism. The many parts form one whole, working under the direction of the intelligent, conscious Thinker, the soul, as far as man is concerned. At the same time, this conscious form is slowly arriving at a point where integration into the larger whole becomes desirable and is finally achieved— again in the waking consciousness. This process of conscious assimilation is carried forward progressively by the gradual integration of the part into the family unit, the nation, the social order, the current civilisation, the world of nations, and finally into humanity itself. This integration is, therefore, both physical in nature, and an attitude of mind. The consciousness of the man is gradually aroused so that it recognises this relation of the part to the whole, with the implied interrelation of all parts within the whole.

The man who has awakened to full consciousness in the various aspects of his nature—emotional, mental and egoic—realises himself first of all as a personality. He integrates his various bodies with their different states of consciousness, into one active reality. He is then definitely a personality, and has passed a major milestone on the Path of Return. This is the first great step. Inevitably, the evolutionary process must bring to pass this phenomenal occurrence in the case of every human being, but it can be produced (and is increasingly so produced today) by a planned mental application to the task, and an intelligent consideration of the relation of the part to the whole. It will be found that the purely selfish, material personality will eventually arrive at the condition wherein the man will be conscious of integrated activity and power, because he

1. Has developed and integrated his own separative "parts" into one whole.

2. Has studied and used his environment, of the whole of which his personality is but a part, in such a way that it contributes to his desire, his success, and his emergence into prominence. In doing this, he necessarily has had to make some living contribution to the whole, in order to evoke its integrating power. His motive, however, being purely selfish and material in objective, can only carry him a certain distance along the path of the higher integration.

The unselfish, spiritually oriented man, also integrates the various aspects of himself into one functioning whole, but the focus of his activity is *contribution,* not acquisition, and, by the working of the higher law, the Law of Service, he becomes integrated, not only as a human being within the radius of the prevalent civilisation, but also into that wider and more inclusive world of conscious activity which we call the Kingdom of God.

The progress of humanity is from one *realised* integration to another; man's basic integrity is, however, in the realm of consciousness. This is a statement of importance. It might be remarked—speaking loosely and generally—that:

1. In Lemurian times, humanity achieved the integration of the vital or etheric body with the physical body.

2. In Atlantean times, humanity added to the already achieved synthesis still another part, that of the astral nature, and psychic man

came definitely into being. He was alive and at the same time sensitive and responsive to his environment in a wider and more specialised sense.

3. Today, in our Aryan race, humanity is occupied with the task of adding still another aspect, that of the mind. To the achieved facts of livingness and sensitivity, he is rapidly adding reason, mental perception, and other qualities of mind and thought life.

4. Advanced humanity upon the Probationary Path is fusing these three divine aspects into one whole, which we call the personality. Many hundreds of thousands stand at this time upon that Path, and are acting, feeling and thinking simultaneously, making of these functions one activity. This personality synthesis comes upon the Path of Discipleship, under the direction of the indwelling entity, the spiritual man.

This integration constitutes alignment and—when a man has achieved this—he passes eventually through a process of re-orientation. This reveals to him, as he slowly changes his direction, the still greater Whole of humanity. Later, upon the Path of Initiation, there will dawn upon his vision, the *Whole* of which humanity itself is only an expression. This is the subjective world of reality, into which we begin definitely to enter as we become members of the Kingdom of God.

5. Upon the Probationary Path, though only during its later stages, he begins to serve humanity consciously through the medium of his integrated personality, and thus the consciousness of the larger and wider whole gradually supersedes his individual and separative consciousness. He knows himself to be but a part.

6. Upon the Path of Discipleship, the process of integration into the Kingdom of God, the Kingdom of Souls, proceeds until the third initiation is undergone.

All these various integrations work out into some definite form of activity. First, there is the service of the personality, selfish and separative, wherein man sacrifices much in the interests of his own desire. Then comes the stage of service of humanity, and, finally, the service of the Plan. (15-348/51)

2. There are in the world today many truly integrated personalities. These, because soul and personality are integrated, can tread the Path of Accepted Discipleship. . . .

Study and meditation combined are the factors which all aspirants should employ if they seek to produce this needed integration and a consequent life of service. Thus the aspirant can test out both his point of integration and the extent of the serving quality produced by this integration. If aspirants would study their physical plane life with care, they would discover that they are either working automatically in response to physical plane conventional ideas of goodwill or of being kind, or they are working emotionally because they like to help, they like to be liked, they like to relieve suffering (owing to their hatred of the discomfort which suffering brings to them), they believe in following the steps of the Christ Who went about doing good, or because of a natural, deep-seated life tendency. This is a hopeful and finalising unfoldment.

Aspirants will eventually find out (when the physical and emotional phases of the integration are over) that there follows a phase of intelligent service, motivated in the first instance by mercy, then by conviction of its essentiality, then by a stage of definitely spiritual ambition, then by a submissive following of the example of the Hierarchy, and finally by the activity of the quality of pure love; this pure love increasingly expresses itself as the higher integration of soul and personality proceeds. All these phases of intention and of techniques are right in their own place, just as long as they have teaching value, and whilst the higher next phases remain vague and nebulous. They become wrong when they are perpetuated and carried on when the next stage is clearly seen but not followed. Ponder on this. It is of value to you to realise the true significance of these varying phases of integration, carried forward—as they are—under evolutionary law.

All these steps upon the way of integration lead to that culminating stage wherein the personality—rich in experience, powerful in expression, reoriented and dedicated—becomes simply the mediator of soul life between the Hierarchy and Humanity. Again—ponder on this. (17-509/10)

36. AT-ONE-MENT THE RESULT OF INITIATION

A point that we need to grasp is that each successive initiation brings about a more complete unification of the personality and the Ego, and on higher levels still, with the Monad. The whole evolution of the human spirit is a progressive at-one-ment. In the at-one-ment between the Ego and the personality lies hid the mystery of the Christian doctrine of the Atonement. One unification takes place at the moment of individualisation, when man becomes a conscious rational entity, in contradistinction to the animals. As evolution proceeds successive at-one-ments occur.

At-one-ment on all levels—emotional, intuitional, spiritual and Divine —consists in conscious, continuous functioning. In all cases it is preceded by a burning, through the medium of the inner fire, and by the destruction, through sacrifice, of all that separates. The approach to unity is through destruction of the lower, and of all that forms a barrier. Take, in illustration, the web that separates the etheric body and the emotional. When that web has been burned away by the inner fire, the communication between the bodies of the personality becomes continuous and complete, and the three lower vehicles function as one. You have a somewhat analogous situation on the higher levels, though the parallel cannot be pushed to detail. The intuition corresponds to the emotional, and the four higher levels of the mental plane, to the etheric. In the destruction of the causal body at the time of the fourth initiation (called symbolically "the Crucifixion") you have a process analogous to the burning of the web that leads to the unification of the bodies of the personality. The disintegration that is a part of the arhat initiation, leads to unity between the Ego and the Monad, expressing itself in the Triad. It is the perfect at-one-ment.

The whole process is therefore for the purpose of making man consciously one:

First: with himself, and those in incarnation with him.

Second: with his Higher Self, and thus with all selves.

Third: with his Spirit, or "Father in Heaven", and thus with all Monads.

Fourth: with the Logos, the Three in One, and the One in Three.

Man becomes a conscious human being through the instrumentality of the Lords of the Flame, through Their enduring sacrifice.

Man becomes a conscious Ego, with the consciousness of the Higher Self, at the third initiation, through the instrumentality of the Masters and of the Christ, and through Their sacrifice in taking physical incarnation for the helping of the world.

Man unites with the Monad at the fifth initiation, through the instrumentality of the Lord of the World, the Solitary Watcher, the Great Sacrifice.

Man becomes one with the Logos through the instrumentality of *One about Whom naught may be said.* (1-18/9)

37. SPIRITUAL EVOLUTION

1. The means of development are ever the same: Occult meditation and service; the inner life of concentration and the outer life of practice; the inner ability to contact the higher, and the outer ability to express that faculty in terms of holy living; the inner irradiation from the Spirit, and the outer shining before men. (2-273)

2. That is spiritual which lies beyond the point of present achievement; it is that which embodies the vision, and which urges the man on towards a goal higher than the one attained. (6-234)

3. The time has now come when the great rhythm of meditation, ranging from desire, through prayer, to worship, and from thence to meditation and invocation, can be imposed by men upon their own thinking.

This is the immediate task of the New Group of World Servers, co-operating everywhere with the men of goodwill; each member of the New Group has to ascertain for himself where he stands, where his meditative responsibility lies, and in what field destiny indicates his service to the race of men must be found. This is no easy task, brother of mine. Men are frequently so spiritually ambitious and waste their time in doing that which is not their destined task because in so doing they satisfy their spiritual pride. (6-235)

4. Because the senior disciples and initiates have reached a goal which has seemed for long quite unattainable to the average aspirant, it is assumed that they have attained; the fact that they have only passed a milestone upon the endless Way of Bliss is entirely forgotten. But, owing to

the impulsion of life itself, progress ever continues; knowledge must ever be transmuted into wisdom; love must ever be accompanied by divine purpose; light must ever be succeeded by life; from the Hierarchy, the initiate must pass to Shamballa, and from Shamballa he will follow one or other of the seven Paths; the Path of Evolution gives place to the Way of the Higher Evolution; planetary recognitions eventually expand into solar contacts; the Christ-consciousness eventually unfolds into something so all-inclusive, that we have as yet no word for it or any need of words; recognition of the Father and of the monadic being causes all lesser recognitions to fade out, and soul-consciousness and progressive life in form are no longer goals, but are left far behind.

In spite of all this, it is necessary to remember that the gain of all experience for ever persists, nothing is ever lost; that which life in form has conferred is still in the possession of the immortal spiritual entity; that which the soul-consciousness has enfolded and included, is still the rich endowment of Being, centred now in the Monad; hierarchical experience is merged into the purposes of the Council Chamber at Shamballa, but ability to work in the Hierarchy ever lasts, because the hierarchical constitution and institution condition all manifestation—for what reason this is so, no one knows, but so is the divine Will.   (13-559/60)

5. It takes the soul itself to reveal to the poised and peaceful mind the next step to be taken in the work of world evolution, through the impartation of ideas. Such is the Plan for humanity.   (15-136)

(a) MAN

1. We might consider the microcosm, or man, evolving in the three worlds. Man is the product of the approximation (at present imperfect) of the two poles of Spirit (the Father in Heaven) and of matter (the Mother). The result of this union is an individualised Son of God, or unit of the divine Self, an exact replica in miniature on the lowest plane, of the great Son of God, the All-Self, Who is in Himself the totality of all the miniature sons, of all the individualised Selves, and of each and every unit. The microcosm, expressed in other terms or from the subjective point of view, is a miniature sun, distinguished by the qualities of heat and light. At present that light is "under the bushel", or deeply hidden by a veil of matter, but in due process of evolution it will shine forth to such an extent that the veils will be lost from sight in a blaze of exceeding glory. At present the microcosmic heat is of small degree, or the magnetic radiation between the microcosmic units is but little *felt* (in the occult significance of the

term), but as time proceeds, the emanations of heat—due to intensification of the inner flame, coupled with the assimilated radiation of other
units—will increase, and become of such proportions that the interaction
between the individualised Selves will result in the merging to perfection
of the flame within each one, and a blending of the heat; this will proceed
until there is "one flame with countless sparks" within it, until the heat is
general and balanced. When this is the case and each Son of God is a
perfected Sun, characterised by perfectly expressed light and heat, then
the entire solar system, the greater Son of God, will be the perfected
Sun.   (3-228/9)

2. During the life cycle of a man, he expresses what is in him at his particular stage, and gradually develops from the stage of the ante-natal period
wherein the Self overshadows the matter aspect, until the period wherein
that Higher Self takes full possession of the prepared form. This stage
varies with every individual. From that time on, fuller self-consciousness
is sought, and the man (if proceeding normally) expresses himself through
the form ever more adequately. Each life or lesser cycle in the great
cycle of the Ego or Self, sees that expression more complete, brings the
form more under control and develops a conscious realisation of the Self,
until there comes a culminating cycle of lives in which the Self within
rapidly dominates, and takes full authority. The form becomes wholly
adequate; the fusion of the two poles of Spirit and matter is fully brought
about; and the light (fire) and heat (radiation) is seen and felt systematically. Then the form is either consciously utilised for specific ends or is
vacated, and the man is liberated.   (3-231)

3. Man, in essential essence, is the Higher Triad demonstrating through
a gradually evolving form, the egoic or causal body, and utilising the
lower threefold personality as a means to contact the lower three planes.
All this has for purpose the development of perfect self-consciousness.
(3-260/1)

4. Man might be defined as a unit of conscious life, swept into tangible
expression through the discriminating love of God. Through his life experiences he is presented with innumerable choices which gradually shift
from the realm of the tangible into that of the intangible. As he attracts,
or is attracted by the life of his environment, he becomes increasingly
conscious of a series of shifting values, until he reaches that point in his
development when the pull or the magnetic attraction of the subjective
world and the intangible mental and spiritual values are more potent than

the factors which have hitherto enticed him on. His sense of values is no longer determined by:

1. The satisfaction of his instinctual animal nature.

2. The desires of a more emotional and sentimental kind which his astral body demands.

3. The pull and pleasures of the mind nature, and of intellectual appetites.

He becomes potently attracted by his soul, and this produces a tremendous revolution in his entire life, regarding the word "revolution" in its true sense, as a complete turning around. This revolution is happening now, on such a universal scale in the lives of individuals in the world, that it is one of the main factors producing the present potency of experimental ideas in the world of modern times. The attractive power of the soul grows steadily, and the pull of the personality weakens as steadily. All this has been brought about by the process of experiment leading to experience; by experience, leading to a wiser use of the powers of the personality; by a growing appreciation of a truer world of values and of reality, and by an effort on man's part to identify himself with the world of spiritual values and not with a world of material values. The world of meaning and of causes becomes gradually the world in which he finds happiness, and his selection of his major interests and the use to which he decides to put his time and powers, are finally conditioned by the truer spiritual values. He then is on the path of illumination.   (14-339/40)

(b) TREADING THE RAZOR-EDGED PATH

1. No glamour, no illusion can long hold the man who has set himself the task of treading the razor-edged Path which leads through the wilderness, through the thick-set forest, through the deep waters of sorrow and distress, through the valley of sacrifice and over the mountains of vision to the gate of Deliverance. He may travel sometimes in the dark (and the illusion of darkness is very real); he may travel sometimes in a light so dazzling and bewildering that he can scarcely see the way ahead; he may know what it is to falter on the Path, and to drop under the fatigue of service and of strife; he may be temporarily sidetracked and wander down the by-paths of ambition, of self-interest and of material enchantment, but the lapse will be but brief. Nothing in heaven or hell, on earth or elsewhere can prevent the progress of the man who has awakened to the illusion, who has glimpsed the reality beyond the glamour of the

astral plane, and who has heard, even if only once, the clarion call of his own soul.   (4-223)

2. Students are begged to deal drastically and potently with their emotional natures, remembering that victory descends from above and cannot be worked up to from below. The soul *must* govern and its instrument in the warfare is the consecrated mind.

It is interesting to note the occult sequence in the description given of this plane in the rule under consideration (Rule Seven).

It is first of all the plane of dual forces. The first thing the aspirant becomes aware of is duality. The little evolved man is aware of synthesis, but it is the synthesis of his material nature. The highly spiritual man is aware also of synthesis but it is that of his soul, whose consciousness is that of unity. But in between is the wretched aspirant, conscious of duality above all else, and pulled hither and thither between the two. His first step has for its objective to make him aware of the pairs of opposites and of the necessity to choose between them. Through the light which he has discovered in himself, he becomes aware of the dark. Through the good which attracts him, he sees the evil which is for him the line of least resistance. Through the activity of pain, he can visualise and become aware of pleasure, and heaven and hell become to him realities. Through the activity of the attractive life of his soul, he realises the attraction of matter and of form, and is forced to recognise the urge and pull of both of them. He learns to feel himself as "pendant 'twixt the two great forces", and, once the dualities are grasped, it dawns on him slowly and surely that the deciding factor in the struggle is his divine will, in contradistinction to his selfish will. Thus the dual forces play their part until they are seen as two great streams of divine energy, pulling in opposite directions, and he becomes then aware of the two paths mentioned in our rule. One path leads back into the dreary land of rebirth, and the other leads through the golden gate to the city of free souls. One is therefore involutionary and involves him in deepest matter; the other leads him out of the body nature, and makes him eventually aware of his spiritual body, through which he can function in the kingdom of the soul. One path, later on (when he is a true and pledged chela) is known to him as the left hand path, and the other the path of right activity. On one path he becomes proficient in black magic, which is only the developed powers of the personality, subordinated to the selfish purposes of a man whose motives are those of self interest and worldly ambition. These confine him to the three worlds and shut the door which opens on to life. On the other path he subordinates his personality and exercises the magic of the White Brotherhood, working always in the light of the soul with the soul in all forms, and laying no emphasis upon the ambitions of the personal self. Clear discrimination of these two paths reveals what is called in some occult books that *"narrow razor-edged Path"* which lies between the two. This is the "noble middle Path" of the Buddha and marks the fine line of demarcation between the pairs of opposites, and between the two streams which he has learnt to recognise—one going up unto the gates of Heaven, and the other passing down into the nethermost hell.   (4-228/9)

(c) THE DEVELOPMENT OF THE HUMAN BEING

1. The development of the human being is but the passing from one state of consciousness to another. It is a succession of expansions, a growth of that faculty of *awareness* that constitutes the predominant characteristic of the indwelling Thinker. It is the progressing from consciousness polarised in the personality, lower self or body, to that polarised in the higher self, ego, or soul, thence to polarisation in the Monad, or Spirit till the consciousness eventually is Divine. As the human being develops, the faculty of awareness extends first of all beyond the circumscribing walls that confine it within the lower kingdoms of nature (the mineral, vegetable and animal) to the three worlds of the evolving personality, to the planet whereon he plays his part, to the system wherein that planet revolves, until it finally escapes from the solar system itself, and becomes universal.   (1-7/8)

2. For a long period of lives the Ego remains practically unconscious of the Personality. The magnetic link exists, but that is all until the time comes when the personal life reaches a point where it has somewhat to add to the content of the causal body—a body at first small, colourless and insignificant. But the hour comes when the stones are first brought perfected from the quarry of the personal life, and the first colours are painted in by the man, the builder and the artist. Then the Ego begins to give attention, rarely at first, but with increasing frequency, until lives come around in which the Ego definitely works at the subjugation of the lower self, at the enlargement of the communicating channel, and at the transmission to the physical brain consciousness of the fact of its existence and the goal of its being. Once that is accomplished, and the inner fire is freer in its passage, lives are then given to the stabilising of that impression, and to the making of that inner consciousness a part

of the conscious life. The flame radiates downward more and more until gradually the different vehicles come into line, and the man stands on the Probationary Path. He is ignorant yet of what lies ahead, and is conscious only of wild and earnest aspiration and of innate divine longings. He is eager to make good, longing to *know,* and dreaming always of someone or something higher than himself. All this is backed by the profound conviction that in service to humanity will the dreamed-of goal be reached, will the vision become reality, the longing fructify into satis faction, and aspiration be merged in sight.

The Hierarchy begins to take action and his instruction is carried out as aforesaid. . . . Until now the Teachers have only watched and guided without definitely dealing with the man himself; all has been left to the Ego and the life divine to carry out the plan, the attention of the Masters being directed to the Ego on his own plane. The Ego bends every effort to quicken vibration, and to force the oft rebelling lower vehicles to respond and measure up to the rapidly increasing force. It is largely a matter of increased fire or heat, and consequent intensification of vibratory capacity. The egoic fire waxes ever greater until the work is done, and the purificatory fire becomes the Light of Illumination. Ponder on this sentence. As above, so below; on each rung of the ladder the process is repeated; the Monad at the third Initiation, begins itself to be conscious of the Ego. The work, then, is more rapid owing to the rarity of the material and to the fact that resistance is a factor in the three worlds but not elsewhere.

Hence pain ceases for a Master. That is, pain as we know it on earth, which is largely *pain in matter.* The pain that lies hid in comprehension, not resistance, is left to the highest circles, yea, it reaches to the Logos Himself. But this is beside the point and wellnigh incomprehensible to you who are yet trammelled by matter. . . .

The Ego seeks to bring about the desired end in three ways :

1. By definite work on abstract levels. It aspires to contact and enclose the permanent atom, its first direct approach to the Triad.

2. By definite work on colour and sound with the aim in view of stimulation and vivification, working thus in groups and under the guidance of a Master.

3. By frequent attempts to definitely control the lower self, a thing distasteful to the Ego, whose tendency is to rest content with consciousness and aspiration on its own plane. Forget not that the Ego itself

has somewhat to wrestle with. The refusal to incarnate is not found only on spiritual levels, but is found also on that of the Higher Self. (2-35/7)

3. Souls, cycling through various forms of life in the long evolutionary process, arrive eventually at full, self-conscious existence. By this we mean that they are self-determined, self-conditioned, and self-aware. They are also conscious of and responsive to their environment.

Once this conscious awareness is achieved, then progress becomes more rapid. It should be borne in mind that many human beings are not thus aware. The groupings which arise out of this awareness (limiting our ideas entirely to those within the radius of the human family) can be expressed as follows:

1. The souls who live but whose consciousness sleeps. These are the dormant human beings whose intelligence is of such a low order, and their awareness of themselves and of life is so dim and nebulous, that only the lowest forms of human existence come into this category. Racially, nationally, and tribally they do not exist as pure types, but occasionally such a person emerges in the slums of our great cities. They are like a "throw back" and never appear among what are called the natural savages, or the peasantry.

2. The souls who are simply aware of physical plane life and of sensation. These people are slow, inert, inarticulate, bewildered *by their environment,* but they are not bewildered, as are the more advanced and emotional types, *by events.* They have no sense of time or of purpose; they rarely exhibit skill in any direction. They can dig and carry, under direction; they eat, sleep and procreate, following the natural instincts of the animal body. Emotionally, however, they are asleep, and mentally they are totally unawakened. These too are relatively rare, though several thousands of them can be found upon our planet. They can be recognised through their complete incapacity to respond to emotional and mental training and culture.

3. The souls who are beginning to integrate and who are emotionally and psychically alive. In them, of course, the animal nature is awake and the desire nature is becoming rampant. These people are to be found in all races to a small extent, and a number of them can be found among the negroes, which race contains a large number of those who are today relatively children. These are child souls, and though the mental equipment is there, and some of them can be trained to use it,

the preponderance of life emphasis is entirely upon physical activity as it is motivated by the desire for satisfaction of some kind, and by a shallow "wish-life" or desire nature, almost entirely oriented towards the physical life. These souls are the modern correspondences to the old Lemurian cultures.

4. The souls who are primarily emotional. The mind nature is not functioning strongly, and only rarely does it swing into activity, and the physical body is slipping steadily into the realm of the unconscious. In every race and nation there are millions of such souls in existence. They may be regarded as the modern Atlanteans.

5. Those souls who can now be classed as intelligent human beings, capable of mental application, if trained, and showing that they can think when need arises. They are still, nevertheless, predominantly emotional. They constitute the bulk of modern humanity at this time. They are the average citizens of our modern world—good, well-intentioned, capable of intense emotional activity, with the feeling nature almost over-developed, and oscillating between the life of the senses and that of the mind. They swing between the poles of experience. Their lives are spent in an astral turmoil, but they have steadily increasing interludes wherein the mind can momentarily make itself felt, and thus at need effect important decisions. These are the nice, good people, who are, nevertheless, largely controlled by the mass consciousness, because they are relatively unthinking. They can be regimented and standardised with facility by orthodox religion and government, and are the "sheep" of the human family.

6. The souls who think, and who are minds. These are steadily increasing in number and gaining in power as our educational processes and our scientific discoveries bring results, and expand human awareness. They constitute the cream of the human family, and are the people who are achieving success in some department of human life. They are the writers, artists, thinkers in various fields of human knowledge and aspiration, politicians, religious leaders, scientists, skilled workers and artisans, and all those who, though in the front rank, yet take ideas and propositions and work with them for the ultimate benefit of the human family. They are the world aspirants, and those who are beginning to get the ideal of service into their consciousness.

7. Those souls whose sense of awareness on the physical plane is now of such an order that they can pass on to the Probationary Path. They

are the mystics, conscious of duality, torn between the pairs of opposites, but who are yet unable to rest until they are polarised in the
soul. These are the sensitive, struggling people, who long for release
from failure and from existence in the world today. Their mind natures
are alive and active, but they cannot yet control them as they should,
and the higher illumination remains as yet a joyous hope and final possibility.

8. Souls whose intelligence and love nature is becoming so awakened
and integrated, that they can begin to tread the Path of Discipleship.
They are the practical mystics, or the occultists of modern times.

9. The souls who are initiate into the mysteries of the kingdom of God.
These are souls who are not only conscious of their vehicles of expression, the integrated personality, and conscious also of themselves
as souls, but they know, past all controversy, that there is no such
thing as "my soul and your soul", but simply "the SOUL". They know
this not only as a mental proposition, and as a sensed reality, but also
as a fact in their own consciousness.

10. The souls who have achieved release from all the limitations of
the form nature, and who dwell eternally in the consciousness of the
One Soul, withdrawn from identification with any aspiration of the
form life, no matter how highly developed. They can and do use the
form at will for the purposes of the general good. These are the Masters of Life, the perfected adepts.   (15-203/7)

4. The life of a *personality* falls into the following stages:

1. Its slow and gradual construction over a long period of time. For
many cycles of incarnations, a man is not a personality. He is just a
member of the mass.

2. The conscious identification of the soul with the personality during
this stage, is practically non-existent. The aspect of the soul which is
concealed within the sheaths, is for a long, long period dominated by
the life of those sheaths, only making its presence felt through what
is called "the voice of the conscience". However, as time goes on, the
active intelligent life of the person is gradually enhanced and co-ordinated by the energy which streams from the knowledge petals of the
egoic lotus, or from the intelligent perceptive nature of the soul on its
own plane. This produces eventually the integration of the three lower
sheaths into one functioning whole. The man is then a personality.

3. The personality life of the now co-ordinated individual persists for a large number of lives, and falls into three phases:

(a) The phase of a dominant, aggressive personality life, basically conditioned by its ray type, selfish in nature, and very individualistic.

(b) A transitional phase wherein a conflict rages between personality and soul. The soul begins to seek liberation from form life and yet —in the last analysis—the personality is dependent upon the life principle, conferred by the soul. Wording it otherwise, the conflict between the soul ray and the personality ray starts, and the war is on between two focussed aspects of energy. This conflict terminates at the third initiation.

(c) The control by the soul is the final phase, leading to the death and destruction of the personality. This death begins when the personality, the Dweller on the Threshold, stands before the Angel of the Presence. The Light of the solar Angel then obliterates the light of matter.

The "control" phase is conditioned by the complete identification of the personality with the soul; this is a reversal of the previous identification of the soul with the personality. This also is what we mean when speaking of the integration of these two; the two are now one. It was of this phase that St. Paul was speaking when he referred (in the Epistle to the Ephesians) to Christ making "out of two, one new man". It is primarily the phase of the final stages of the Probationary Path (where the work consciously begins) and its carrying forward to completion upon the Path of Discipleship. It is the stage of the practical and successful server; it is that wherein the entire focus and output of the life of the man is dedicated to the fulfilment of hierarchical intent. The man begins to work on and from levels not included in the three worlds of ordinary evolution, but which nevertheless have their effects and their planned objectives within those three worlds.   (17-506/8)

See also: "Five Evolutionary Periods"—(2-23/9), and (4-467/70), (15-268/9), (15-332/3)

(d) POINTS OF CRISIS IN LIFE

We have five points of crisis in the life of the individual. . . . The reflection of this fivefold experience in any individual life takes place in the following order in the life of the average intelligent aspirant, who responds to, and takes advantage of the civilisation and education of the present time.

1. Appropriation of the physical sheath.
This takes place between the fourth and seventh year, when the soul, hitherto overshadowing, takes possession of the physical vehicle.

2. A crisis during adolescence, wherein the soul appropriates the astral vehicle. This crisis is not recognised by the general public and is only dimly sensed, from its evidenced temporary abnormalities, by the average psychologist. They do not recognise the cause, but only the effects.

3. A similar crisis between the twenty-first and twenty-fifth years, wherein the mind vehicle is appropriated. The man should then begin to respond to egoic influences, and in the case of advanced man, he frequently does.

4. A crisis between the thirty-fifth and forty-second years, wherein conscious contact with the soul is established; the threefold personality then begins to respond, as a unit, to soul impulse.

5. For the remaining years of life, there should be an increasingly strong relationship between the soul and its vehicles, leading to another crisis between the fifty-sixth or the sixty-third years. According to that crisis will depend the future usefulness of the person, and whether the ego continues to use the vehicles on into old age, or whether there is a gradual withdrawal of the indwelling entity.

There are many corresponding cycles of crisis in the life history of any soul down through the ages, but these major five crises can be traced with clarity from the standpoint of the higher vision.   (15-52/3)

(e)   RATE OF PROGRESS

I would . . . emphasise to you the need of ever remembering that in all work that is truly occult, expected effects are very slowly achieved. Should a man seem in any one incarnation to make spectacular progress, it is due to the fact that he is but demonstrating what has already been earlier acquired (the manifesting forth of innate faculty, acquired in previous incarnations) and is preparing for a fresh period of slow, careful and painstaking endeavour. He recapitulates in the present life the processes surmounted in the past, and thus lays the foundation for renewed effort. This slow and laborious effort, which is the consistent method of all that evolves, is after all but an *illusion of time* and is due to the fact that consciousness is at present, for the majority, polarised in the lower vehicles and not in the causal. The states of consciousness succeed each other apparently slowly, and in their slow progression lies the chance for the Ego to assimilate the fruit of these stages.

It takes a long time to establish a stable vibration, and it takes as long to shatter it, and to impose another and still higher rhythm. Growth is one long period of building in order to destroy, of constructing in order to disorganise later, of developing certain rhythmic processes in order to later disrupt them, and to force the old rhythm to give place to the new. What the Personality spends many thousands of lives in establishing, is not going to be lightly altered when the Ego—working in the lower consciousness—seeks to effect a change. The shifting of polarisation from emotional to mental, and thence to the causal, and later to the threefold Spirit, inevitably entails a period of great difficulty, of violent conflict, both internally and with the environment, intense suffering and apparent darkness and disruption—all these things characterise the life of the aspirant or the disciple.   (2-81/2)

(f) LEARNING FROM EXPERIENCE

1. Lift not too much (from the shoulders of your associates). It is the right of their souls to learn the same lessons as you have had to learn, and an over-pitiful heart is not always the most helpful of possessions. A loving heart is always helpful. . . . Take not away from others this right to stand alone, by too great a display of shielding love. . . . Let them stand up to the issues of the soul which are brought to their attention through the medium of the material lesson, and thus enable them to enter upon their next life better equipped to love, to work, and to live unselfishly. . . . True love has sometimes to stand aside and look on peacefully whilst others learn their lessons. . . . Refuse then to be overwhelmed and regard not yourself as failing in some respect when others fail to meet the issues as they should. The reactions of others are not your responsibility. It is your responsibility to give them strength and detachment. Shoulder not, therefore, responsibilities which are not yours. (But at the same time do not use this motivation—out of context—as an excuse to shirk taking action where and when it is your responsibility to act, and to play that part as planned by your soul—*Compiler.*) (5-404/5)

2. Under the occult law, doing ever precedes knowledge, because knowledge is gained through experiment and experience. The disciple or aspirant works always in the dark, particularly in the early stages of his

unfoldment, following a deep and hidden instinct towards right activity. By that hard and persistent performance of duty, under the pressure of conscience at first, under the impulse of his awakening soul, and under the influences of the Master, he moves forward from darkness to light; he discovers that obedience to his spiritual instincts leads him inevitably into the realm of knowledge, and that knowledge—when acquired—is transformed eventually into wisdom. He then becomes a Master and walks no longer in the dark.

Aspirants usually bitterly resent the many cycles of darkness through which they seem to go; they complain of the difficulty of working in the dark and of seeing no light anywhere; they forget that the ability to work in the dark or in the light is all one inherent capacity. The reason for this is that the soul knows nothing but *being*, and light and dark are—to the soul—one and the same thing. Above everything else, knowledge comes through conscious experiment, and where there is no experimental activity, no experience can be gained. Knowledge is the reward of both these factors—a knowledge which is not theoretical, but which is proven, factual, and the intelligent result of hard work; it is also the result of frequent distress (rightly handled) and of spiritual anticipation.

The above is true of the life and work of the individual aspirant as he tackles the problem of his own lower nature and prepares for the stage of becoming a soul-infused personality; it is true also of the working disciple, seeking knowledge and wisdom as he works out the hierarchical Plan as best he can. He must perforce experiment and gain practical experience; he must learn the meaning of both success and failure, and the knowledge which can be gained thereby. Knowledge comes at first through the struggle to move forward into greater and clearer light; then it comes as the aspirant (seeking soul expression) learns to forget himself in the need of others as they demand whatever light and knowledge he may possess; wisdom takes the place of knowledge when, in the transmuting fires of struggle, pain and hard work, the aspirant transforms himself into the working disciple, and is gradually absorbed into the ranks of the Hierarchy.   (6-393/5)

38. DISCIPLESHIP

1. A disciple is one who above all else, is pledged to do three things:

(a) To serve humanity.

(b) To co-operate with the Plan of the Great Ones as he sees it and as best he may.

(c) To develop the powers of the Ego, to expand his consciousness until he can function on the three planes in the three worlds, and in the causal body, and to follow the guidance of the higher Self and not the dictates of his three-fold lower manifestation.

A disciple is one who is beginning to comprehend group work, and to change his centre of activity from himself (as the pivot around which everything revolves) to the group centre.

A disciple is one who realises simultaneously the relative insignificance of each unit of consciousness, and also its vast importance. His sense of proportion is adjusted, and he sees things as they are; he sees people as they are; he sees himself as he inherently is, and seeks then to become that which he is.

A disciple realises the life or force side of nature, and to him the form makes no appeal. He works with force and through force; he recognises himself as a force centre within a greater force centre, and his is the responsibility of directing the energy which may pour through him into channels through which the group can be benefitted.

The disciple knows himself to be—to a greater or less degree—an outpost of the Master's consciousness, viewing the Master in a twofold sense:

(a) As his own egoic consciousness.

(b) As the centre of his group; the force animating the units of the group, and binding them into a homogeneous whole.

A disciple is one who is transferring his consciousness out of the personal into the impersonal, and during the transition stage much of difficulty and of suffering is necessarily endured. These difficulties arise from various causes:

(a) The disciple's lower self, which rebels at being transmuted.

(b) A man's immediate group, friends, or family, who rebel at his growing impersonality. They do not like to be acknowledged as one with him on the life side, and yet separate from him where desires and interests lie. Yet the law holds good, and only in the essential life of the soul can true unity be cognised. In the discovery as to what is form lies much of sorrow for the disciple, but the road leads to perfect union eventually.

The disciple is one who realises his responsibility to all units who come under his influence—a responsibility of co-operating with the plan of evolution as it exists for them, and thus to expand their consciousness and teach them the difference between the real and the unreal, between life and form. This he does most easily by a demonstration in his own life as to his goal, his object, and his centre of consciousness.   (1-71/2)

2. Just as in the past the instrument and its relation to the outer world has been the paramount fact in the experience of the spritual man, so now it is possible for a readjustment to take place wherein the outstanding fact will be the spiritual man, the solar angel or soul. It will also be realised that his relationship (through the form side) will be to the inner as well as the outer worlds. Man has included in his relation only the form side of the field of average human evolution.

He has used it and has been dominated by it. He has also suffered from it and consequently in time revolted, through utter satiety, from all that pertains to the material world. Dissatisfaction, disgust, distaste, and a deep fatigue are characteristic very frequently of those who are on the verge of discipleship. For *what is a disciple?* He is one who seeks to learn a new rhythm, to enter a new field of experience, and to follow the steps of that advanced humanity who have trodden ahead of him the path, leading from darkness to light, from the unreal to the real. He has tasted the joys of life in the world of illusion, and has learnt their powerlessness to satisfy and hold him. Now he is in a state of transition between the new and the old states of being. He is vibrating between the condition of soul awareness and form awareness. He is "seeing double".

His spiritual perception grows slowly and surely as the brain becomes capable of illumination from the soul, via the mind. As the intuition develops, the radius of awareness grows and new fields of knowledge unfold.

The first field of knowledge receiving illumination might be described as comprising the totality of forms to be found in the three worlds of human endeavour, etheric, astral and mental. The would-be disciple, through this process, becomes aware of his lower nature and begins to realise the extent of his imprisonment and (as Patanjali puts it) "the modifications of the versatile psychic nature". The hindrances to achievement and the obstacles to progress are revealed to him, and his problem becomes specific. Frequently then he reaches the position in which Arjuna found himself, confronted by enemies who are those of his own household, confused as to his duty and discouraged as he seeks to balance himself between the pairs of opposites. His prayer then should be the famous prayer of India, uttered by the heart, comprehended by the head, and supplemented by an ardent life of service to humanity:

> "Unveil to us the face of the true spiritual sun,
> Hidden by a disk of golden light,
> That we may know the truth and do our whole duty
> As we journey to Thy sacred feet."

As he perseveres and struggles, surmounts his problems, and brings his desires and thoughts under control, the second field of knowledge is revealed—knowledge of the self in the spiritual body, knowledge of the Ego as it expresses itself through the medium of the causal body, . . . and awareness of that source of spiritual energy which is the motivating impulse behind the lower manifestation. The "disk of golden light" is pierced; the true sun is seen; the path is found and the aspirant struggles forward into ever clearer light.

As the knowledge of the self and as the consciousness of that which the self sees, hears, knows and contacts, is stabilised, the Master is found; his group of disciples is contacted; the plan for the immediate share of work he must assume is realised and gradually worked out on the physical plane. Thus the activity of the lower nature decreases, and the man little by little enters into conscious contact with his Master and his group. But this follows upon the "lighting of the lamp"—the aligning of the lower and the higher and the downflow of illumination to the brain. . . . Every step of the way has to be carved out by a man himself, and there is no short and easy road out of darkness into light.   (4-58/60)

3. You have been told that the soul is in deep meditation for the greater part of the cycle of lives of any one individual, and that it is only when a fair measure of personality integration is set up that the soul's attention is drawn away from its own interior considerations and egoic affairs to those of its shadow. When this happens, the egoic group is definitely affected and the Master (upon the same ray as that of the soul concerned) becomes aware of what is esoterically called "a downward gazing soul". On the Path of Discipleship, the Ego is all the time consciously aware of the striving personality, and there comes a stage when (towards the end of the Path of Evolution) the soul recapitulates the evolutionary processes of involution and evolution. Soul energy descends and personality

force ascends, and this takes place through a process of conscious descents and ascents. I refer here to the process which is undertaken by the soul under hierarchical impulse, and not to that in which the personality invokes the soul under the desperate need brought about in the lower consciousness by the gradual cessation of desire. (5-714)

39. THE DUAL LIFE OF THE DISCIPLE

1. In connection with the dual life of the disciple, the factors involved are the threefold *personality* (with an awakening or onlooking consciousness, centred or focussed in the brain); the *soul*, which seems at first the ultimate goal of attainment, but is later seen as simply a system or collection of fusing spiritual attributes; and the lowest aspect of the Spiritual Triad, the *abstract mind*. The disciple feels that, if he can attain the immediate and fused consciousness of the three, he has attained; he realises also that this involves the construction of the antahkarana. All these factors, for one who has just been admitted to the Path of Discipleship, and who is just finding his place within an Ashram, seem an adequately difficult undertaking and one that engrosses every power which he possesses.

This, for the time being, is true and—until the third initiation—these objectives, their conscious fusion, plus a recognition of the divine planes of awareness to which they all admit him, indicate the disciple's task and keep him fully occupied. To the recognition entailed, he has to add a growing capacity to work on the levels of consciousness involved, remembering always that a plane and a state of consciousness, are synonymous terms, and that he is making progress, becoming aware, building the antahkarana, training as a hierarchical worker within an Ashram, familiarising himself with new and opening spiritual environments, widening his horizon, stabilising himself upon the Path, and living upon the physical plane the life of an intelligent man within the world of men. He is demonstrating also no freakish peculiarities, but appears as a man of goodwill, of benevolent intelligence, of unalterable goodness, and of stern and unchangeable spiritual purpose. Is that enough of a goal for a disciple? Does it seem well-nigh impossible of accomplishment? Can you undertake such a proposition and make good your undertaking?

Most assuredly you can, for the factor of time enters in and the disciple is free to submit to its conditioning, particularly in the early stages of his discipleship; this he usually does at first, knowing nothing else to do, but the speed or the sattvic or rhythmic nature of the spiritual life eventually changes this attitude; he then works with no true consciousness of time, except as it affects other people and his associates upon the physical plane.

At first, his registration of that which is sensed or seen upon the subtler planes or the soul plane, is slow; it takes time for contacts and for knowledge gained to penetrate from the higher levels to his physical brain. This fact (when he discovers it) tends to upset his time-awareness, and the first step is therefore taken on the path of timelessness, speaking symbolically. He gains also the capacity to work with greater rapidity and mental co-ordination than does the average intelligent man; in this way he learns the limitations of time as a brain condition, and learns also how to offset it and to work in such a way that he does more within a set limit than is possible to the average man, no matter how ardently he may pursue the effort. The overcoming of time and the demonstration of spiritual speed, are indications that the dual life of discipleship is superseding the integrated life of the personality, though leading in its turn to a still greater synthesis and higher integration.

The dual life which all disciples lead, produces also a rapidity of mental interpretation which is essential to the sane registration of the phenomenal life of the various higher planes and states of consciousness. Forget not that all our planes are subplanes of the cosmic physical plane, and are therefore phenomenal in nature. As they are contacted and recorded, and the knowledge is transmitted to the physical brain, via the mind, there must always accompany them a true interpretation and a correct recognition of "things as they are". It is here that the non-disciple and the psychic go wrong, for their interpretation is almost always fundamentally in error, and it takes time (coming within that cycle of limitation) intelligently to interpret and truly register what the perceiving consciousness has contacted. When the time factor no longer controls, the interpretations registered by the brain, are infallibly correct. I have here given you a major piece of information.

You will see, therefore, that in the earlier initiatory process, the factor of time is noted by the initiate and also by the presenting Masters. An instance of a slow permeation of information from the plane of initiation to the physical brain can be seen in the fact that very few aspirants and disciples register *the fact* that they have already taken the first initiation, the birth of the Christ in the cave of the heart. That they have taken it is evidenced by their deliberate treading of the Way, by their love of the Christ—no matter by what name they may call Him—and by their effort to serve and help their fellow men; they are still, however, surprised when told that the first initiation lies behind them. This is due entirely to the factor of time, leading to their inability to "bring through" past events with accuracy, by a false humility as well (inculcated by the Christian Church, as it attempts to keep people subjugated by the sin idea), and by the intensely forward-looking anticipatory consciousness of the average aspirant. When a true perspective and a balanced point of view have been attained, and some awareness of the Eternal Now is beginning to penetrate into their understanding, then the past, the present and the future will be lost to sight in the consciousness of *the inclusiveness of the moment that IS;* then the limitations of time will be ending and the Law of Karma will be negated; it is at present so closely related to past and future. The dual life of the disciple will then be ended, giving place to the cosmic dualism of the Master. The Master is free from the limitations of time, though not of space, because space is an eternal Entity.

You will see, therefore, the great necessity for a constant emphasis, at this stage in the training of the average aspirant, on the need for *alignment,* or for the creation of a channel of direct relation from the brain to the desired point of contact. To this trained alignment must eventually be added the building of the antahkarana and its subsequent use in a growing system of alignments. The antahkarana must be completed and direct contact must be established with the Spiritual Triad by the time the third initiation has been taken. Then follows the fourth initiation with its destruction of the egoic, causal or soul body, owing to the complete fusion of the soul and personality. The dual life of the disciple ends. (18-434/7)

2. It is proper . . . to see a duality existing in the consciousness of the disciple, and both of its aspects existing side by side :

Firstly: The life of awareness in which he expresses the soul attitude, soul awareness and soul consciousness, through the medium of *the personality upon the physical plane;* this he learns to register and express *consciously.*

Secondly: The intensely private and purely subjective life in which he —the soul-infused personality—oriented upon the mental plane, brings into increasing rapport :

(a) His lower concrete mind, and the higher abstract mind.

(b) Himself and the Master of his ray group, thus developing the ashramic consciousness.

(c) Himself and the Hierarchy as a whole, becoming increasingly aware of the spiritual synthesis underlying the united Ashrams. He thus consciously and steadily approaches the radiant Centre of this solar Ashram, the Christ Himself, the first Initiator.   (18-441)

40.   THE WHITE MAGICIAN

1.   1. The white magician is one who is in touch with his soul.

2. He is receptive to and aware of the purpose and the plan of his soul.

3. He is capable of receiving impressions from the realm of spirit and of registering them in his physical brain.

4. It is stated also that white magic :

(a) Works from above downwards.

(b) Is the result of solar vibration, and therefore of egoic energy.

(c) Is not an effect of the vibration of the form side of life, being divorced from emotion and mental impulse.   (4-57)

2. The white magician is ever one who, through conscious alignment with his ego, with his "angel", is receptive to his plans and purposes, and therefore capable of receiving the higher impression. We must remember that while magic works from above downwards, and is the result of solar vibration, and not the impulses emanating from one or the other of the lunar pitris, the downflow of the impressing energy from the solar pitri is the result of his internal recollectedness, the indrawing of his forces, prior to sending them concentratedly to his shadow, man, and his steady meditation upon the purpose and the plan. It may be of use to the student if he here remembers that the ego (as well as the Logos) is in deep meditation during the whole cycle of physical incarnation. This meditation is cyclic in nature, the pitri involved sending out to his "re-flection" rhythmic streams of energy, which streams are recognised by the man concerned as his "high impulses", his dreams and aspirations. There-fore, it will be apparent why workers in white magic are ever advanced

and spiritual men, for the "reflection" is seldom responsive to the ego or the solar angel until many cycles of incarnation have transpired. The solar pitri communicates with his "shadow" or reflection by means of the sutratma, which passes down through the bodies to a point of entrance in the physical brain, if I might so express it, but the man, as yet, cannot focus or see clearly in any direction.

If he looks backward he can see only the fogs and miasmas of the planes of illusion, and fails to be interested. If he looks forward he sees a distant light which attracts him, but he cannot as yet see that which the light reveals. If he looks around, he sees but shifting forms and the cinematograph of the form side of life. If he looks within, he sees the shadows cast by the light, and becomes aware of much impedimenta which must be discarded before the light he sees in the distance can be approached, and then enter within him. Then he can know himself as light itself, and walk in that light and transmit it likewise to others.

It is perhaps well to remember that the stage of discipleship is in many ways the most difficult part of the entire ladder of evolution. The solar angel is unceasingly in deep meditation. The impulses of energy, emanating from him are increasing in vibratory rate, and are becoming more and more powerful. The energy is affecting more and more the forms through which the soul is seeking expression, and endeavouring control. (4-60/2)

3. White magic . . . is concerned with the unfoldment of the soul in form and its gaining needed experience thereby. It is not concerned with direct work upon the form, but with the indirect influence of the soul, functioning in any form in every kingdom in nature as it brings the form under its control, thereby effecting needed and developing changes in the apparatus of contact. The white magician knows that when the proper and correct ray stimulation is applied to the centre which we call the soul in any form but not to the form itself, that then the soul thus stimulated, will do its own work of destruction, of attraction, of rebuilding and of a consequent renewed life manifestation. This is true of the soul of man, of the soul of a nation, and of the soul of humanity itself. Bear this in mind, for I have here stated a basic and fundamental rule by which all white magic is agelessly governed.   (9-122/3)

41. THE CREATIVE NATURE OF THE SOUL

1. The unfolding of the creative nature of the conscious, spiritual man . . . takes place through right use of the mind, with its power to intuit ideas, to respond to impact, to translate, analyse, and to construct forms for revelation. Thus the soul of man creates. This creative process can be described, as far as its steps are concerned, as follows:

(a) The soul creates its physical body, its phenomenal appearance, its outer form.

(b) The soul creates, in time and space, in line with its desires. Thus the secondary world of phenomenal things comes into being, and our modern civilisation is the result of this creative activity of the soul's desire nature, limited by form. Ponder on this.

(c) The soul creates through the direct agency of the lower mind and hence the appearance of the world of symbols which fill our united lives with interest, concepts, ideas and beauty, through the written word, and the creative arts. These are the products of the thought of the thinkers of the race.

The right direction of this already developed tendency, is the aim of all true education. The nature of ideas, the modes of intuiting them, and the laws which should govern all creative work, are its goals and objectives. (12-20/1)

2. On its own plane, the soul knows no separation, and the factor of synthesis governs all soul relations. The soul is occupied not only with the form that the vision of its objective may take, but with the quality or the meaning which that vision veils or hides. The soul knows the Plan; its form, outline, methods and objective are known. Through the use of the creative imagination, the soul creates; it builds thought-forms on the mental plane and objectifies desire on the astral plane. It proceeds then to externalise its thought and its desire upon the physical plane through applied force, creatively actuated by the imagination of the etheric or vital vehicle. Yet because the soul is intelligence, motivated by love, it can (within the realised synthesis which governs its activities) analyse, discriminate and divide. The soul likewise aspires to that which is greater than itself, and reaches out to the world of divine ideas, and thus itself occupies a midway position between the world of ideation and the world of forms. This is its difficulty and its opportunity. (15-243)

3. Much is heard today of the New Age, of the coming revelation, of the imminent leap forward into an intuitive recognition of that which has hitherto been only dimly sensed by the mystics, the seer, the inspired poet, the intuitive scientist, and the occult investigator who is not too occupied with the technicalities and the academic activities of the lower mind. But one thing is oft forgotten in the great expectancy. There is no need for too great an upward straining or too intense an outward looking, to use terms which the usual limited point of view can grasp. That which is to be revealed lies all around us, and within us. It is the significance of all that is embodied in form, the meaning behind the appearance, the reality veiled by the symbol, the truth expressed in substance.

Only two things will enable man to penetrate into this inner realm of causes and of revelation. These are :

First, the constant effort, based on a subjective impulse, to create those forms which will express some sensed truth; for thereby and through this effort, the emphasis is constantly shifted from the outer world of seeming to the inner side of phenomena. By this means, a focusing of consciousness is produced which eventually becomes stable and withdrawn from its present intense exteriorisation. An initiate is essentially one whose sense of awareness is occupied with subjective contacts and impacts, and is not predominantly preoccupied with the world of outer sense perceptions. This cultivated interest in the inner world of meaning will produce not only a pronounced effect upon the spiritual seeker himself, but will eventually bring about the emphasis, recognised in the brain consciousness of the race, that the world of meaning is the sole world of reality for humanity. . . .

Secondly, the constant effort to render oneself sensitive to the world of significant realities and to produce, therefore, those forms on the outer plane which will run true to the hidden impulse. This is brought about by the cultivation of the creative imagination. As yet, humanity knows little about this faculty, latent in all men. A flash of light breaks through to the aspiring mind; a sense of unveiled splendour for a moment sweeps through the aspirant, tensed for revelation; a sudden realisation of colour, a beauty, a wisdom and glory beyond words break out before the attuned consciousness of the artist, in a high moment of applied attention, and life is then seen for a second as it essentially is. But the vision is gone and the fervour departs, and the beauty fades out. The man is left with a sense of bereavement, of loss, and yet with a certainty of knowledge and a desire to express that which he has contacted, such as he has never experienced before. He must recover that which he has seen; he must discover it to those who have not had his secret moment of revelation; he must express it in some form, and reveal to others the realised significance behind the phenomenal appearance. How can he do this? How can he recover that which he has once had and which seems to have disappeared, and to have retired out of his field of consciousness? He must realise that that which he has seen and touched is still there and embodies reality; that it is he who has withdrawn and not the vision. The pain in all moments of intensity must be undergone and lived again and again, until the mechanism of contact is accustomed to the heightened vibration and can not only sense and touch, but can hold and contact at will this hidden world of beauty. The cultivation of this power to enter, hold and transmit, is dependent upon three things:

1. A willingness to bear the pain of revelation.

2. The power to hold on to the high point of consciousness at which the revelation comes.

3. The focusing of the faculty of the imagination upon the revelation, or upon as much of it as the brain consciousness can bring through into the lighted area of external knowledge. It is the imagination of the picture-making faculty which links the mind and brain together and thus produces the exteriorisation of the veiled splendour.

If the creative artist will ponder upon these three requirements—endurance, meditation, and imagination—he will develop in himself the power to respond to this . . . rule of soul control, and will know the soul eventually as the secret of persistence, the revealer of the rewards of contemplation and the creator of all forms upon the physical plane. (15-246/9)

42. RHYTHMIC NATURE OF SOUL IMPULSES

1. I said "The soul's meditation is rhythmic and cyclic in its nature, as is all else in the cosmos. The soul breathes and its form lives thereby". The rhythmic nature of the soul's meditation must not be overlooked in the life of the aspirant. There is an ebb and flow in all nature, and in the tides of the ocean we have a wonderful picturing of an eternal law. As the aspirant adjusts himself to the tides of the soul life, he begins to realise that there is ever a flowing in, a vitalising and a stimulating which is followed by a flowing out as sure and as inevitable as the immutable laws of force. This ebb and flow can be seen functioning in the processes of death and incarnation. It can be seen also over the entire process of a man's lives, for some lives can be seen to be apparently static and uneventful, slow and inert from the angle of the soul's experience, whilst others are vibrant, full of experience and of growth. This should be remembered by all of you who are workers, when you are seeking to help others to live rightly. Are they on the ebb or are they being subjected to the flow of the soul energy? Are they passing through a period of temporary quiescence, preparatory to greater impulse and effort, so that work to be done must be that of strengthening and stabilising in order to enable them to "stand in spiritual being", or are they being subjected to a cyclic inflow of forces? In this case the worker must seek to aid in the direction and utilisation of the energy which (if misdirected) will eventuate in wrecked lives, but which when wisely utilised will produce a full and fruitful service.

The above thoughts can also be applied by the student of humanity to the great racial cycles, and much of interest will be discovered. Again, and of more vital importance to us, these cyclic impulses in the life of the disciple are of a greater frequency and speed and forcefulness than in the life of the average man. They alternate with a distressing rapidity. The hill and valley experience of the mystic is but one way of expressing this ebb and flow. Sometimes the disciple is walking in the sunlight and at other times in the dark; sometimes he knows the joy of full communion and again all seems dull and sterile; his service is on occasion a fruitful and satisfying experience and he seems to be able to really aid; at other times he feels that he has naught to offer, and his service is arid and apparently without results. All is clear to him some days and he seems to stand on the mountain top looking out over a sunlit landscape, where all is clear to his vision. He knows and feels himself to be a son of God.

Later, however, the clouds seem to descend and he is sure of nothing, and seems to know nothing. He walks in the sunlight and is almost over-powered by the brilliance and heat of the solar rays, and wonders how long this uneven experience and the violent alternation of these opposites is to go on.

Once however that he grasps the fact (that) he is watching the effect of the cyclic impulses and the effect of the soul's meditation upon his form nature, the meaning becomes clearer and he realises that it is that form aspect which is failing in its response, and reacting to energy with unevenness. He then learns that once he can live in the soul consciousness and attain that "high altitude" (if I might so express it) at will, the fluctuations of the form life will not touch him. He then perceives the narrow-edged razor path which leads from the plane of physical life to the soul realm, and finds that when he can tread it with steadiness, it leads him out of the ever changing world of the senses into the clear light of day and into the world of reality.

The form side of life then becomes to him simply a field of service and not a field of sensuous perception. Let the student ponder upon this last sentence. Let him aim to live as a soul. Then the cyclic impulses, emanating from the soul, are known to be impulses for which he himself is responsible and which he has sent forth; he then knows himself to be the initiating cause and is not subject to the effects. (4-62/4)

2. May there be a full and steady play of cyclic force from the kingdom of spirit upon each one of us, calling us forth into the realm of light, love and service, and producing a cyclic response from each one! May there be a constant interchange between those who teach and the disciple who seeks instruction! (4-64/5)

3. The moment a man sets his hand to the plough and starts upon his ploughing, from that moment until he has completed his task, he remains internally free but outwardly bound. So it must ever be with the servers in our work.

But climaxing moments are of importance and the pursuit of an even tenor is not usually good for a disciple, if overlong perpetuated. . . . The crises of the soul are expansions, registered by the inflow of love and light. They are mentally recognised crises of inclusiveness. These lead one on and prepare one for the later more vast expansions which we call initiations. (5-228/9)

4. A constant succession of spiritual enlightenments and an unabated keying-up to high contacts would eventually dull the instrument so that

true recognitions would fade out. Ponder on this, my brother, and be grateful for the days of coming duty, of quiet living, of steadfast orientation towards the light, of silent communication with your soul, of study and of thought.   (5-323/4)

5. All life is cyclic, and this is a point which disciples are apt to forget and overlook; they then find themselves discouraged when the *intensity of feeling* leaves them. The initiate walks ever a straight course between the pairs of opposites, serene and unafraid.   (5-448)

43.   VISION

1. Those who see a vision that is withheld from those lacking the necessary equipment for its apprehension, are regarded as fanciful, and unreliable. When many see the vision, its possibility is admitted, but when humanity itself has the awakened and open eye, the vision is no longer emphasised, but a fact is stated and a law enunciated. Such has been the history of the past and such will be the process in the future.   (4-16)

2. The true disciple sees the vision. He then seeks to keep so closely in touch with his soul that he can stand with steadiness whilst he endeavours to make that vision a reality; he aims to achieve what, from the standpoint of the world seems to be impossible, knowing that the vision is not materialised through expediency and undue adaptation of the suggested ideas of worldly or intellectual counsellors.   (4-630/1)

3. *The vision is a symbolic way of experiencing revelation.* The gradual unfoldment of each of the five senses brought a steady emerging revelation of God's world, and a constantly extending vision. The development of sight brought a synthetic aptitude to focus the results of all lesser visions brought to the point of revelation by the four senses. Then comes a vision, revealed by the "common sense" of the mind. This demonstrates in its most developed stage as world perception where human affairs are concerned, and frequently works out in the vast personality plans of the world leaders in the various fields of human living. But the vision with which you should be concerned, is to become aware of what the soul knows and what the soul sees, through the use of the key to soul vision— the *intuition.* That key can only be used intelligently and consciously

when personality affairs are dropping below the threshold of consciousness.

. . . A disciple becomes an Accepted Disciple when he starts climbing towards the vision, towards the mountain top; he can also register consciously what he has seen, and then begins to do something constructive towards materialising it. This, many throughout the world are beginning to do. A man becomes a World Disciple in the technical sense when the vision is to him an important and determining fact in his consciousness, and one to which all his daily efforts are subordinated. He needs no one to reveal the Plan to him. *He knows.* His sense of proportion is adjusted to the revelation and his life is dedicated to bringing the vision into factual existence—in collaboration with his group.

It is, therefore, a gradually unfolding process up to a certain stage. After that stage has been reached, it is no longer the vision which is the dominant factor, but the field of experience, of service, and of achievement. Ponder on this.   (5-687/8)

4. Sight is the greatest of all the developments in this world period in which the Logos is seeking to bring the subhuman kingdoms to the point where *human* vision is theirs, to bring humanity to the point where *spiritual* vision is developed and hierarchical insight is the normal quality of the initiate sight, and to bring the Members of the Hierarchy to the point where *universal* perception is Theirs. Therefore, it might be said that:

1. *Through the door of individualisation* the subhuman kingdoms pass to human vision, leading to mental contact and intelligent impression.

2. *Through the door of initiation* humanity passes to spiritual vision, leading to soul contact and spiritual impression.

3. *Through the door of identification* the Hierarchy passes to universal vision, leading to monadic contact and extra-planetary impression. (11-56)

See also: (4-368)

44. THE EYE OF THE SOUL

As a result of focussed thinking "in the heart" the spiritual eye opens and becomes the directing agent, employed consciously by the initiate. . . . What is meant here by the words "in the heart"? The soul is the heart of the system of the spiritual man; it is the seat of the life and consciousness which animate the personality, and it is the motivating potency in every incarnation, according to the experience conditioning the expression of the spiritual man in any particular rebirth. In the early stages of experience, this "eye" remains closed; there is present no capacity for thought and no ability to think in the heart; i.e. from soul levels. As the intellect develops and the power to focus upon the mental plane grows, the fact of the soul's existence becomes known, and the goal of attention changes. There follows the ability to focus in the soul-consciousness and so to fuse the soul and the mind, that an at-one-ment takes place and a man can then begin to think "in his heart". Then also the "eye of the soul" opens, and energy from soul levels, intelligently utilised, becomes directed from those levels and pours into what is now ambiguously called "the third eye". Immediately the personality in the three worlds begins to express itself as the soul upon the physical plane, and will, purpose and love begin to control. . . .

Let me now expand the concept further, reminding you of the phrase so oft employed, "the All-seeing Eye". This refers to the power of the planetary Logos to see into all parts, aspects and phases (in time and space) of His planetary vehicle, which is His physical body, and to identify Himself with all the reactions and sensitivities of His created world and to participate with full knowledge in all events and happenings. Through what medium does He, on His own high levels, do this? Through what mechanism does He thus "see"? What is His organ of vision? What is the nature of the sight whereby He contacts the seven planes of His manifested universe? What is the organ employed by Him, which corresponds to the third eye in man? The answer is as follows: The Monad is to the planetary Logos what the third eye is to man; this will become clearer to you if you will bear in mind that our seven planes are only the seven subplanes of the *cosmic physical plane*. The monadic world—so-called—is His organ of vision; it is also His directing agent for the life and light which must be poured into the phenomenal world. In the same way, the Monad is to the personality in the three worlds, also the source of its life and light.

There are, therefore, three organs of revelation, as far as the spiritual man is concerned:

1. *The human eye,* giving "in-sight" into the phenomenal world, letting in the light, and bringing revelation of the environment.

2. *The eye of the soul,* bringing revelation of the nature of the interior worlds, of the Kingdom of God, and of the divine Plan.

3. The centre within the One Life which we call by the unmeaning word *"Monad",* the spark within the one Flame. In the final stages of initiation, the Monad becomes the revealer of the Purpose of God, of the Will of the planetary Logos, and of the door which opens on the Way of the Higher Evolution. This Way leads a man off the cosmic physical plane on to the cosmic astral plane, and therefore into the world of divine sentiency, of which we can have no possible understanding, but for which the development of consciousness has given us the initial steps.

Man has learnt to use the physical eye and to find his way by its means around and through his environment. The stage in human evolution wherein he learnt first to "see" lies far behind, but when man saw and could focus and direct his course *by sight,* it marked a stupendous unfoldment, and his first real entrance upon the Path of Light. Ponder on this. It has also interior repercussions and was indeed the result of an invocative interplay between inner centres of power and the groping creature in the phenomenal world.

Man is now learning to use the eye of the soul, and as he does so he brings its correspondence in the head also into functioning activity; this produces fusion and identification, and brings the pineal gland into action. The major result, however, is to enable the disciple to become aware, whilst in the physical body, of a new range of contacts and perceptions. This marks a crisis in his unfoldment of as drastic and important a nature as the attaining of physical sight and the use of the physical eye was in the unfoldment of the curious creature which antedated the most primitive animal man. Things unknown can now be sensed, searched for, and finally seen; a new world of being stands apparent, which has always been present, though never before known; the life, nature, quality and the phenomena of the kingdom of souls, or of the Hierarchy, become as patent to his vision and as real as is the world of the five physical senses.

Then later, upon the Path of Initiation, the initiate develops his tiny correspondence to the planetary "All-seeing Eye". He unfolds the powers of the Monad. These are related to divine Purpose and to the world in which Sanat Kumara moves, and which we call Shamballa. I have impressed upon you elsewhere that the state of being of the Monad has naught to do with what we call consciousness; in the same way, there is naught in the world of Shamballa which is of the same nature as the phenomenal world of man in the three worlds, or even of the soul world. It is a world of pure energy, of light and of directed force; it can be seen as streams and centres of force, all forming a pattern of consummate beauty, all potently invocative of the world of the soul and of the world of phenomena; it therefore constitutes in a very real sense, the world of causes and of initiation.

As man the human being, man the disciple, and man the initiate, gradually move forward on the stream of life, revelation comes step by step, moving from one great point of focus to another, until naught more remains to be revealed.

In all these spiritual points of crisis or of opportunity for vision, for fresh spiritual insight, and for revelation (for that is what they are in reality), the thought of struggle is the first one to warrant attention. I used, in this connection, the words "stage of penetration"; the thought which this conveys to the initiate understanding, signifies an extension of the struggle which the neophyte makes in order to achieve inner control, and then to use the mind as a searchlight so as to penetrate into new fields of awareness and of recognition. Forget not that recognition involves right interpretation and right relation to that which is seen and contacted. Into all revelation enters the concept of "whole vision" or a synthesis of perception, and then comes recognition of that which is visioned and perceived. It is the mind (the common sense, as it used to be called) which utilises the physical senses of perception, and through their united contribution gets a "whole vision" and a synthesis of perception of the phenomenal world, according to man's point of development, his mental capacity to recognise, rightly interpret, and rightly relate that which has been conveyed to him by the activity of the five senses. This is what is meant when we use the phrase "the mind's eye", and this ability is the common possession of humanity in varying degrees of availability.

Later, man uses the "eye of the soul", as we have noted above; it reveals to him a world of subtler phenomena, the Kingdom of God, or the world of souls. Then the light of the intuition pours in, bringing the power to recognise and rightly interpret and relate.

As the disciple and the initiate progress from stage to stage of revelation, it becomes increasingly difficult to make clear not only what is revealed, but also the processes of revelation, and the methods used to bring the stage of revelation about. The vast mass of mankind throughout the world have no clear idea as to the function of the mind as an organ of vision illumined by the soul; still fewer, only the disciples and initiates, are able to glimpse the purpose of the spiritual eye and its functioning in the light of the intuition. When we come, therefore, to the great organ of universal revelation, the monadic principle, functioning through the medium of an extra-planetary light, we enter realms which are indefinable and for which no terminology has been created, and which only initiates above the third degree are able to consider.   (6-289/94)

45. THE THIRD EYE

1. No man is a magician or worker in white magic until the third eye is opened, or in process of opening, for it is by means of that eye that the thought form is energised, directed and controlled, and the lesser builders are swept into any particular line of activity. . . .

The *"Eye of Shiva"* in the human being has its position . . . in the centre of the forehead, between the two physical eyes.   (3-1008)

2. . . . It is the eye of the inner vision, and he who has opened it can direct and control the energy of matter, see all things in the Eternal Now, and therefore be in touch with causes more than with effects, read the akashic records, and see clairvoyantly. Therefore, its possessor can control the builders of low degree.   (3-1011)

3. Through the practice of the power of visualisation, the third eye is developed. The forms visualised, and the ideas and abstractions which are, in the process, mentally clothed and vehicled, are pictured a few inches from the third eye. It is the knowledge of this which causes the Eastern Yogi to speak of "concentration upon the tip of the nose". Behind this misleading phrase a great truth is veiled.   (3-1012)

4. The centre between the eyebrows, commonly called the "third eye", has a unique and peculiar function. . . . Students must not confound the pineal gland with the third eye. They are related but not the same. . . . The third eye manifests as a result of the vibratory interaction between the forces of the soul, working through the pineal gland, and the forces of the person-

ality, working through the pituitary body. These negative and positive forces interact, and when potent enough, produce the light in the head. Just as the physical eye came into being in response to the light of the sun, so the spiritual eye equally comes into being in response to the light of the spiritual sun. As the aspirant develops, he becomes aware of the light. I refer to the light in all forms, veiled by all sheaths and expressions of the divine life, and not just to the light within the aspirant himself. As his awareness of this light increases, so does the apparatus of vision develop, and the mechanism whereby he can see things in the spiritual light comes into being in the etheric body.

This is the "Eye of Shiva", for it is only fully utilised in the magical work when the monadic aspect, the will aspect, is controlling.

By means of the third eye the soul accomplishes three activities:

1. *It is the eye of vision.* By its means, the spiritual man sees behind the forms of all aspects of divine expression. He becomes aware of the light of the world, and contacts the soul within all forms. Just as the physical eye registers forms, so does the spiritual eye register the illumination within those forms, which "illumination" indicates a specific state of being. It opens up the world of radiance.

2. *It is the controlling factor of the magical work.* All white magical work is carried forward with a definite constructive purpose, made possible through the use of the intelligent will. In other words, the soul knows the Plan, and when the alignment is right and the attitude correct, the will aspect of the divine man can function and bring about results in the three worlds. The organ used is the third eye. The analogy to this can be seen in the often noticed power of the human eye as it controls other human beings and animals by a look, and through steady gazing can act magnetically. Force flows through the focussed human eye. Force flows through the focussed third eye.

3. *It has a destructive aspect* and the energy flowing through the third eye can have a disintegrating and destroying effect. It can, through its focussed attention, directed by the intelligent will, drive out physical matter. It is the agent of the soul in the purificatory work.

. . . In a most mysterious sense, the soul is the eye of the Monad, enabling the Monad, which is pure Being, to work, to contact, to know, and to see.   (4-212/5)

46. IMPRESSION

For the aspirant, and particularly for the conscious disciple, the impression to be considered, comes from four sources:

1. From the disciple's own soul.
2. From the Ashram with which he is to be affiliated.
3. Direct from the Master.
4. From the Spiritual Triad, via the antahkarana.

The first two stages cover the period of the first two initiations; the third precedes the third initiation, and persists until the disciple is himself a Master; the fourth type of informative impression can be registered after the third initiation and reach the disciple *in the Ashram;* he then has the task himself of impressing his mind with what he has been told and known within the Ashram; eventually, as a Master of an Ashram, he starts upon one of the major hierarchical tasks of mastering the Science of Impression. There are therefore, two aspects to this work of impression: one deals with the capacity to be impressed; the other with the ability to be an impressing agent. The disciple is not permitted to practise the art of impressing until he himself is among those who receive Triadal impression, and therefore impression from Shamballa, within the protective area or aura of the Ashram with which he is affiliated. It must be remembered that this Science of Impression is in reality the science of thoughtform making, thoughtform vitalisation, and thoughtform direction; and only a disciple who has passed through the processes of Transfiguration and is no longer the victim of his own personality, can be entrusted with so dangerous a cycle of powers. As long as there exists any desire for selfish power, for unspiritual control, and for influence over the minds of other human beings, or over groups, the disciple cannot be trusted, under the hierarchical rules, with the deliberate creation of thoughtforms designed to produce specific effects, and with their dispersal to men and groups. After he has passed the tests of the Transfiguration Initiation he may do so.

The Science of Impression is the bedrock or the foundation for the practice of telepathy. (11-86/7)

(a) TELEPATHY

1. Telepathic communication . . . is the registry in the physical brain consciousness of information imparted:

(a) Direct from Master to Pupil; from disciple to disciple; from student to student.

(b) From Master or disciple to the Ego and thence to the personality, via the atomic sub-planes. You will note therefore that only those in whose bodies atomic sub-plane matter is found, can work this way. Safety and accuracy lie in this equipment.

(c) From ego to ego via the causal body and transmitted direct according to the preceding method or stored up to work through gradually and at need.   (4-179)

2. (*Telepathic work from soul to soul*) is the highest type of telepathic work possible to humanity, and is that form of communication which has been responsible for all the inspirational writings of real power, the world Scriptures, the illumined utterances, the inspired speakers, and the language of symbolism. It only becomes possible where there is an integrated personality, and at the same time, the power to focus oneself in the soul consciousness. The mind and the brain have, at the same time, to be brought into perfect rapport and alignment.   (11-12)

3. When a man can begin, as a soul, to respond to other souls and their impacts and impressions, then he is rapidly becoming ready for the processes which lead to initiation. . . .

Telepathic work between soul and mind. This is the technique whereby the mind is "held steady in the light", and then becomes aware of the content of the soul's consciousness, an innate content, or that which is part of the group life of the soul on its own level, and when in telepathic communication with other souls. . . . This is the true meaning of intuitional telepathy. Through this means of communication, the mind of the disciple is fertilised with the new and spiritual ideas; he becomes aware of the great Plan; his intuition is awakened. One point should here be borne in mind, which is oft forgotten : The inflow of the new ideas from the buddhic levels, thus awakening the intuitional aspect of the disciple, indicates that his soul is beginning to integrate consciously and definitely with the Spiritual Triad, and therefore to identify itself less and less with the lower reflection, the personality. This mental sensitivity and rapport between soul and mind remains for a long time relatively inchoate on the mental plane. That which is sensed remains too vague or too abstract for formulation. It is the stage of the mystical vision and of mystical unfoldment.

Telepathic work between soul, mind and brain. In this stage the mind still remains the recipient of impression from the soul, but in its turn, it becomes a "transmitting agent" or communicator. The impressions re-

ceived from the soul, and the intuitions registered as coming from the
Spiritual Triad, via the soul, are now formulated into thoughts; the vague
ideas and the vision hitherto unexpressed, can now be clothed in form and
sent out as embodied thoughtforms to the brain of the disciple. In time,
and as the result of technical training, the disciple can in this way reach
the mind and brains of other disciples. This is an exceedingly interesting
stage. It constitutes one of the major rewards of right meditation and
involves much true responsibility. . . .

*Telepathic work between a Master (the focal point of a group) and the
disciple in the world.* It is an occult truth that no man is really admitted
into a Master's group as an accepted disciple, until he has become spiritually impressionable and can function as a mind in collaboration with his
own soul. Prior to that he cannot be a conscious part of a functioning
group on the inner planes gathered around a personalised force, the
Master; he cannot work in true rapport with his fellow disciples. But
when he can work somewhat as a conscious soul, then the Master can begin to impress him with group ideas via his own soul. He hovers then for
quite a while upon the periphery of the group. Eventually, as his spiritual
sensitivity increases, he can be definitely impressed by the Master and
taught the technique of contact. Later, the group of disciples, functioning
as one synthetic thoughtform, can reach him, and thus automatically he
becomes one of them. To those who have the true esoteric sense, the
above paragraph will convey a good deal of information, hitherto
hidden. (11-21/3)

4. *Intuitional telepathy* begins to manifest increasingly among advanced
human beings in all lands and all races. This indicates soul contact and
the consequent awakening of group consciousness, for sensitivity to intuitional impressions has to do *only* with group concerns. (11-68)

5. *Love* (not sentiment) is the clue to successful telepathic work. Therefore love one another with a fresh enthusiasm and devotion; seek to express that love in every possible way—upon the physical plane, upon the
levels of emotion, and through right thought. Let the love of the soul
sweep through all like a regenerating force. (11-26)

6. The truly telepathic man is the man who is responsive to impressions
coming to him from all forms of life in the three worlds, but he is also
equally responsive to impressions coming to him from the world of souls
and the world of the intuition. It is the development of the telepathic
instinct which will eventually make a man a master in the three worlds,

and also in the five worlds of human and superhuman development.   (11-35)

7. I am not indicating in any way how an individual can become telepathic. All those developments within the area or region of progressive contacts are only useful and truly available, when they are developed normally and naturally, and are not the result of premature unfoldment. When the development is premature, there is always the danger of wrong, erroneous and self-centered interpretations. The telepathic information can be of purely selfish and personal import, and that type of telepathy has no place in what I am seeking to impart. People today frequently evidence a telepathic tendency or capacity. They tune in (a phrase they regard as more euphonious than the words "telepathic rapport") with something or someone, though they know not what it is. Everything that they purport to register is regarded by them as of major importance: it is usually self-related and not due to their high point of spiritual unfoldment which warrants their being the custodians of mysterious spiritual messages—usually of a most unimportant and platitudinous nature. There are many sources of these messages, and it might be useful if I here mentioned some of them; what I have to say may prove to be of value to the general occult public:

1. Messages emanating from the relatively nice, well-trained subconscious nature of the recipient. These well up from the subconscious, but are regarded by the recipient as coming from an outside source. . . . It accounts for eighty-five per cent (85%) of the so-called telepathic or inspired writings so prevalent at this time.

2. Impressions from the soul, which are translated into concepts and written down by the personality; the recipient is deeply impressed by the relatively high vibration which accompanies them, forgetting that the vibration of the soul is that of a Master, for the soul is a Master on its own plane. These are true soul impressions but usually have in them nothing new or of major importance; they are again the result of past ages of soul development (as far as the personality is concerned); they are, therefore, that which an awakening personality has contributed to the soul of the good, the true and the beautiful, plus that which has entered into the personality consciousness as a result of soul contact. This accounts for eight per cent (8%) of the writings and communications put before the general public by aspirants today.

3. Teachings given by a senior or more advanced disciple on the inner planes to a disciple under training, or who has just been admitted into

an Ashram. . . . They will account for five per cent (5%) of the teaching given. . . .

4. Communications from a Master to His disciple. This accounts for two per cent (2%) of the entire telepathic receptivity, demonstrated by humanity as a whole throughout the entire world. (11-75/7)

(b) SENSITIVITY TO IMPRESSION

1. The disciple on the physical plane and the inner teacher (whether one of the Great Ones or the "Master within the Heart") need to know each other somewhat, and to accustom themselves to each other's vibration. Teachers on the inner planes have much to contend with owing to the slowness of the mental processes of students in physical bodies. But confidence and trust will set up the right vibration which will produce eventually accurate work. Lack of faith, of calmness, of application, and the presence of emotional unrest will hinder. Long patience those on the inner side need in dealing with all who must, for lack of other and better material, be utilised. Some physical injudiciousness may make the physical body non-receptive; some worry or care may cause the astral body to vibrate to a rhythm impossible for the right reception of the inner purpose; some prejudice, some criticism, some pride, may be present that will make the mental vehicle of no use. Aspirants to this difficult work must watch themselves with infinite care, and keep the inner serenity and peace and a mental pliability that will tend to make them of some use in the guarding and guiding of humanity.

The following rules might therefore be given:

1. It is essential that there should be an endeavour to arrive at absolute purity of motive.

2. The ability to enter the silence of the high places will follow next. The stilling of the mind depends upon the law of rhythm. If you are vibrating in many directions and registering thoughts from all sides, this law will be unable to touch you. Balance and poise must be restored before equilibrium can be reached. The law of vibration and the study of atomic substance are closely intertwined. When more is known about these atoms and their action, reaction and inter-action, then people will control their bodies scientifically, synchronising the laws of vibration and rhythm. They are the same and yet unlike. . . .

3. Remember always that lack of calm in the daily life prevents the teachers on egoic levels from reaching you. Endeavour therefore to re-

main quiescent as life unrolls; work, toil, strive, aspire, and hold the inner calm. Withdraw steadily into interior work and so cultivate a responsiveness with the higher planes. A perfect steadiness of inner poise is what the Masters need in those whom They seek to use. It is an inner poise that holds to the vision yet does its outer work on the physical plane with a concentrated physical brain attention which is in no way deviated by the inner receptiveness. It involves a dual activity.

4. Learn to control thought. It is necessary to guard what you think. These are days when the race as a whole is becoming sensitive and telepathic and responsive to thought interplay. The time is approaching when thought will become public property, and others will sense what you think. Thought has, therefore, to be carefully guarded. Those who are contacting the higher truths and becoming sensitive to the Universal Mind, must protect some of their knowledge from the intrusion of other minds. Aspirants must learn to inhibit certain thoughts, and prevent certain knowledge from leaking out into the public consciousness when in contact with their fellow men.   (4-65/7)

2. *Sensitivity* . . . does not mean primarily that you are a "sensitive soul"—the connotation of which usually means that you are thin-skinned, self-centred and always on the defensive! Rather do I refer to the capacity whereby you are enabled to expand your consciousness so that you become aware of ever-widening ranges of contact. I refer to the ability to be alive, alert, keen to recognise relationships, quick to react to need, mentally, emotionally and physically attentive to life and rapidly developing the power to observe upon all three planes in the three worlds simultaneously. I am not interested in your personal relations where they concern your wrong personality sensitivity to depression, to self-pity, your defences, your so-called sensitivity to slights, to misunderstandings, your dislike of your environing conditions, your hurt pride, and qualities of this kind. These all cause you bewilderment and let loose in you the floodgates of compassion for yourself. But you do not need me to deal with them; of them you are well aware and can handle them *if you choose*. These faults are interesting only in so far as they affect the life of your group; they must be handled by you with care and with the open eye that senses danger from afar and seeks to avoid it. The sensitivity which I want to see developed, is alertness to soul contact, impressionability to the "voice of the Teacher", an aliveness to the impact of new ideas, and to the delicacy of intuitional responsiveness. These are ever

the hallmark of the true disciple. It is spiritual sensitivity which must be cultivated; this is only truly possible when you learn to work through the centres above the diaphragm and to transmute solar plexus activity (which is so dominant in the average person), turning it into heart activity and the service of your fellow men. (5-47/8)

3. Growth in sensitivity is difficult to understand. The members of a Master's group and of His Ashram have to become increasingly sensitive —sensitive to the Master and to His pledged workers. You cannot be made sensitive or be rendered sensitive by some type of process or ordered training. Men and women *are* sensitive, only they do not know it, being so preoccupied with outer matters, with form life and objective things. Let me put it this way: What you say to yourself and to others—through your spoken words or your life—is so noisy that it is not easy to be what you are, and to be recognised as a spiritual being. The Master is guided by what He knows of you in your quiet moments of aspiration, by what you have demonstrated for years to be your fixed life tendency, and by the manner in which you react at moments of crisis or tension. The task of the Master is to stimulate the disciple to be at all times what He knows him to be at his highest times. That is a simple and almost child-ish way of putting it, but it serves to express the general idea. A Master does this because the need of the world for decentralised, forward-look-ing, loving and intelligent workers is so great, particularly at this time. Many have reached the point where they may become sensitive if the loud assertions of personality are dimmed and the light of the soul is permitted to pour through. Then the Master can be known and contacted. When you can get away from yourselves and your personal reactions, your own interpretations, and your personal demands, you will discover for yourselves how and in what manner the Master is seeking to impress you and the group with which you may be affiliated. You will become sensitive to that impression. You can then facilitate (as it is called) the activity of the Master by a profound and deep interest in the esoteric life, to the exclusion of your own and also of the Master's individuality. There are many ways which can then be revealed which will aid the interplay between you, the disciple, and the Master. (5-710/1)

4. Gradually as the disciple acquires true freedom of thought and the power to be receptive to the impression of the abstract mind, he creates for himself a reservoir of thought which becomes available at need for the helping of other people and for the necessities of his growing world service. Later, he becomes sensitive to impression from the Hierarchy.

This is at first purely ashramic, but is later transformed into total hierarchical impression by the time the disciple is a Master; *the Plan is then the dynamic substance providing the content of the reservoir of thought upon which he can draw.* This is a statement of unique and unusual importance. Later still, he becomes sensitive to impression from Shamballa, and the quality of the Will which implements planetary Purpose, is added to the content of his available knowledge. The point which I seek to make here, however, is the fact of the existence of a growing reservoir of thought which the disciple has created in response to the many varying impressions to which he is becoming increasingly sensitive; the ideas, concepts, and spiritual objectives of which he is becoming aware, are steadily being formulated by him into thoughts with their appropriated thoughtforms, and upon these he learns to draw as he seeks to serve his fellow men. He finds himself in possession of a reservoir or pool of thoughtsubstance which is the result of his own mental activity, of his innate receptivity, and which provides the material for teaching and the "fount of knowledge" upon which he can draw when he seeks to aid other people.

The essential point to be grasped is that sensitivity to impression is a normal and natural unfoldment, paralleling spiritual development. I gave you a clue to the entire process when I said that:

"Sensitivity to impression involves the engendering of a magnetic aura upon which the highest impressions can play."

I would have you give the deepest consideration to these words. As the disciple begins to demonstrate soul quality, and the second divine aspect takes possession of him, and controls and colours his entire life, automatically the higher sensitivity is developed; he becomes a magnet for spiritual ideas and concepts; he attracts into his field of consciousness the outline, and later the details, of the hierarchical Plan; he becomes aware eventually of the planetary Purpose; all these impressions are not things which he must seek out and learn laboriously to ascertain, to hold and seize upon. They drop into his field of consciousness *because* he has created a *magnetic aura* which invokes them and brings them "into his mind". This magnetic aura begins to form itself from the first moment he makes a contact with his soul; it deepens and grows as those contacts increase in frequency, and become eventually an habitual state of consciousness; then, at will and at all times, he is *en rapport* with his soul, the second divine aspect.

It is this aura which is in reality the reservoir of thought-substance upon which he can spiritually rely. This point of focus is upon the mental plane. He is no longer controlled by the astral nature; he is successfully constructing the antahkarana along which the higher impressions can flow; he learns not to dissipate this inflow, but to accumulate within the aura (with which he has surrounded himself) the knowledge and the wisdom which he realises his service to his fellow men requires. A disciple is a magnetic centre of light and knowledge just in so far as the magnetic aura is held by him in a state of receptivity. It is then constantly invocative of the higher range of impressions; it can be evoked and set into "distributing activity" by that which is lower and which is demanding aid. The disciple therefore, in due time, becomes a tiny or minute correspondence of the Hierarchy—invocative as it is to Shamballa and easily evoked by human demand.   (11-94/6)

5. The *aura* which each of you has created around the central nucleus of your incarnated self or soul, is a fragment of the overshadowing soul which brought you into manifestation.   (11-97)

(c) REGISTRATION OF IMPRESSIONS

1. The *capacity to interpret* recorded impressions is . . . learnt as the mental aura develops under the influence of the "mind held steady in the light" of the soul; the disciple learns that all recorded truth is susceptible to many interpretations, and that these unfold with increasing clarity as he takes one initiation after another, and as he develops conscious responsiveness. The *ability to invoke* demonstrates from life to life, and involves the invocation of conscious response from the anima mundi or from the subconscious soul of all things, as well as from the human consciousness and from the world of super-conscious contact.

This ability (to invoke) develops steadily as the aspirant treads the Path of Discipleship; it is frequently prefaced in the earlier stages by much confusion, much astral psychism, and frequent wrong interpretations. There is no need at this stage, however, for undue distress, because all that is needed is experience, and that experience is gained through experiment and its expression in the daily life. In no case is the truism of learning through a system of trial and error proved more correct than it is in the life and experience of the accepting disciple. When he is an accepted disciple, the errors decrease in number, even though the trials (or the experimental use of the many varying energies) become more extensive and, therefore, cover a much wider range of activities.

The *Processes of Registration* are founded upon what I might call invocative approaches from a wide area of possible contacts. The disciple has to learn to distinguish between these many impacts upon his sensitive aura. In the early stages the majority of them are unconsciously registered, though the registration is acute and accurate; the goal, nevertheless, is *conscious* registration; this is brought about through the constant and steady holding of the attitude of the Observer. It is developed through the attainment of detachment—the detachment of the Observer from all desires and longings which concern the separated self.   (11-100/1)

2. Usually in the early stages, the one desire of the disciple is to register impressions from the Hierarchy; he much prefers that idea to the idea of registering impressions from his own soul or from the surrounding human factors, his fellow men, and the environment and the circumstances which they create. He longs for what might be called "vertical impression". This motive, being very largely self-centredness, turns the disciple introspectively in upon himself, and it is in this stage that many aspirants become prisoners, astrally speaking, because they register in their magnetic aura the many astrally motivated thoughtforms of what they believe and hope "vertical impression" supposedly would convey. They contact with facility the astral counterparts of the higher worlds, which are reflected (and thereby distorted) into the astral plane; the world there registered is glamoured by wrong and selfish desires, and by the wishful thinking of well meaning devotees. Upon this I need not enlarge. All disciples—at some point or another in their training—have to work through this phase of glamour; in so doing they clarify and intensify the magnetic aura, and simultaneously, clarify the surrounding astral world with which they are in contact. They learn also that the longing to register impressions from the Hierarchy *must* give place to the determination to place their magnetic aura at the disposal of humanity; they then learn to register human need and to understand thereby where help is possible and their fellow men can be served. By means of this conscious registration of invocative appeals from the world of horizontal contacts, the magnetic aura of the disciple is cleared of the hindering and engrossing thoughtforms, and from the aspirational desires and longings which have hitherto prevented right registration. The disciple then ceases to create them, and those which have been created die out, or atrophy for lack of attention.

    Later on, when the accepting disciple becomes the accepted disciple, and is permitted to participate in ashramic activity, he adds the ability to register hierarchical impression; this however is only possible *after* he has learnt to register impression coming to him from his own soul (the vertical impression) and from the surrounding world of men (the horizontal impression). When he has taken certain important initiations, his magnetic aura will be capable of registering impression from the sub-human kingdoms in nature. Again, later on, when he is a Master of the Wisdom, and therefore a full member of the fifth kingdom in nature, the world of hierarchical life and activity will be the world from which *horizontal* impression will be made upon his magnetic aura, and *vertical* impression will come from the higher levels of the Spiritual Triad, and still later, from Shamballa. Then the world of humanity will be to him what the sub-human kingdoms were when the fourth kingdom, the human, was the field of his registered horizontal impression. (11-102/3)

(d) INSPIRATION

1. (Inspiration) involves another aspect of development. Inspiration is analogous to mediumship, but is entirely egoic. It utilises the mind as the medium of transmission to the brain of that which the soul knows. Mediumship usually describes the process when confined entirely to astral levels. On the egoic plane this involves inspiration. Ponder on this explanation for it explains much. (4-179)

2. *Sources of Inspiration:* Those who are in preparation for initiation *must* inevitably work alone. I would have you remember this. There are, as you know, three sources of inspiration which indicate to the disciple, struggling on the physical plane, his goal :

1. His own soul . . . . through direct contact, as the result of alignment.

2. The Master . . . . through impression, as a result of sensitivity.

3. The Ashram group . . . . through service, as a result of interplay.

Later, as the initiate-disciple makes progress, and as he builds the antahkarana, the energy of the One Life emanating from the Monad, brings in the fourth type of inspiration. To these spiritual sources of inspiration must be added lesser ones, such as mental impression, telepathically registered and coming from a multitude of thinkers and minds. (6-30/1)

47. THE INNER VOICE

1. Men deaden the inner voice that bears witness to the life hereafter, and they drown the words that echo in the silence by the noise and whirl of business, pleasure and excitement.

The whole secret of success in treading the occult path depends upon an attitude of mind; when the attitude is one of concrete materialism, of concentration upon form, and a desire for the things for the present moment, little progress can be made in apprehending the higher esoteric truth.   (4-84)

2. The Path (of Initiation) . . . is a path on which steady expansion of consciousness is undergone, with increasing sensitivity to the higher vibrations. This works out at first as sensitiveness to the inner voice and this is one of the most necessary faculties in a disciple. The Great Ones are looking for those who can rapidly obey the inner voice of their soul. (4-353)

3. Nothing satisfies (the true enquirer) until he finds the Way, and nothing appeases the desire at the centre of his being except that which is found in the house of his Father. He is what he is because he has tried all lesser ways and found them wanting, and has submitted to many guides only to find them "blind leaders of the blind". Nothing is left to him but to become his own guide and to find his own way home *alone*. In the loneliness which is the lot of every true disciple, are born that self-knowledge and self-reliance which will fit him in his turn to be a Master. This loneliness is not due to any separative spirit, but to the conditions of the Way itself. Aspirants must carefully bear this distinction in mind.

. . . The true enquirer is one whose courage is of that rare kind which enables its possessor to stand upright and to sound his own clear note in the very midst of the turmoil of the world. He is one who has the eye trained to see beyond the fogs and miasmas of the earth to that centre of peace which presides over all earth's happenings, and that trained attentive ear which (having caught a whisper of the Voice of the Silence) is kept tuned to that high vibration and is thus deaf to all lesser alluring voices. This again brings loneliness and produces that aloofness which all less evolved souls feel when in the presence of those who are forging ahead.

A paradoxical situation is brought about from the fact that the disciple is told to enquire the Way and yet there is none to tell him. Those who know the Way may not speak, knowing that the Path is constructed by the aspirant as the spider spins its web out of the centre of his own being. Thus only those souls flower forth into adepts in any specific generation, who have "trodden the wine press of the wrath of God alone", or who (in other words) have worked out their karma alone and who have intelligently taken up the task of treading the Path.

Obey the inward impulses of the Soul. Well do the teachers of the race instruct the budding initiate to practise discrimination and train him in the arduous task of distinguishing between :

(a) Instinct and intuition.

(b) Higher and lower mind.

(c) Desire and spiritual impulse.

(d) Selfish aspiration and divine incentive.

(e) The urge emanating from the lunar lords, and the unfoldment of the solar Lord.

It is no easy or flattering task to find oneself out and to discover that perhaps even the service we have rendered and our longing to study and work, has had a basically selfish origin, and resting on a desire for liberation or a distaste for the humdrum duties of everyday. He who seeks to obey the impulses of the soul, has to cultivate an accuracy of summation and a truthfulness with himself which is rare indeed these days. Let him say to himself "I must to my own Self be true" and in the private moments of his life, and in the secrecy of his own meditation, let him not gloss over one fault, nor excuse himself along a single line. Let him learn to diagnose his own words, deeds, and motives, and to call things by their true names. Only thus will he train himself in spiritual discrimination and learn to recognise truth in all things. Only thus will the reality be arrived at and the true Self known.

Pay no consideration to the prudential considerations of worldly science and sagacity. If the aspirant has need to cultivate a capacity to walk alone, if he has to develop the ability to be truthful in all things, he has likewise need to cultivate courage. It will be needful for him to run counter consistently to the world's opinion, and to the very best expression of that opinion, and this with frequency. He has to learn to do the right thing as he sees and knows it, irrespective of the opinion of earth's greatest and most quoted. He must depend upon himself and upon the conclusions he himself has come to in his moments of spiritual communion and illumination. It is here that so many aspirants fail. They do *not* do the very best they know; they fail to act in detail as their Inner Voice tells them; they leave undone certain things which they are prompted to do in their moments of meditation, and fail to speak the word which their spiritual mentor, the Self, urges them to speak. *It is in the aggregate of these unaccomplished details that the big failures are seen.* (4-584/6)

48. OBEDIENCE TO THE SOUL

1. If any command may ever emanate from the subjective band of teachers . . . let it be to follow the dictates of your own soul, and the promptings of your higher self.   (4-104)

2. Go your own way with strength and silence, and do that which your soul demands. Let not the lesser voices of the loved and near deflect you from your progress upon the path of service. You belong now to the world, and not to a handful of your fellow men. This is not an easy · lesson to learn, my brother, but all disciples have some day to learn it. (5-140/1)

3. What is this occult obedience which a Master is supposed to exact? Today, the Masters are dealing with the highly mental type of disciple who believes in the freedom of the human will and consciousness, and who resents the imposition of any so-called authority. The intellectual man will not accept any infringement of his freedom, and in this he is basically right. He objects to having to obey. . . .

The obedience required is obedience to the Plan. It is *not* obedience to the Master, no matter what many old style occult schools may say. The obedience which is asked of you is based on your growing recognition of the Plan for humanity, as it emerges in your consciousness through the process of meditation and through definite service, based upon a growing love of your fellow men.

The obedience demanded is that of the personality to the soul, as soul knowledge, soul light, and soul control become increasingly potent in the mind and brain reactions of the disciple. This whole problem of occult obedience would not arise at all if the rapport between soul and personality, or between the disciple and the Master was complete and soundly established. The entire question is based upon the blindness and lack of knowledge of the disciple. As the rapport becomes more firmly established, no fundamental divergences of opinion can appear; the aims of the soul and the personality blend and fuse; the objectives before the disciple and the Master become identical, and the group life conditions the service rendered by both of them. It is, therefore, the limitations of the disciple which prompt the question, and his fear that too much may be asked of him by the Master and his soul. (5-686/7)

4. The difficulty at present is that relatively few people are soul-conscious, and consequently most men remain unaware of the "occult commands" of their own souls. (17-435)

49. RELIANCE ON THE SOUL

1. Could you but see it, the unrest and difficulty everywhere is producing a good which far outweighs the seeming evil. Souls are finding themselves and learning dependence upon the inner Ruler. When all outward props fail, and when all the apparent authorities differ in the solution proffered, then souls are thrown back upon themselves and learn to seek within. This inner contact with the higher self is becoming apparent in gradually unfolding degree, and leads to that self-reliance and inward calm which is based upon the rule of the inner God and which, therefore, makes a man an instrument for service in the word. (4-130)

2. The disciple has to take himself as he is at any given time, with any given equipment, and under any given circumstances; then he proceeds to subordinate himself, his affairs and his time to the need of the hour, particularly during a phase of group, national or world crisis. When he does this within his own consciousness, and is therefore thinking along lines of the true values, he will discover that his own private affairs are taken care of, his capacities are increased and his limitations are forgotten. (6-44)

50. GUIDANCE BY THE SOUL

1. Guidance can come, as you well know, from a man's own soul when through meditation, discipline and service, he has established contact, and there is consequently a direct channel of communication from soul to brain, via the mind. This, when clear and direct, is true divine guidance, coming from the inner divinity. It can, however, be distorted and misinterpreted if the mind is not developed, the character is not purified, and the man is not free from undue personality control. The mind must make right application of the imparted truth or guidance. Where there is true and right apprehension of the inner divine voice, then—and only then—do you have infallible guidance, and the voice of the inner God can then speak with clarity to its instrument, man upon the physical plane.

Once this latter form of guidance has been established, stabilised, fostered, developed and understood, other forms of spiritual guidance then become possible. The reason for this is that they will pass through, or be submitted to the standard of values which the factor of the soul itself constitutes. The awareness of the soul is a part of all awarenesses. The recognition of this soul awareness is a gradual and progressive happening where the man upon the physical plane is concerned. The brain cells must be gradually awakened and the correct interpretative response developed. As, for instance, a man becomes aware of the Plan of God, he may regard that Plan as being imparted to him by a Master or by some Member of the Hierarchy; he may regard the knowledge as coming to him through his own immediate contact with a thoughtform of the Plan. If he achieves and interprets this knowledge in a truly right way, he is perforce simply achieving recognition of that which his own soul inevitably knows, because his soul is an aspect of the Universal Soul, and an integral part of the planetary Hierarchy. (15-491/2)

2. How easily unimportant people and beginners interpret calls and messages they hear or receive as coming to them from some high and elevated source, whereas they are in all probability hearing that which emanates from their own souls, or from some teacher (not a Master) who is attempting to help them. (17-688)

51. THE RAINCLOUD OF KNOWABLE THINGS

1. (The initiate) has learnt through life in the three worlds, to penetrate into the world of mind, and the lower concrete mind has become his instrument, integrating his personality, opening up to him the world of thought, and putting into his power the processes of thoughtform creation; he has learnt through meditation to make contact with the soul, the Son of Mind, who is himself, and has in time identified himself with that soul; he becomes the soul in fact, and can create in the world of thought those living forms which bring light and help and truth to others; thus he serves; he learns also, through unfolding perception, to penetrate into the levels of abstract thought, the antechamber to the world of pure reason, and through these three aspects of mind he discovers that he possesses the "three keys" which will permit him to delve into the knowledge, wisdom and reason of the Universal Mind. This is what is revealed to him as he penetrates deeper into what is called the Arcana of Wisdom, the Mind of God, the third divine Aspect. This is essentially what is covered by the symbolic and pictorial phrase *"the raincloud of knowable things"*. The raincloud is a symbol of that area of the as yet unrevealed purposes of God which can be immediately revealed if the world disciples and initiates care to "penetrate to the point of precipitation".

This idea should in the future lie behind all you do in your meditation work. Your meditation should now be regarded by you as a process of penetration, carried forward as an act of service, with the intent to bring enlightenment to others.   (6-313)

2. By the *super-conscious,* I mean those potencies and knowledges which are available but which are as yet uncontacted and unrecognised and, therefore, of no immediate use. These are the wisdom, love and abstract idealism which are inherent in the nature of the soul, but which are not yet, and never have been a part of the equipment available for use. Eventually all these powers will be recognised and used by the man. These potencies and realisations are called in *The Yoga Sutras of Patanjali* by the interesting name of "the raincloud of knowable things". These "knowable things" will eventually drop into the conscious aspect of a man's nature and become an integral part of his intellectual equipment. Finally, as evolution proceeds and the ages pass away, they will drop into the subconscious aspect of his nature, as his power to grasp the super-conscious grows in capacity. I might make this point clearer to you if I

219

pointed out that just as the instinctual nature is today found largely in the realm of the subconscious, so in due time, the intellectual part of man (of which he is at this time becoming increasingly aware) will be relegated to a similar position, and will drop below the threshold of consciousness. The intuition will then take its place. For most people, the free use of the intuition is not possible, because it lies in the realm of the super-conscious. (15-440/1)

52. ESOTERIC SENSE

By the words "esoteric sense", I mean essentially the power to live and to function subjectively, to possess a constant inner contact with the soul and the world in which it is found, and this must work out subjectively through love, actively shown; through wisdom, steadily outpoured; and through that capacity to include and to identify oneself with all that breathes and feels, which is the outstanding characteristic of all truly functioning sons of God. I mean, therefore, an interiorly held attitude of mind which can orient itself at will in any direction. It can govern and control the emotional sensitiveness, not only of the disciple himself, but of all whom he may contact. By the strength of his silent thought, he can bring light and peace to all. Through that mental power, he can tune in on the world thought, and upon the realm of ideas and can discriminate between and choose those mental agencies and those concepts which will enable him, as a worker under the Plan, to influence his environment and to clothe the new ideals in that thought matter which will enable them to be more easily recognised in the world of ordinary everyday thinking and living. This attitude of mind will enable the disciple also to orient himself to the world of souls and in that high place of inspiration and of light, discover his fellow workers, communicate with them and—in union with them—collaborate in the working out of divine intentions.

This esoteric sense is the main need of the aspirant at this time of the world history. Until aspirants have somewhat grasped it and can use it, they can never form part of the New Group; they can never work as white magicians, and these Instructions will remain for them theoretical and mainly intellectual, instead of being practical and effective.

To cultivate this inner esoteric sense, meditation is needed, and continuous meditation, in the early stages of development. But as time elapses and a man grows spiritually, this daily meditation will perforce give way to a steady spiritual orientation, and then mediation as now understood and needed will no longer be required. The detachment between a man and his usable forms will be so complete, that he will live ever in the "seat of the Observer", and from that point and attitude will direct the activities of the mind and of the emotions and of the energies which make physical expression possible and useful.

The first stage in this development and culture of the esoteric sense, consists in the holding of the attitude of constant detached observation. (4-603/4)

53. GLAMOUR AND ILLUSION

1. Only the intuition can dispel illusion, and hence the need of training intuitives. (10-23)

2. The *Problem of Illusion* lies in the fact that it is a soul activity, and the result of the mind aspect of all the souls in manifestation. It is the soul which is submerged in the illusion and the soul that fails to see with clarity until such time as it has learnt to pour the light of the soul through into the mind and the brain.

The *Problem of Glamour* is found when the mental illusion is intensified by desire. What the theosophist calls "kama-manas" produces glamour. It is illusion on the astral plane. (10-21)

3. In the process of *dissipating glamour,* the way of the greatest potency is to realise the necessity to act purely as a channel for the energy of the soul. If the disciple can make right alignment and consequent contact with his soul, the results show as *increased light.* This light pours down and irradiates not only the mind, but the brain consciousness as well. He sees the situation more clearly: he realises the facts of the case as against his "vain imaginings"; and so the "light shines upon his way". He is not yet able to see truly in the larger sweeps of consciousness; the group glamour, and of course, the world glamour remain to him as yet a binding and bewildering mystery, but his own immediate way begins to clear, and he stands relatively free from the fog of his ancient and distorting emotional miasmas. Alignment, contact with his soul, and then steadfastness, are the key-notes to success. (10-37)

4. The *Illusion of Power* is perhaps one of the first and most serious tests which comes to an aspirant. It is also one of the best examples of this "great mistake", and I therefore bring it to your attention as being one against which I beg you most carefully to guard yourself. It is rare indeed for any disciple to escape the effects of this error of illusion for it is, curiously, based upon right success and right motive. Hence the specious nature of the problem. It might be expressed thus:

An aspirant succeeds in contacting his soul or ego through right effort. Through meditation, good intention, and correct technique, plus the desire to serve and to love, he achieves alignment. He becomes then aware of the results of his successful work. His mind is illumined. A sense of power flows through his vehicles. He is, temporarily at least, made aware of the Plan. The need of the world and the capacity of the soul to meet that need flood his consciousness. His dedication, consecration and right purpose enhance the directed inflow of spiritual energy. He knows. He loves. He seeks to serve, and does all three more or less successfully. The result of all this is that he becomes more engrossed with the sense of power, and with the part he is to play in aiding humanity, than he is with the realisation of a due and proper sense of proportion and of spiritual values. He over-estimates his experience and himself. Instead of redoubling his efforts and thus establishing a closer contact with the kingdom of souls, and loving all being more deeply, he begins to call attention to himself, to the mission he is to develop, and to the confidence that the Master and even the planetary Logos apparently have in him. He talks about himself; he gestures and attracts notice, demanding recognition. As he does so, his alignment is steadily impaired; his contact lessens, and he joins the ranks of the many who have succumbed to the illusion of sensed power.

This form of illusion is becoming increasingly prevalent among disciples and those who have taken the first two initiations. There are today many people in the world who have taken the first initiation in a previous life. At some period in the present life cycle, recurring and recapitulating as it does the events of an earlier development, they again reach a point in their realisation which they earlier reached. The significance of their attainment pours in upon them, and the sense of their responsibility and their knowledge. Again they over-estimate themselves, regarding their missions and themselves as unique among the sons of men, and their esoteric and subjective demand for recognition enters in and spoils what might otherwise have been a fruitful service. Any emphasis upon the personality can distort most easily the pure light of the soul as it seeks to pour through the lower self. Any effort to call attention to the mission or task which the personality has undertaken, detracts from that mission and handicaps the man in his task; it leads to the deferring of its fulfilment until such time when the disciple can be naught but a channel through which love can pour, and light can shine. This pouring through and shining forth has to be a spontaneous happening, and contain no self-reference. (10-51/3)

5. Only as the disciple learns to hold his mind "steady in the light", and as the rays of pure light stream forth from the soul, can the glamour be discovered, discerned, recognised for what it essentially is and thus be made to disappear, as the mists of the earth dissolve in the rays of the rising sun. Therefore, I would counsel you to pay more adequate attention to your meditation, cultivating ever the ability to reflect and to assume the attitude of reflection—held steady throughout the day. (10-81)

6. It is the soul itself which dispels illusion, through the use of the faculty of the intuition. It is the illumined mind which dissipates glamour. (10-83)

7. The vehicles through which the soul is seeking experience and expression, are normally and naturally subject to world glamours, and to the glamours of humanity as well as illusion. When the soul, in the early stages of experience, falls into the snare of maya, of glamour, and eventually of illusion, the reason is that the soul is identifying itself with those forms, and therefore with the surrounding glamour, and thus failing to achieve identification with itself. As evolution proceeds, the nature of the problem becomes apparent to the soul in incarnation, and a process is then instituted whereby the soul frees itself from the results of wrong identification. Every soul in incarnation which succeeds in releasing its consciousness from the world of illusion and of glamour, is definitely serving the race, and helping to free humanity from this ancient and potent thraldom. (10-114)

8. The only light which can dissipate the fogs of glamour, and rid the life of its ill effects, is that of the soul, which—like a pure dispelling beam —possesses the curious and unique quality of revelation, of immediate dissipation, and of illumination. The revelation vouchsafed is different to that of the intuition, for it is the revelation of that which the glamour veils and hides, which is a revelation unique to the astral plane and conditioned by its laws. (10-139)

9. The *Problem of Illusion* lies in the fact that it is a soul activity, and is the result of the mind aspect of all the souls in manifestation. It is the

soul which is submerged in the illusion, and the soul that fails to see with clarity until such time as it has learnt to pour the light of the soul through into the mind and brain.   (15-472)

54. THE PAIRS OF OPPOSITES

1. For so many disciples . . . the lesson has been to learn to move forward in spite of the activity of the pairs of opposites, paying no attention to the reactions of the senses and standing free and unafraid, whether the experience being undergone is one of high import and of spiritual satisfaction, or is one of the "dead-level" happenings, where nothing brings joy and where only pain, fear and suspense are to be found. You must learn to move forward steadily *between* the pairs of opposites, saying to yourself: I am not this; I am not that; eternally, I am the *Self*. (5-664)

2. The constitution of the ego, or soul, is the factor of paramount importance to the Master in the task of training the disciple for hierarchical work. This necessarily involves the three higher centres (head, heart and throat). It is with the so-called egoic lotus that He is concerned, and this is a point which the disciple is very apt to forget. The soul is preoccupied with its own life; the details of the personality life (its inadequate expression or shadow in the three worlds) simply make no impact whatsoever upon the soul consciousness. As the violence of the personality life grows, the soul which has been increasingly the recipient of the best the aspiring personality has to offer, and which has been slowly turning its attention towards the mind of the personality, becomes also aware of an opposing factor to true soul expression upon the outer periphery of life. Then the battle of the higher pairs of opposites begins—the battle between soul and personality, *consciously waged* on both sides. That is the point to have in mind. This conflict terminates, prior to each of the first three initiations, in the confronting of the two opponents; the Dweller on the Threshold (of initiation) and the Angel of the Presence stand face to face.   (5-762)

55. THE DWELLER ON THE THRESHOLD

1. A question now arises in your minds: "How can I overcome this Dweller and yet at the same time refuse to concentrate upon myself and my problems? This I am told by you not to do, and yet the Dweller is the sum total of all personality holds and defects, all potencies—emotional, mental and physical—which limit my expression as a soul. What can I therefore do?"

My answer would be: You must first of all accept the fact of the Dweller, and then relegate that Dweller to its rightful place as part of the Great Illusion, the great phantasmagoria of existence and as an integral part of the life of the three worlds. You must then proceed upon your planned life service (What definite plan or plans have you, my brother?) and act as if the Dweller existed not, thus freeing yourself from all personality influence in due time, and leaving your mind free for the task in hand. I could perhaps word it another way. When your interest in hierarchical work and the programme of the Ashram with which you are connected is adequately strong, it will then dominate all your actions, and all your thoughts (waking or sleeping); you will then find that the grip of the Dweller will be broken, that its *life* has been destroyed by the force of attrition, and its *form* destroyed in the fires of sacrifice. Such briefly is the story.   (6-47/8)

2. The Dweller on the Threshold is oft regarded as a disaster, as a horror to be avoided, and as a final and culminating evil. I would remind you nevertheless that the Dweller is the "one who stands before the Gate of God", who dwells in the shadow of the portal of initiation, and who faces the Angel of the Presence open-eyed, as the ancient scripture calls it. The Dweller can be defined as the sum total of the forces of the lower nature as expressed in the personality prior to illumination, to inspiration, and to initiation. The personality, at this stage, is exceedingly potent, and the Dweller embodies all the psychic and mental forces which down the ages have been unfolded in a man, and nurtured with care; it can be looked upon as the potency of the threefold material form, prior to its consecration and dedication to the life of the soul and to the service of the Hierarchy, of God and humanity.

The Dweller on the Threshold is all that a man is, apart from the higher spiritual self; it is the third aspect of divinity as expressed in the human mechanism, and this third aspect must eventually be sub-ordinated to the second aspect, the soul.   (10-90/1), (15-312)

225

3. (About the nature of the Dweller) I would like . . . to enlarge upon one or two points, and give one or two new suggestions which—for the sake of clarity and for your more rapid comprehension—we will tabulate as follows:

1. The Dweller on the Threshold is essentially the personality; it is an integrated unity composed of physical forces, vital energy, astral forces and mental energies, constituting the sum total of the lower nature.

2. The Dweller takes form when a reorientation of man's life has taken place consciously and under soul impression; the whole personality is then theoretically directed towards *liberation into service*. The problem is to make the theory and the aspiration facts in experience.

3. For a great length of time the forces of the personality do not constitute the Dweller. The man is not on the threshold of divinity; he is not consciously aware of the Angel. His forces are inchoate; he works unconsciously in his environment, the victim of circumstance and of his own nature apparently, and under the lure and the urge of desire for physical plane activity and existence. When, however, the life of the man is ruled from the mental plane, plus desire or ambition, and he is controlled at least to some large extent by mental influence, then the Dweller begins to take shape as a unified force.

4. The stages wherein the Dweller on the Threshold is recognised, subjected to a discriminating discipline, and finally controlled and mastered, are mainly three:

(a) The stage wherein the personality dominates and rules the life and ambitions and the goals of man's life-endeavour. The Dweller then controls.

(b) The stage of a growing cleavage in the consciousness of the disciple. The Dweller or the personality is then urged in two directions: *one*, towards the pursuit of personal ambitions and desires in the three worlds; *the other*, in which the effort is made by the Dweller (note this statement) to take a stand upon the threshold of divinity and before the Portal of Initiation.

(c) The stage wherein the Dweller consciously seeks the co-operation of the soul and, though still in itself essentially constituting a barrier to spiritual progress, is more and more influenced by the soul than by its lower nature.

5. When the final stage is reached (and many are now reaching it today) the disciple strives with more or less success to steady the Dweller (by

learning to "hold the mind steady in the light" and thus controlling the lower nature). In this way the constant, fluid, changefulness of the Dweller is gradually overcome; its orientation towards reality and away from the Great Illusion is made effective, and the Angel and the Dweller are slowly brought into a close rapport.

6. In the earlier stages of effort and of attempted control, the Dweller is positive and the Soul is negative in their effects in the three worlds of human endeavour. Then there is a period of oscillation, leading to a life of equilibrium, wherein neither aspect appears to dominate; after that the balance changes and the personality steadily becomes negative and the soul or psyche becomes dominant and positive. (10-153/5)

4. There are some cycles wherein the Dweller on the Threshold appears and confronts the aspirant, challenging his purpose and progress, and blocking the door which leads to expanded life and liberation. The Dweller challenges the freedom of the human soul. So it is also in the life of a nation, a race, and humanity as a whole.

The Angel of the Presence indicates divine possibility, reveals to the attentive disciple the next step towards liberation which must be made, and throws light upon the immediate stage of the Path to Light which must be trodden. . . .

The Dweller on the Threshold summarises in itself the evil tendencies, the accumulated limitation and the sum total of the selfish habits and desires which are characteristic of the material nature of the disciple. The Angel of the Presence indicates *the future* possibility and the divine nature. . . . The Dweller on the Threshold indicates *the past* with its limitations and evil habits. . . .

Some cycles in a disciple's life present one aspect of a "confrontation" and some another. In one life he may be entirely occupied with fighting the Dweller on the Threshold, or with orienting himself to the Angel of the Presence, and permitting the divine conditioning energy to flow into him; he may be succumbing to the influence of the dread sum total of his evil and material desires, or he may be drawing gradually nearer to the Angel. But—and this is the point of importance—*it is he himself who evokes one or other of these manifestations*. . . . It is the magnetic appeal . . . of the disciple . . . which produces the manifestation. In other lives, the disciple may simply swing between the two poles of his being, with no conscious effort, no direct confrontation and no clear understanding of life purpose. . . .

Eventually, however, there comes a life wherein the disciple is confronted by both the Dweller and the Angel simultaneously, and the major conflict of his experience takes place. So it is today in the world. The spiritual and the material are in conflict, and humanity itself is the battleground.

. . . When (the disciple) has achieved right desire, and has made true effort towards correct orientation, then—when the conflict between good and evil is at its height—there comes a moment when he demands more light, more power, more understanding, and liberation to take his next forward step. When he can make this demand with firm intent, and can stand steady and unafraid, response will inevitably come from the very Presence itself. A manifestation of light and love and power will stream forth. Recognition of need has then evoked response. The conflict ceases; the Dweller departs to his own place; the Path ahead lies clear; the disciple can move forward with assurance, and a better life dawns for him. (13-293/5)

56.   THE SOUL AND PSYCHIC POWERS

When a man is firmly polarised upon the mental plane, and when he has achieved some measure of contact with the soul, and when his entire orientation is towards the world of spiritual realities, and his life is one of discipline and service, then, at times, and when necessary, he can at will call into use these lower psychic powers in the service of the Plan, and in order to do some special work upon the astral plane. But this is a case where the greater consciousness includes normally the lesser consciousness. This is however seldom done even by adepts, for the powers of the soul— spiritual perception, telepathic sensitivity and psychometrical facility—are usually adequate to the demand and the need to be met. I interject these remarks, as there are some enlightened men who use these powers, but it is always along the line of some specific service to the Hierarchy and humanity, and *not* along any line connected with the individual. (15-477)

57. THE SUTRATMA

1. The "silver thread" which incarnates from the beginning of a period of manifestation until the end, stringing upon itself the pearls of human existence. It is the line of energy which connects the lower personal man with his Father in Heaven via the Ego, the mediating middle principle. Upon it are found those focal points of energy we call the permanent atoms.   (3-114)

2. The soul dominates its form through the medium of the sutratma or life thread, and (through it) vitalises its triple instrument (mental, emotional and physical) and thus sets up a communication with the brain. Through the brain, consciously controlled, the man is galvanised into intelligent activity on the physical plane.   (4-57/8)

3. The purpose and will of the soul, the spiritual determination to be and to do, utilises the thread soul, the sutratma, the life current as its means of expression in form. This life current differentiates into threads when it reaches the body and is "anchored", if I might so express it, in two locations in that body. This is symbolic of the differentiations of Atma, or Spirit, into its two reflections, soul and body. The soul, or consciousness aspect, that which makes a human being a rational, thinking entity, is "anchored" by one aspect of this thread soul to a "seat" in the brain, found in the region of the pineal gland. The other aspect of the life which animates every atom of the body and which constitutes the principle of coherence or of integration, finds its way to the heart and is focused or 'anchored" there. From these two points, the spiritual man seeks to control the mechanism. Thus functioning on the physical plane becomes possible, and objective existence becomes a temporary mode of expression. The soul, seated in the brain, makes man an intelligent rational entity, self-conscious and self-directing; he is aware in varying degree of the world in which he lives, according to the point in evolution and the consequent development of the mechanism. The mechanism is triple in expression. There are first of all the nadis and the seven centres of force; then the nervous system in its three divisions: cerebro-spinal, sympathetic, and peripheral; and then there is the endocrine system, which might be regarded as the densest aspect or externalisation of the other two.
  The soul, seated in the heart, is the life principle, the principle of self-determination, the central nucleus of positive energy, by means of which all the atoms of the body are held in their right place and subordinated

to the "will-to-be" of the soul. This principle of life utilises the blood stream as its mode of expression and as its controlling agency, and through the close relation of the endocrine system to the blood stream, we have the two aspects of soul activity brought together in order to make man a living, conscious, functioning entity, governed by the soul, and expressing the purpose of the soul in all the activities of daily living.   (4-495/6)

4. Students should train themselves to distinguish between the sutratma and the antahkarana, between the life thread and the thread of consciousness. One thread is the basis of immortality, and the other the basis of continuity. Herein lies a fine distinction for the investigator. One thread (the sutratma), links and vivifies all forms into one functioning whole, and embodies in itself the will and the purpose of the expressing entity, be it man, God or crystal. The other thread (the antahkarana) embodies the response of the consciousness within the form to a steadily expanding range of contacts within the environing whole.

The sutratma is the direct stream of life, unbroken and immutable, which can be regarded symbolically as a direct stream of living energy flowing from the centre to the periphery, and from the source to the outer expression or the phenomenal appearance. It is the *life*. It produces the individual process and the evolutionary unfoldment of all forms. It is, therefore, the path of life, which reaches from the Monad to the personality, via the soul. This is the thread soul, and it is one and indivisible. It conveys the energy of life and finds its final anchor in the centre of the human heart and at some central focal point in all forms of divine expression. Naught is and naught remains but life.   (12-26/7)

58.   THE ANTAHKARANA

1. The symbology of the antahkarana tends badly to complicate the grasp of its real nature. . . . The antahkarana is not a series of energy threads, slowly woven by the soul-infused personality, and met by corresponding threads projected by the Spiritual Triad, but is in reality a state of awareness. . . .

H.P.B. taught that the antahkarana was primarily the channel of energy relating forms and their forces to their originating sources, and that across the mental plane (with its three aspects of mind) the life thread necessarily passed, linking Monad, soul and personality into one living whole. Technically speaking, therefore, there is no need for the so-called bridge, except for one important factor: there is, on the part of the soul-infused personality, a definite break *in consciousness* between the lower mind and the abstract mind. The higher mind (being the lowest aspect of the Spiritual Triad) can be regarded as a door admitting the consciousness of the soul-infused personality into a higher realm of contact and awareness. But again—as you can well see—there is nothing here but symbolism; there is no door, but simply a symbol indicating means of access.

In the total evolution of the spiritual man through physical incarnation during untold hundreds of lives, the entire process is simply one of expanding consciousness and of attaining—sequentially and stage by stage—an ever more inclusive awareness. This is good to bear in mind, for eventually all this symbolic picturing will give place to reality. The task—and it is a real one—of building the antahkarana and creating that which will bridge the gap, is in truth the planned and conscious effort to project the focused thought of the spiritual man from the lower mental plane into areas of awareness which have been *sensed but not contacted;* it entails using the totality of the awareness already developed and already "enlightened" by the soul, and (with deliberation) making it increasingly sensitive to the focused activity of the world of the higher spiritual realities; it is directing the stream of conscious thought towards the sensed and theoretically recognised world of the Masters, of the Spiritual Triad and, finally, of Shamballa. Disciples should remember that the Higher way of Evolution is far simpler than the lower way, and that therefore, the teaching on the significance and the meaning of the antahkarana—which is the first creation of the soul-infused personality acting as a unitary being—is far simpler than that relating to the personality in the three worlds of human evolution. (6-193/5)

2. The antahkarana is now being built by all soul-infused personalities (or constructed unconsciously by all struggling to attain spiritual orientation and stature), and is rapidly becoming a strong cable, composed of all the many threads of living light, of consciousness and of life; these threads are blended and fused so that no one can truly say: "my thread, or my bridge, or my antahkarana". This, in ignorance, they ofttimes do. All soul-infused personalities are creating *the* human antahkarana, which will unite, in an indissoluble unity, the three aspects or energies of the Spiritual Triad, and the three aspects of the soul-infused personality in the three worlds. In time to come, the phrase "life in the three worlds" will be

discontinued; men will talk in terms of "life in the five worlds of the manifested Kingdom of God". Think in these terms today if you can, and begin to grasp somewhat the significance of the truth therein embodied. In the beautiful Eastern symbology, "The Bridge of Sighs" which links the animal world with the human world, and leads all men into the vale of tears, of woe, of discipline, and of loneliness, is rapidly being replaced by the radiant *Rainbow Bridge,* constructed by the sons of men who seek pure light. "They pass across the bridge into the Light serene which there awaits them, and bring the radiant light down to the world of men, revealing the new kingdom of the soul; souls disappear, and only the Soul is seen".   (6-408)

3. The clarity of the vision and the grasp of the Plan . . . are dependent upon the conscious and intelligent construction of the antahkarana. (6-667)

4. When the antahkarana is constructed and the higher three are directly related to the lower three, then the soul is no longer needed.   (11-157)

5. *The Science of the Antahkarana.* This deals with the mode of bridging the gap which exists in man's consciousness between the world of ordinary human experience, the threefold world of physical—emotional—mental functioning, and the higher levels of so-called spiritual development, which is the world of ideas, of intuitive perception, of spiritual insight and understanding. . . . This leads to the overcoming of the limitations— physical and psychological—which restrict man's free expression of his innate divinity.   (12-2)

6. Education is . . . the Science of the Antahkarana. This science and this term is the esoteric way of expressing the truth of this bridging necessity. The antahkarana is the bridge the man builds—through meditation, understanding, and the magical creative work of the soul—between the three aspects of his mind nature. Therefore, the primary objectives of the coming education will be:

   1. To produce alignment between mind and brain, through a correct understanding of the inner constitution of man, particularly of the etheric body and the force centres.

   2. To build or construct a bridge between the brain-mind-soul, thus producing an integrated personality which is a steady developing expression of the indwelling soul.

   3. To build the bridge between the lower mind, soul, higher mind, so that the illumination of the personality becomes possible.

The true education is consequently the science of linking up the integral parts of man, and also of linking him up in turn with his immediate environment, and then with the greater whole in which he has to play his part. (12-6)

7. The consciousness thread (antahkarana) is the result of the union of life and substance. . . . It is the thread which is woven as a result of the appearance of life in form upon the physical plane. Speaking again symbolically, it might be said that the *sutratma* works from above downward, and is the precipitation of life into the outer manifestation. The *antahkarana* is woven, evolved, and created as the result of this primary creation, and works from below upwards, from the without to the within, from the world of exoteric phenomena into the world of subjective realities and of meaning.

This "Path of Return", by means of which the race is withdrawn from outer emphasis and begins to recognise and register those inner conscious knowledges of that which is not phenomenal, has already (through the evolutionary process) reached a point of development wherein some human beings can follow along this path from the physical consciousness to the emotional, and from the emotional to the mental. That part of the work is already accomplished in many thousands of cases and what is now required is facility and right use of this power. This thread of energy, coloured by conscious sentient response, is later coloured by the discriminating consciousness of the mind, and this produces that inner integration which makes man eventually an efficient thinking being. At first, this thread is used purely for lower selfish interests; it steadily gets stronger and more potent as time goes on, until it is a definite, clear, strong thread, reaching from the outer physical life, from a point within the brain, straight through to the inner mechanism. This thread, however, is not identified with the mechanism, but with the consciousness in man. Through the means of this thread a man becomes aware of his emotional life in its many forms (note this phraseology), and through it he becomes aware of the world of thought; he learns to think and begins to function consciously on the mental plane, in which the thinkers of the race—a steadily increasing number—live and move and have their being. Increasingly he learns to tread this path of consciousness, and thereby ceases to be identified with the animal outer form and learns to identify himself with the inner qualities and attributes. He lives first the life of dreams, and then the life of thought. Then the time comes when this lower aspect of the antahkarana is completed, and the first great conscious unity is consummated. The man is an integrated, conscious, living personality. The thread of continuity between the three lower aspects of the man is established and can be used. It stretches, if such a term can be used (my intent being entirely pictorial), from the centre of the head to the mind, which is in its turn a centre of energy in the world of thought. At the same time, this antahkarana is interwoven with the thread of life or the sutratma, which emerges from the heart centre. The objective of evolution in form is now relatively complete.

When this stage has been reached, the sensitive feeling-out into the environing universe, still continues. Man weaves a thread which is like the thread the spider weaves so amazingly. He reaches out still further into his possible environment, and then discovers an aspect of himself of which he had little dreamt in the early stages of his development. He discovers the *soul* and then passes through the illusion of duality. This is a necessary but not a permanent stage. It is one which characterises the aspirant of this world cycle, perhaps I should say this manvantara or world period. He seeks to merge himself with the soul, to identify himself, the conscious personality, with that overshadowing soul. It is at this point, technically speaking, that the true building of the antahkarana must be begun. It is the bridge between the personality and the soul.   (12-27/9)

8. *The Science of the Antahkarana.* This is the new and true science of the mind, which will utilise mental substance for the building of the bridge between personality and soul, and then between the soul and the Spiritual Triad. This constitutes active work in substance subtler than the substance of the three worlds of ordinary human evolution. It concerns the substance of the three higher levels of the mental plane. These symbolic bridges, when constructed, will facilitate the stream or flow of consciousness, or that sense of unimpeded awareness, which will finally end the fear of death, negate all sense of separateness, and make a man responsive in his brain consciousness to impressions coming to him from the higher spiritual realms or from the Mind of God. Thus he will more easily be initiated into the purposes and plans of the Creator.   (12-95/6)

9. I would have you bear in mind that the "threads of lighted consciousness" which we unfailingly create, and which eventually form the antahkarana, have to be woven between each and every hierarchical unit, and that within the human kingdom itself, these connecting relationships and bridging factors, have to be established between unit and unit, and between group and group.   (12-126)

10. The Science of the Antahkarana . . . deals with the threefold thread which connects:

1. The Monad, the soul and the personality, linking all three periodical vehicles and unifying all seven principles.

2. The triple personality and its environment in the three worlds of human enterprise, and later in the other two worlds (making five) of super-human expression.

3. The consciously creative man, and the world of ideas. These he must contact and express through creative work, thus bridging with the light:

(a) Between the world of souls and the world of phenomena.

(b) Between the realm of subjective beauty and reality, and the outer tangible world of nature.

(c) Between himself and others.

(d) Between group and group.

(e) Later, when the divine Plan has become a reality to him, between the fourth kingdom (the human) and the fifth kingdom (the Kingdom of God).

(f) Finally, between humanity and the Hierarchy.

(This science) is the science of the triple thread which exists from the very beginning of time, and links individual man with his monadic source. The recognition of this thread and its use, consciously, as the Path and the means of ever expanding contacts, comes relatively late in the evolutionary process. The goal of all aspirants and disciples, is to become aware of this stream of energy in its various diversifications, and consciously to employ these energies in two ways: interiorly in self-unfoldment, and in the service of the Plan for humanity.

. . . (It) deals, therefore, with the entire incoming system of energy, with the processes of usage and transformation and fusion. It deals also with the outgoing energies and their relationship to the environment, and is the basis of the science of the force centres. The incoming and the outgoing energies constitute finally two great stations of energy, one characterised by power and the other by love, and all directed to the illumination of the individual and of humanity as a whole, through the medium of the Hierarchy composed of individuals. This is basically the Science of the Path.

The antahkarana, therefore, is the *thread of consciousness,* of intelligence, and the responsive agent in all sentient reactions. The interesting point to bear in mind, and where we must now lay the emphasis, is that this thread of consciousness *is evolved by the soul* and not by the Monad. The World Soul pours its gossamer thread of sentient consciousness into all forms, into all body cells, and into all atoms. The human soul, the solar angel, repeats the process in relation to its shadow and reflection, the personality. This is part of the creative work of the soul. But, in its turn, the human being has also to become creative in the mental sense of the term, and must repeat the process, for in all points the microcosm resembles the macrocosm. Therefore, through the life thread, the soul creates and reproduces a personality through which to function. Then through the building of the antahkarana, the soul first of all develops sentiency down upon the physical plane, and later bridges the gap—through meditation and service—between the three mental aspects. It thus completes the creation of the path of return to the Centre, which must parallel the path of outgoing.   (12-145/8)

11. The human soul (in contradistinction to the soul as it functions in its own kingdom, free from the limitations of human life) is imprisoned and subject to the control of the lower three energies for the major part of its experience. Then, upon the Path of Probation, the dual energy of soul begins to be increasingly active, and the man seeks to use his mind consciously, and to express love-wisdom on the physical plane. This is a simple statement of the objective of all aspirants. When the five energies are begining to be used, consciously and wisely in service, rhythm is then set up between the Personality and the Soul. It is as if a magnetic field were then established and these two vibrating and magnetic units or grouped energies, swung into each other's field of influence. This happens only occasionally and rarely in the early stages; later it occurs more constantly, and thus a path of contact is established which eventually becomes the line of least resistance, "the way of familiar approach", as it is sometimes called. Thus is the first half of the "bridge", the antahkarana, constructed. By the time the third initiation is completed, this Way is completed, and the initiate can "pass to higher worlds at will, leaving the lower worlds far behind; or he can come again and pass upon the way that leads from dark to light, from light to dark, and from the under lower worlds into the realms of light".

Thus the two are one, and the first great union upon the Path of Return is completed. A second stage of the Way has then to be trodden, leading to a second union of still further importance, in that it leads to complete liberation from the three worlds. It must be remembered that the soul, in its turn, is a union of three energies of which the lower three are the reflection. It is a synthesis of the energy of Life itself (which demonstrates as the life-principle within the world of forms), of the energy of the intuition or spiritual love-wisdom or understanding (this demonstrates as sensitivity and feeling in the astral body), and spiritual mind, whose reflection in the lower nature is the mind or the principle of intelligence in the form world. In these three we have the atma-buddhi-manas of the theosophical literature—that higher triplicity which is reflected in the lower three, and which focuses through the soul body on the higher levels of the mental plane before being precipitated into incarnation—as it is esoterically called.

Modernising the concept, we might say that the energies which animate the physical body and the intelligent life of the atom, the sensitive emotional states, and the intelligent mind, have eventually to be blended with and transmuted into the energies which animate the soul. These are the spiritual mind, conveying illumination; the intuitive nature, conferring spiritual perception; and divine livingness.

After the third initiation the "Way" is carried forward with great rapidity, and the "bridge" is finished which links perfectly the higher Spiritual Triad and the lower material reflection. The three worlds of the Soul and the three worlds of the Personality, become one world wherein the initiate works and functions, seeing no distinction, regarding one world as the world of inspiration and the other world as constituting the field of service, yet regarding both together as forming one world of activity. Of these two worlds, the subjective etheric body (or the body of vital inspiration) and dense physical body, are symbols on the external plane. (18-444/5)

12. It is with the work of the "bridge-builders" that we are concerned. *First, let me assure you that the real building of the antahkarana takes place only when the disciple is beginning to be definitely focused upon mental levels,* and when therefore, his mind is intelligently and consciously functioning. He must begin at this stage to have some more exact idea than has hitherto been the case as to the distinctions existing between the thinker, the apparatus of thought, and thought itself, beginning with its dual esoteric function, which is:

1. The recognition and receptivity to *Ideas*.

2. The creative faculty of conscious thoughtform building.

This necessarily involves a strong mental attitude and reorientation of the mind to reality. As the disciple begins to focus himself on the mental

plane (and this is the prime intent of the meditation work), he starts working in mental matter and trains himself in the powers and uses of thought.
He achieves a measure of mind control; he can turn the searchlight of the
mind in two directions, into the world of human endeavour, and into the
world of soul activity. Just as the soul makes a way for itself by project-
ing itself in a thread or stream of energy into the three worlds, so the
disciple begins consciously to project himself into the higher worlds. His
energy goes forth, through the medium of the controlled and directed
mind, into the world of the higher spiritual mind, and into the realm
of the intuition. A reciprocal activity is thus set up. This response between the higher and the lower mind is symbolically spoken of in terms
of light, and the "lighted way" comes into being between the personality
and the Spiritual Triad, via the soul body, just as the soul came into
definite contact with the brain via the mind. This "lighted way" is the
illumined bridge. *It is built through meditation;* it is constructed through
the constant effort to draw forth the intuition, through subservience and
obedience to the Plan (which begins to be recognised as soon as the intuition and the mind are *en rapport*), and through a conscious incorpora-
tion into the group in service, and for purposes of assimilation into the
whole. All these qualities and activities are based upon the foundation
of good character and the qualities developed upon the Probationary
Path.

The effort to draw forth the intuition, requires directed occult (but not
aspirational) meditation. It requires a trained intelligence, so that the line
of demarcation between intuitive realisation and the forms of the higher
psychism may be clearly seen. It requires a constant disciplining of the
mind, so that it can "hold itself steady in the light", and the development of a cultured right interpretation, so that the intuitive knowledge
achieved may then clothe itself in the right thoughtforms.

It might also be stated here that the construction of the bridge whereby
the consciousness can function with facility, both in the higher worlds and
in the lower, is *primarily brought about by a definitely directed life-ten-
dency,* which steadily sends the man in the direction of the world of spiritual realities, plus certain movements of planned and carefully timed and
directed reorientation or focusing. In this last process the *gain* of the
past months or years is closely assessed; the *effect* of that gain upon the
daily life and in the bodily mechanism is as carefully studied; and the
will-to-live as a spiritual being is brought into the consciousness with a
definiteness and a determination that makes for immediate progress.

This building of the antahkarana is most assuredly proceeding in the case of every ernest student. When the work is carried on intelligently and with full awareness of the desired purpose, and when the aspirant is not only aware of the process, but alert and active in its fulfilment, then the work proceeds apace and the bridge is built.   (18-446/8)

13. *The Bridge between the Three Aspects of the Mind:*

There is one point which I would like to clarify if I can, for—on this point—there is much confusion in the minds of aspirants, and this is necessarily so.

Let us for a moment, therefore, consider just where the aspirant stands when he starts consciously to build the antahkarana. Behind him lie a long series of existences, the experience of which has brought him to the point where he is able consciously to assess his condition and arrive at some understanding of his point in evolution. He can consequently undertake—in co-operation with his steadily awakening and focusing consciousness—to take the next step, which is that of accepted discipleship. In the present, he is oriented towards the soul; he, through meditation and the mystical experience, does have occasional contact with the soul, and this happens with increasing frequency; he is becoming somewhat creative upon the physical plane, both in his thinking and in his actions; at times, even if rarely, he has a genuine intuitive experience. This intuitive experience serves to anchor the "first tenuous thread spun by the Weaver in fohatic enterprise", as the *Old Commentary* puts it. It is the first cable, projected from the Spiritual Triad in response to the emanation of the personality, and this is the result of the growing magnetic potency of both these aspects of the Monad in manifestation.

It will be obvious to you that when the personality is becoming adequately magnetised from the spiritual angle, its note or sound will go forth and will evoke response from the soul on its own plane. Later the personality note and the soul note in unison will produce a definitely attractive effect upon the Spiritual Triad. This Spiritual Triad in its turn has been exerting an increasingly magnetic effect upon the personality. This begins at the time of the first *conscious* soul contact. This response of the Triad is transmitted necessarily, in this early stage, via the sutratma and produces inevitably the awakening of the head centre. That is why the heart doctrine begins to supersede the doctrine of the eye. The heart doctrine governs occult development; the eye doctrine—which is the doctrine of the eye of vision—governs the mystical experience; the

240 THE SOUL

heart doctrine is based upon the universal nature of the soul, conditioned by the Monad, the One, and involves reality; the eye doctrine is based on the dual relation between soul and personality. It involves the spiritual relationships, but the attitude of dualism or of the recognition of the polar opposites is implicit in it. These are important points to remember, as this new science becomes more widely known.

The aspirant eventually arrives at the point where the three threads—of life, of consciousness, and of creativity—are being focused, recognised as energy streams, and utilised deliberately by the aspiring disciple upon the *lower mental plane*. There—esoterically speaking—"he takes his stand, and looking upward sees a promised land of beauty, love and future vision".

But there exists a *gap in consciousness,* though not in fact. The sutratmic strand of energy bridges the gap, and tenuously relates Monad, soul and personality. But the consciousness thread extends only from soul to personality—from the involutionary sense. From the evolutionary angle (using a paradoxical phrase) there is only a very little *conscious awareness* existing between the soul and the personality, from the standpoint of the personality upon the evolutionary arc of the Path of Return. A man's whole effort is to become aware of the soul and to transmute his consciousness into that of the soul, whilst still preserving the consciousness of the personality. As the fusion of soul and personality is strengthened, the creative thread becomes increasingly active, and thus the three threads steadily fuse, blend, become dominant, and the aspirant is then ready to bridge the gap and unite the Spiritual Triad and the personality, through the medium of the soul. This involves a direct effort at divine creative work. The clue to understanding lies perhaps in the thought that hitherto the relation between soul and personality has been steadily carried forward, primarily by the soul, as it stimulated the personality to effort, vision and expansion. Now—at this stage—the integrated, rapidly developing personality becomes consciously active, and (in unison with the soul) starts building the antahkarana—a fusion of the three threads and a projection of them into the "higher, wider reaches" of the mental plane, until the abstract mind and the lower concrete mind are related by the triple cable.

It is to this process that our studies are related; earlier experience in relation to the three threads is logically regarded as having occurred normally. The man now stands, holding the mind steady in the light; he has some knowledge of meditation, much devotion, and also recognition of the next step. Knowledge of process gradually becomes clearer; a growing soul contact is established; occasional flashes of intuitive perception from the Triad occur. All these recognitions are not present in the case of every disciple; some are present; some are not. I am seeking to give a general picture. Individual application and future realisation have to be worked out by the disciple in the crucible of experience.   (18-457/9)

14. One of the points which it is essential that students should grasp, is the deeply esoteric fact that this antahkarana is built through the medium of a conscious effort *within consciousness itself,* and not just by attempting to be good, or to express goodwill, or to demonstrate the qualities of unselfishness and high aspiration. Many esotericists seem to regard the treading of the Path as the conscious effort to overcome the lower nature and to express life in terms of right living and thinking, love and intelligent understanding. It is all that, but *it is something far more.* Good character and good spiritual aspiration are basic essentials. But these are taken for granted by the Master Who has a disciple under training; their foundation and their recognition and development are the objectives upon the Path of Probation.

But to build the antahkarana is to relate the three divine aspects. This involves intense mental activity; it necessitates the power to imagine and to visualise, plus a dramatic attempt to build the Lighted Way in mental substance. . . . It is essentially, however, an activity of the integrated and dedicated personality. Esotericists must not take the position that all they have to do is to await negatively some activity by the soul which will automatically take place after a certain measure of soul contact has been achieved, and that consequently and in time this activity will evo. e response both from the personality and the Triad. This is *not* the case. The work of the building of the antahkarana is primarily an activity of the personality, aided by the soul; this in time evokes a reaction from the Triad. There is far too much inertia demonstrated by aspirants at this time.   (18-467/8)

See also: (18-441/530)

59. MEDITATION

1. The basis of all occult growth is meditation, or those periods of silent gestation in which the soul grows in the silence. (2-326)

2. What results in meditation? By dint of strenuous effort and due attention to rules laid down, the aspirant succeeds in touching matter of a quality rarer than is his usual custom. He contacts his causal body, in time he contacts the matter of the buddhic plane. By means of this touch his own vibration is temporarily and briefly quickened. (3-197)

3. By means of meditation a man finds freedom from the delusion of the senses and their vibratory lure; he finds his own positive centre of energy and becomes consciously able to use it; he becomes, therefore, aware of his real Self, functioning freely and consciously beyond the planes of sense; he enters into the plans of the greater Entity within Whose radiatory capacity he has a place; he can then consciously proceed to carry out those plans as he can grasp them at varying stages of realisation; and he becomes aware of essential unity. (3-746)

4. The main function of meditation is to bring the lower instrument into such a condition of receptivity and vibratory response that the Ego, or solar Angel, can use it and produce specific results. This involves, therefore, a downflow of force from the upper levels of the mental plane (the habitat of the real Man) and a reciprocal vibration, emanating from Man, the Reflection. When these two vibrations are attuned, and the interplay is rhythmic, then the two meditations proceed synchronously, and the work of magic and of creation can proceed unimpeded. . . . The first thing the solar Angel does, is to form a triangle, consisting of himself, the man on the physical plane, and the tiny point of force which is the result of their united endeavour. It will be of value to students of meditation to ponder upon this procedure. (3-998/9)

5. One of the objectives of the daily meditation is to enable the brain and mind to vibrate in unison with the soul as it seeks "in meditation deep" to communicate with its reflection. (4-74)

6. Let every effort be made to bring mind and brain into such a functioning condition that a man can slip out of his own meditation and (losing sight of his own thoughts) become the soul, the thinker in the kingdom of the soul. (4-89)

7. Meditation is so oft regarded as the means for establishing soul contact. People oft forget, however, that this contact is brought about very frequently by an inner reflective attitude of mind, by a life given to service and seflessness, and by a determination to discipline the lower nature so that it may become a true channel for the soul. When these three methods of development are fully expressed and become a life tendency or permanent habits, then meditation can be shifted into another category of usefulness, and serve as a technique for the development of the intuition and for the solution of group problems. To this use of meditation I seek to direct your attention.   (5-349)

8. *The Science of Meditation*. At present meditation is associated in the minds of men with religious matters. But that relates only to theme. The science can be applied to every possible life process. In reality, this science is a subsidiary branch, preparatory to the Science of the Antahkarana. It is really the true science of the occult bridge building or bridging in consciousness. By its means, particularly in the early stages, the building process is facilitated. It is one of the major ways of spiritual functioning; it is one of the many ways of God; it relates the individual mind eventually to the higher mind, and later to the Universal Mind. It is one of the major building techniques, and will eventually dominate the new education methods in schools and colleges. It is intended primarily to:

(a) Produce sensitivity to the higher impressions.

(b) Build the first half of the antahkarana, that between the personality and the soul.

(c) Produce an eventual continuity of consciousness. Meditation is essentially the science of light, because it works in the substance of light. One branch of it is concerned with the science of visualisation, because as the light continues to bring revelation, the power to visualise can grow with the aid of the illumined mind, and the later work of training the disciple to create is then possible. It might be added here that the building of the second half of the antahkarana (that which bridges the gap in consciousness between the soul and the Spiritual Triad) is called the Science of Vision, because just as the first half of the bridge is built through the use of mental substance, so the second half is built through the use of light substance.   (12-96/7)

9. The emphasis in all esoteric schools is necessarily, and rightly, laid upon meditation. Technically speaking, meditation is the process whereby

the head centre is awakened, brought under control, and used. When this is the case, the soul and the personality are co-ordinated and fused, and at-one-ment takes place, producing in the aspirant a tremendous inflow of spiritual energy, galvanising his whole being into activity, and bringing to the surface the latent good and also evil. Herein lies much of the danger. Hence also the stress laid in such true schools upon the need of purity and truth. Over-emphasis has been laid upon the need for physical purity, and not sufficient emphasis laid upon the avoidance of all fanaticism and intolerance. These two qualities hinder the student far more than can wrong diet, and they feed the fires of separativeness more than any other one factor.

Meditation involves the living of a one-pointed life, always and every day. This perforce puts an undue strain on the brain cells, for it brings quiescent cells into activity and awakens the brain consciousness to the light of the soul. This process of ordered meditation, when carried forward over a period of years, and supplemented by meditative living and one-pointed service, will successfully arouse the entire system, and bring the lower man under the influence and control of the spiritual man; it will awaken also the centres of force in the etheric body and stimulate into activity that mysterious stream of energy which sleeps at the base of the spinal column. When this process is carried forward with care and due safeguards, and under direction, and when the process is spread over a long period of time, there is little risk of danger, and the awakening will take place normally and under the law of being itself. If, however, the tuning up and awakening is forced, or is brought about by exercises of various kinds before the student is ready, and before the bodies are co-ordinated and developed, then the aspirant is headed towards disaster. Breathing exercises or pranayama training should never be undertaken without expert guidance, and only after years of spiritual application, devotion and service; concentration upon the centres in the force body (with a view to their awakening) is ever to be avoided; it will cause over-stimulation and the opening of doors on to the astral plane which the student may have difficulty in closing. I cannot impress too strongly upon aspirants in all occult schools, that the yoga of this transition period is the yoga of one-pointed intent, of directed purpose, of a constant practice of the Presence of God, and of ordered, regular meditation carried forward systematically and steadily over years of effort.

When this is done with detachment, and is paralleled by a life of loving service, the awakening of the centres and the raising of the sleeping fire of kundalini will go forward with safety, and the whole system will be brought to the requisite stage of "aliveness". I cannot too strongly advise students against the following of intensive meditation processes for hours at a time, or against practices which have for their objective the arousing of the fires of the body, the awakening of a particular centre, and the moving of the serpent fire. The general world stimulation is so great at this time, and the average aspirant is so sensitive and finely organised, that excessive meditation, a fanatical diet, the curtailing of the hours of sleep, or undue interest in, and emphasis upon psychic experience, will upset the mental balance and often do irretrievable harm.

Let the students in esoteric schools settle down to steady, quiet, unemotional work. Let them refrain from prolonged hours of study and of meditation. Their bodies are as yet incapable of the requisite tension, and they only damage themselves. Let them lead normal busy lives, remembering in the press of daily duties and service who they are essentially, and what are their goal and objectives. Let them meditate regularly every morning, beginning with a period of fifteen minutes and never exceeding forty minutes. Let them forget themselves in service, and let them not concentrate their interest upon their own psychic development. Let them train their minds with a normal measure of study, and learn to think intelligently, so that their minds can balance their emotions, and enable them to interpret correctly that which they contact as their measure of awareness increases and their consciousness expands.

Students need to remember that devotion to the Path or to the Master is not enough. The Great Ones are looking for *intelligent* co-operators and workers more than They are looking for devotion to Their Personalities, and a student who is walking independently in the light of his own soul is regarded by Them as a more dependable instrument than a devoted fanatic. The *light of his soul* will reveal to the earnest aspirant the unity underlying all groups, and enable him to eliminate the poison of intolerance which taints and hinders so many; it will cause him to recognise the spiritual fundamentals which guide the steps of humanity; it will force him to overlook the intolerance and the fanaticism and separativeness which characterise the small mind and the beginner upon the Path, and help him so to love them that they will begin to see more truly and enlarge their horizon; it will enable him to estimate truly the esoteric value of service, and teach him above all to practise that *harmlessness* which is the outstanding quality of every son of God. A harmlessness that speaks no word that can damage another person, that thinks no thought which could poison or produce misunderstanding, and which does no action which could hurt the least of his brethren—this is the main virtue which will enable the esoteric student to tread with safety the difficult path of development. Where the emphasis is laid upon service to one's fellow men and the trend of the life force is outward to the world, then there is freedom from danger, and the aspirant can safely meditate and aspire and work. His motive is pure, and he is seeking to decentralise his personality and shift the focus of his attention away from himself to the group. Thus the life of the soul can pour through him, and express itself as love to all beings. He knows himself to be a part of a whole, and the life of that whole can flow through him consciously, leading him to a realisation of brotherhood and of his oneness in relation to all manifested lives.   (13-17/20)

10. Forget not that *meditation* clarifies the mind as to the fact and nature of the Plan, that *understanding* brings that Plan into the world of desire, and that *love* releases the form which will make the Plan materialise upon the physical plane. To these three expressions of your soul I call you. All of you, without exception, can serve in these three ways, if you so desire.   (13-23)

11. The man's efforts in meditation have opened a door through which he can pass at will (and eventually with facility) into a new world of phenomena, of directed activity, and of different ideals. He has unlatched a window through which light can pour in, revealing that which is, and always has been, existent within the consciousness of man, and throwing illumination into the dark places of his life; into other lives; and into the environment in which he moves. He has released within himself a world of sound and of impressions which are at first so new and so different that he does not know what to make of them. His situation becomes one requiring much care and balanced adjustment.

It will be obvious to you that if there is a good mental equipment, and a sound educational training, that there will be a balancing sense of proportion, an interpretative capacity, patience to wait till right understanding can be developed, and a happy sense of humour. Where, however, these are not present, there will be (according to the type and the sense of vision) bewilderment, a failure to comprehend what is happening, undue emphasis upon personality reactions and phenomena, pride in achievement, a tremendous sense of inferiority, too much speech, a running hither and thither for explanation, comfort, assurance, and a sense of comradeship, or perhaps a complete breakdown of the mental forces, or the disruption of the brain cells through the strain to which they have been subjected.

Exhilaration is also sometimes found as a result of the contact with a new world, and strong mental stimulation. Depression is as frequently a result, based upon a sensed incapacity to measure up to the realised opportunity. The man sees and knows too much. He can no longer be satisfied with the old measure of living, with the old satisfactions, and with the old idealisms. He has touched and now longs for the larger measures, for the new and vibrant ideas, and for the broader vision. The way of life of the soul has gripped and attracts him. But his nature, his environment, his equipment and his opportunitites appear somehow to frustrate him consistently, and he feels he cannot march forward into this new and wonderful world. He feels the need to temporise and to live in the same state of mind as heretofore, or so he thinks, and so he decides. (15-465/6)

See also: "Meditation on the Path of the Inner Light". (5-546/7)

(a) MEDITATION TO ASSIST ALIGNMENT

1. Fundamentally, meditation is to assist alignment and so permit of contact with the Higher Self; hence its institution. . . .

The emphasis upon the importance of meditation follows naturally upon the realisation by the student of the absolute necessity for the domination of the Personality by the Ego.

Man at this time is engaged in many pursuits and through the force of circumstances he is polarised entirely in the lower self, that polarisation being in either the emotional or mental body. One point of interest I would indicate : As long as the polarisation is purely physical, or purely emotional, no need for meditation is ever felt. Even when the mental body is active, no urge arises until the man has run through many changes and many lives, has tasted the cup of pleasure and of pain through many incarnations, has sounded the depths of the life lived entirely for the lower self and found it unsatisfying. Then he begins to turn his thought to other things, to aspire to that which is unknown, to realise and sense within himself the pairs of opposites, and to contact within his consciousness possibilities and ideals undreamt of hitherto. He has come to a point where success, popularity and diverse gifts are his, and yet from their use he derives no content; always the urge within persists, until the pain is so severe that the desire to reach out and up, to ascertain something and someone beyond, overcomes all obstacles. The man begins to turn within and to seek the source from whence he came. Then he begins to meditate, to ponder, to intensify vibration, until in process of time he garners the fruits of meditation. . . .

(Meditation) enables a man to contact the Ego and to align the three lower bodies.

. . . (Meditation) puts a man into an attitude of equilibrium, neither utterly receptive and negative, nor utterly positive, but at the point of balance. Thus is afforded opportunity to the Ego, and later to the Master, to disturb that equilibrium and tune the quiescent vibration to a higher note than heretofore; to cause the consciousness to vibrate to a newer and higher measure, and to swing (if I may so express it) into the periphery of the threefold Spirit. By the constant practice of this, the whole point of equilibrium is gradually shifted higher and higher, until the time comes when the lower point of attraction in the swinging and adjustment, is not the physical, touches not the emotional, contacts not the mental (the causal body even escaping) and the man is polarised in the spiritual consciousness from henceforth.   (2-9/11)

2. Early in experience, after the attainment of the highest the lower nature has to offer, man begins to meditate. Disorderly at first are his attempts, and sometimes several incarnations may go by in which the Higher Self only forces the man to think and seriously to meditate, at rare and separated intervals. More frequently come the occasions of withdrawing within, until there arises for the man several lives given to mystic meditation and aspiration, culminating usually in a life given entirely to it. It marks the point of the highest emotional aspiration, apart from the scientific application of the law, via the mental body. These laws are those governing the true occult meditation.

Behind each of you who are working definitely under one of the Masters, lie two lives of culmination—the life of worldly apotheosis, and the life of intensest meditation along the mystic or emotional—institutional line. This meditative life was taken either in a monastery or nunnery in middle Europe, by those linked with the Master Jesus and His disciples, or in India, Tibet or China by the pupils of the Master M. or the Master K.H.

Now comes to all of you the most important series of lives, to which the previous points of culmination were but stepping stones. In the lives immediately ahead of those upon the Path, will come final achievement through the instrumentality of the ordered occult meditation, based on law. For some few may come attainment in this life or the next; for others, shortly in other lives. For a few there lies ahead the attainment of the mystic method, to be the basis later on of the occult or mental method.   (2-12)

3. (The Probationer is supposed to be developing) the faculty of abstract thought, or the power to link up with the higher mind, via the causal body. He must learn to contact the lower mind simply as an instrument whereby he can reach the higher, and thus transcend it, until he becomes polarised in the causal body. Then, through the medium of the causal body he links up with the abstract levels. Until he can do this he cannot really contact the Master, for, as you have been told, the pupil has to raise himself from his world (the lower) into Their world (the higher).

Now both these things—the power to touch the Master and the Master's group, and the power to polarise himself in the causal body and touch abstract levels—are definitely the result of meditation. . . . By strenuous meditation, and the faculty of one-pointed application to the duty in hand (which is after all the fruit of meditation worked out in daily living) will come the increased faculty to hold steadily the higher vibration. Again and again would I reiterate the apparently simple truth, that *only similarity of vibration* will draw a man to the higher group to which he may belong, to the Master Who represents to him the Lord of his Ray, to the World Teacher Who administers to him the mysteries, to the One Initiator Who effects the final liberation, and to the centre within the Heavenly Man in Whose body he finds a place. . . . The work of the Probationer is to attune his vibration to that of the Master, to purify his three lower bodies so that they form no hindrance to that contact, and so to dominate his lower mind that it is no longer a barrier to the downflow of light from the threefold Spirit. Thus he is permitted to touch that Triad and the group on the sub-plane of the higher mental to which he—by right and karma—belongs. All this is brought about by meditation, and there is no other means of achieving these aims. (2-268/9)

4. Students of Meditation would be astounded and perhaps discouraged, could they realise how seldom they provide the right conditions through meditation, which will enable their watching Teacher to bring about certain effects. By the frequency of the student's ability to do this comes indication of progress, and the possibility of carrying him on another step. Emphasise this point in teaching, for it carries with it an incentive to greater diligence and application. If the pupil himself on his side provides not the just conditions, the Master's hands are tied and He can do but little. *Self-effort is the key to progress, coupled to conscious comprehending application to the work laid down.* When that effort is made with perseverence, then comes the opportunity of the Master to carry out His side of the work. (2-277)

5. Meditation is a technique of the mind which eventually produces correct, unimpeded relationship; this is another name for alignment. It is therefore, the establishment of a direct channel, not only between the one source, the Monad, and its expression, the purified and controlled personality, but also between the seven centres in the human etheric vehicle. (17-620)

(b) Danger of Atrophy

Some natures become so polarised on the mental plane that they run the risk of breaking connection with the two lower vehicles. These lower bodies exist for purposes of contact, for the apprehension of knowledge on the lower planes, and for reasons of experience, in order that the content of the causal body may be increased. Therefore, it will be apparent to you that if the indwelling consciousness comes no lower than the mental plane, and neglects the body of emotions and the dense physical, two things will result. The lower vehicles will be neglected and useless and fail in their purposes, atrophying and dying from the point of view of the Ego, whilst the causal body itself will not be built as desired, and so time will be lost. The mental body will be rendered useless likewise, and will become a thing of selfish content, of no use in the world and of little value. A dreamer whose dreams never materialise, a builder who stores up material which he never employs, a visionary whose visions are of no use to gods or men, is a clog upon the system universal. He is in great danger of atrophying.

Meditation should have the effect of bringing all three bodies more completely under the control of the Ego, and lead to a co-ordination and an alignment, to a rounding-out and a symmetrical development that will make a man of real use to the Great Ones. When a man realises that mayhap he is too much centralised on the mental plane, he should definitely aim at making all his mental experiences, aspirations and endeavours matters of *fact* on the physical plane, bringing the two lower vehicles under control of the mental and making them the instruments of his mental creations and activities. (2-97)

(c) Meditation Determined by the Egoic Ray

The ray on which a man's causal body is found, the egoic ray, should determine the type of meditation. Each ray necessitates a different method of approach, for the aim of all meditation is union with the divine. At this

stage, it is union with the Spiritual Triad, that has its lowest reflection
on the mental plane. Let me illustrate briefly :

When the egoic ray is what is termed the *Power Ray,* the method of
approach has to be by the application of the will in a dynamic form to
the lower vehicles; it is largely what we term achievement by an intense
focusing, a terrific one-pointedness, that inhibits all hindrances and literally forces a channel, thus driving itself into the Triad.

When the egoic ray is the second or the *Love-Wisdom Ray,* the path
of least resistance lies along the line of expansion, of a gradual inclusion.
It is not so much a driving forward as it is a gradual expanding from an
inner centre to include the entourage, the environment, the allied souls,
and the affiliated groups of pupils under some one Master, until all are
included in the consciousness. Carried to the point of achievement, this
expansion results in the final shattering of the causal body at the fourth
Initiation. In the first instance—achievement via the Power Ray—the
driving forward and the forcing upward had a like result; the opened
channel admitted the downflow of force or fire from the Spirit, and the
causal in time is equally destroyed.

When the egoic ray is the third or *Activity-Adaptability Ray,* the
method is somewhat different. Not so much the driving forward, not so
much the gradual expansion, as the systematic adaptation of all knowledge and of all means to the end in view. It is in fact the process of the
utilisation of the many for the use of the one; it is more the accumulation
of needed material and quality for the helping of the world, and the
amassing of information through love and discrimination that eventually
causes the shattering of the causal body.

In these "Rays of the Aspect" or of divine expression, if so I may call
them, the shattering is brought about by the widening of the channel, due
to the driving power of will in the first case; by the expansion of the
lower auric egg, the causal body, in the second case, due to the inclusiveness of the synthetic Ray of Love and Wisdom; and by the breaking of
the periphery of the causal body in the third case, due to the accumulative
faculty and systematic absorption of the Adaptability Ray.

All these three different methods have the same result, and are fundamentally all forms of one great method employed in the evolution of
love or wisdom—the goal of endeavour in this present solar system.

You have the *wisdom or love* aspect driving a man on to perfection
of the Higher, and resulting in the service of power through love activity.

You have the *wisdom or love* aspect driving a man on to perfection through the realisation of his oneness with all that breathes, resulting in the service of love through love in activity.

You have the *activity* aspect driving a man on to perfection through the utilisation of all in the service of man; first by the utilisation of all for himself, then by the graded steps of the utilisation of all for the family, of all for those he personally loves, of all for his environing associates, and thus on and up till all is utilised in the service of humanity. (2-15/7)

(d) THE SELF IS FIRE

1. Cosmic fire forms the background of our evolution; the fire of the mental plane, its inner control and dominance and its purifying asset, coupled to its refining effects, is the aim of the evolution of our threefold life. When the inner fire of the mental plane, and the fire latent in the lower vehicles merge with the sacred fire of the Triad, the work is completed, and the man stands adept, the at-one-ment has been made, and the work of aeons is completed.   (2-100)

2. The man who undertakes the practice of occult meditation literally "plays with fire". I wish you to emphasise this statement for it embodies a truth little realised. "Playing with fire" is an old truth that has lost its significance through flippant repetition, yet is absolutely and entirely correct, and is not a symbolic teaching but a plain statement of fact. Fire forms the basis of all—the Self is fire, the intellect is a phase of fire, and latent in the microcosmic physical vehicles lies hid a veritable fire that can either be a destructive force, burning the tissue of the body and stimulating centres of an undesirable character, or be a vivifying factor, acting as a stimulating and awakening agent. When directed along certain prepared channels, this fire may act as a purifier and the great connector between the lower and the Higher Self.

In meditation the student seeks to contact the divine flame that is his Higher Self, and to put himself likewise *en rapport* with the fire of the mental plane. When meditation is forced, or is pursued too violently, before the alignment between the higher and the lower bodies, via the emotional is completed, this fire may act on the fire latent at the base of the spine (that fire called kundalini) and may cause it to circulate too early. This will produce disruption and destruction instead of vivification and stimulation of the higher centres.   (2-102/3)

60. THE EGO AND THE INITIATIONS

1. It is the man, as the soul, in full waking consciousness, who takes initiation. Hence the emphasis upon soul contact when a man is upon the Probationary Path and passing through the early stages of discipleship. This leads later to the emphasis placed upon the need for two major activities—before the man can take the higher initiations:

    (a) Upon alignment.

    (b) Upon the scientific building of the antahkarana.   (6-254)

2. Upon the Path of Initiation, the monadic will (of which the egoic will is the reflection and the individual self-will is the distortion) is gradually transmitted, via the antahkarana, direct to the man upon the physical plane. This produces the higher correspondence of those qualities so glibly spoken of by the well trained but dense esotericist—transmutation and transformation. The result is the assimilation of the individual will and the egoic will into the purpose of the Monad, which is the purpose—undeviating and unalterable—of the One in Whom we live and move and have our being.   (18-31)

3. If you will note your own present attitudes and reactions, you will discover that primarily (I might add almost necessarily) they centre around yourselves, your own recognitions, your own grasp of truth, and your own progress upon the Path. But—as you achieve initiate status —self-interest declines until it disappears and, as an ancient Word has it, "only God is left"; only that remains in consciousness which is THAT, which is beauty, goodness and truth; which is not form but quality, which is that which lies behind the form and that which indicates destiny, soul place, and status. Ponder on these words, for they convey to you where (as evolution goes on) you will later lay the emphasis.   (18-293)

4. The soul, in its own nature, is group conscious and has no individual ambitions or individual interests, and is not at all interested in the aims of its personality. It is the soul which is the initiate. Initiation is a process whereby the spiritual man within the personality becomes aware of himself as the soul, with soul powers, soul relationships, and soul purpose. The moment a man realises this, even in a small measure, it is the group of which he is conscious.   (18-341)

(a) EXPANSION OF CONSCIOUSNESS AND INITIATION

1. The great moment in which a man passed out of the animal kingdom into the human, which is called in many occult textbooks the
"moment of individualisation", was itself one of the greatest of all initiations. Individualisation is the conscious apprehension by the self of its
relation to all that constitutes the not-self, and in this great initiatory process, as in all the later ones, the awakening of consciousness is preceded
by a period of gradual development; the awakening is instantaneous at
the moment of self-realisation for the first time, and is always succeeded
by another period of gradual evolution. This period of gradual evolution,
in its turn, leads up to a later crisis which is called Initiation. In the one
case, we have initiation into self-conscious existence, in the other, initiation into spiritual existence.

These realisations, or apprehended expansions of consciousness, are
under natural law, and come in due course of time to every soul *without
exception*. In a lesser degree they are undergone daily by every human
being, as his mental grip of life and experience gradually grows, but they
only become initiations into the wisdom (as differentiated from expansions of knowledge) when the knowledge gained is:

(a) Consciously sought for.

(b) Self-sacrificingly applied to life.

(c) Willingly used in service for others.

(d) Intelligently utilised on the side of evolution.

Only souls of a certain amount of experience and development do all
these four things consistently and steadily, and thus transmute knowledge into wisdom, and experience into quality. The ordinary average
man transmutes ignorance into knowledge, and experience into faculty. It
would be helpful if all of us pondered upon the difference between inherent quality and innate faculty; one is the very nature of buddhi, or
wisdom, and the other of manas, or mind. The union of these two,
through a man's conscious effort, results in a major initiation.

These results are brought about in two ways: First, by a man's own
unaided effort, which leads him in due course of time to find his own
centre of consciousness, to be guided and led by the inner ruler or Ego
entirely, and to unravel, through strenuous effort and painful endeavour,
the mystery of the universe, which is concealed in material substance
energised by Fohat. Secondly, by a man's efforts, supplemented by the intelligent, loving co-operation of the Knowers of the race, the Masters of

the Wisdom. In this case the process is quicker, for a man comes under instruction—should he so desire—and subsequently, when he has on his part provided the right conditions, there is placed at his disposal the knowledge and the help of Those Who have achieved. In order to avail himself of this help, he has to work with the material of his own body, building right material into an ordered form, and has therefore, to learn discrimination in the choice of matter, and to understand the laws of vibration and of construction. . . .

He has to equip also his mental body, so that it may be an explainer and transmitter, and not a hindering factor as now. He must likewise develop group activity, and learn to work in a co-ordinated manner with other units. These are the main things that a man must accomplish along the path of initiation, but when he has worked at them, he will find the Way, it will be made clear to him, and he will then join the ranks of the Knowers.   (1-176/8)

2. Initiation does not simply enhance and deepen the soul quality; it does not simply enable the personality to express soul powers, and thus emphasise and draw out the best that is in the disciple and his service, but it makes available to him, progressively, forces and energies of which he has had no previous knowledge, and which he must learn to use as an initiate of a certain degree upon the Lighted Way. It reveals to him worlds of being hitherto unsuspected and unrecognised, with which he must learn to co-operate, and it integrates him more definitely into the "lighted area" of our planetary life, bringing fresh revelation and vision, but making the unlighted area dark indeed.   (6-666)

3. Initiation is not a ceremonial procedure, or an accolade conferred upon a successful aspirant; neither is it a penetration into the Mysteries . . . but (it) is simply the result of experiencing "livingness" on all three levels of awareness (physical, emotional and mental) and—through that livingness—bringing into activity those registering and those recording cells within the brain substance which have hitherto not been susceptible to the higher impression. Through this expanding area of registration or, if you prefer it, through the development of a finer recording instrument or responsive apparatus, the mind is enabled to become the transmitter of higher values and of spiritual understanding. Thus the individual becomes aware of areas of divine existence and of states of consciousness which are always eternally present, but which the individual man was constitutionally unable to contact or to register; neither the mind, nor its record-

ing agent, the brain, were able to, from the angle of their evolutionary development.

When the searchlight of the mind is penetrating slowly into hitherto unrecognised aspects of the divine mind, when the magnetic qualities of the heart are awakening and becoming sensitively responsive to both the other aspects, then the man becomes able to function in the new unfolding realms of light, love and service. He is initiate.   (8-128)

4. Initiation is essentially a moving out from under ancient controls into the control of more spiritual and increasingly higher values. Initiation is an expansion of consciousness which leads to a growing recognition of the inner realities. It is equally the recognition of a renewed sense of the need for changes so that real progress can be made; the consciousness is expanded and becomes more generously and divinely inclusive, and there is a fresh and more potent control by the soul as it assumes increasingly the direction of the life of the individual, of a nation and of the world.   (13-136)

5. What . . . is Initiation? Initiation might be defined in two ways:

It is *first* of all the entering into a new and wider dimensional world by the expansion of a man's consciousness, so that he can include and encompass that which he now excludes, and from which he normally separates himself in his thinking and acts.

It is, *secondly,* the entering into man of those energies which are distinctive of the soul and of the soul alone—the forces of intelligent love and of spiritual will.   (15-12)

(b)   THE FIRST INITIATION

1. At the first initiation, the control of the Ego over the physical body must have reached a high degree of attainment. "The sins of the flesh", as the Christian phraseology has it, must be dominated; gluttony, drink, and licentiousness must no longer hold sway. The physical elemental will no longer find its demand obeyed; the control must be complete, and the lure departed. A general attitude of obedience to the Ego must have been achieved, and the *willingness* to obey must be very strong. The channel between the higher and the lower is widened, and the obedience of the flesh practically automatic.   (1-82/3)

2. Many thousands of people in the world today have taken the first initiation and are oriented towards the spiritual life and the service of their fellow men; their lives, however, frequently leave much to be desired, and

the soul is obviously *not* in constant control; a great struggle is still being waged to achieve purification on all three levels. The lives of these initiates are faulty and their inexperience great, and a major attempt is instituted in this particular cycle to achieve soul fusion. (18-385)

(c) THE SECOND INITIATION

1. The second initiation forms the *crisis* in the control of the *astral body*. Just as at the first initiation the control of the dense physical has been demonstrated, so here the control of the astral is similarly demonstrated. Desire itself has been dominated by the Ego, and only that is longed for which is for the good of the whole, and in the line of the will of the Ego and of the Master. The astral elemental is controlled, the emotional body becomes pure and limpid, and the lower nature is rapidly dying. At this time the Ego grips afresh the two lower vehicles and bends them to his will. The aspiration and longing to serve, love, and progress become so strong that rapid development is usually to be seen. This accounts for the fact that this initiation and the third, frequently (though not invariably) follow each other in one single life. At this period of the world's history such stimulus has been given to evolution, that aspiring souls—sensing the dire and crying need of humanity—are sacrificing all in order to meet that need.

. . . At this initiation, should the ordinary course be followed, (which again is not at all certain) the throat centre is vivified. This causes a capacity to turn to account in the Master's service, and for the helping of man, the attainments of the lower mind. It imparts the ability to give forth and utter that which is helpful, possibly in the spoken word, but *surely* in service of some kind. A vision is accorded of the world's need, and a further portion of the plan is shown. The work, then, to be done prior to the taking of the third initiation, is the complete submerging of the personal point of view in the need of the whole. It entails the complete domination of the concrete mind by the Ego. (1-85/6)

2. The second inititiation marks the release of the soul from the prison of the astral body. Henceforth the soul will use the astral body, and mould desire into line with divine purpose. (4-237)

3. Once the second initiation has been taken, the watching Hierarchy can begin to note the constant reorientation of the soul towards the Monad, and the attractive power of that highest aspect over the initiate. Today, so many members of the human family—in incarnation and out of incar-

nation—have taken the first two initiations, that the attention of Shamballa is being increasingly turned to humanity, via the Hierarchy, whilst simultaneously the thoughts of men are being turned to the Plan, to the use of the will in direction and guidance, and to the nature of dynamic force.   (9-120)

(d)   THE THIRD INITIATION

1. At the third initiation, termed sometimes the Transfiguration, the entire personality is flooded with light from above. It is only after this initiation that the Monad is definitely guiding the Ego, pouring His divine life ever more into the prepared and cleansed channel. . . .

The aim of all development is the awakening of the spiritual intuition; when this has been done, when the physical body is pure, the astral stable and steady, and the mental body controlled, then the initiate can safely wield and wisely use the psychic faculties for the helping of the race. Not only can he use these faculties, but he is able now to create and vivify thoughtforms that are clear and well-defined, pulsating with the spirit of service and not controlled by lower mind or desire. These thoughtforms will not be (as is the case with those created by the mass of men) disjointed, unconnected, and uncorrelated, but will attain a fair measure of synthesis. Hard and ceaseless must the work be before this can be done, but when the desire nature has been stabilised and purified, then the control of the mind-body comes more easily.   (1-86/7)

2. At the third Initiation of Transfiguration, the control of the personality in the three worlds is broken in order that the Son of Mind, the soul, may be substituted finally for the concrete and hitherto directing lower mind. Again, through the Law of Sacrifice, the personality is liberated and becomes simply an agent of the soul.   (6-398)

3. (The third initiation) is the *first* initiation in which personality and soul are united and fused so that the two aspects form one unit. . . . Aspiration ends and the intensest conviction takes its place.   (9-140)

4. When the individual antahkarana has been successfully started, and there is even a tenuous thread of living energy connecting the threefold personality and the Spiritual Triad, then the inflow of the will-energy becomes possible. This, in the early stages, can be most dangerous when not offset by the love energy of the soul. . . .

After the third initiation, when the soul body, the causal body, starts to dissipate, the line of relation or of connection can be, and is direct.

The initiate then "stands in the ocean of love, and through him pours that love; his will is love and he can safely work, for love divine will colour all his will, and he can wisely serve". Love and intelligence then become the servants of the will. Soul energy and personality force contribute to the experience of the Monad in the three worlds of life service, and then the age-long task of the incarnating spiritual man is finally accomplished. He is ready for Nirvana, which is but the Way into new fields of spiritual experience and of divine development—incomprehensible as yet, even to the intitiate of the third degree. This Way is revealed only when the antahkarana is built and completed and the man becomes focused in the Triad as consciously as he is now focused in the threefold lower nature.   (18-471/2)

5. At the third initiation the control of the soul-illumined mind is finally established, and the soul itself assumes the dominant position and not the phenomenal form.   (18-674)

(e) THE ELIMINATION OF THE PERSONALITY THOUGHTFORM

In dealing with this subject (and it can only be done very briefly), two things must be borne in mind :

1. That we are considering solely an idea in the mind of the soul and dealing with the basic fact of the illusion which has controlled the entire cycle of incarnation and so held the soul a prisoner to form. To the soul, the personality connotes two things :

    (a) The soul's capacity for identification with form; this is first of all realised by the soul when the personality is beginning to react to a measure of real integration.

    (b) An opportunity for initiation.

2. That the elimination of the thoughtform of the personality, which is consummated at the third initiation, is a great initiation for the soul on its own plane. For this reason, the third initiation is regarded as the first major initiation, since the two previous initiations have very little effect upon the soul and only affect the incarnated soul, the "fragment" of the whole.

These are facts which are little realised and seldom emphasised in any of the literature hitherto published. The emphasis up till now has been upon the initiations as they affect the disciple in the three worlds. But I am specifically dealing with the initiations as they affect or do not affect *the soul,* overshadowing its reflection, the personality, in the three worlds.

What I have said, therefore, will have little meaning for the average reader.

From the angle of the personal self, regarding itself as the Dweller on the Threshold, the attitude or state of mind has been adequately portrayed as one of complete obliteration in the light of the soul; the glory of the Presence, transmuted by the Angel, is such that the personality completely disappears, with its demands and its aspirations. Naught is left but the shell, the sheath, and the instrument through which the solar light can pour for the helping of humanity. This is true to a certain degree, but is only—in the last analysis—man's attempt to put into words the transmuting and the transfiguring effect of the third initiation, which cannot be done.

Infinitely more difficult is the attempt I am here making, to depict the attitude and the reactions of the soul, the one self, the Master in the heart, as it recognises the stupendous fact of its own essential liberation, and realises, once and for all, that it is now incapable of responding in any way to the lower vibrations of the three worlds, as transmitted to the soul by its instrument of contact, the personality form. That form is now incapable of such transmission.

The second reaction of the soul, once this realisation has been focused and admitted, is that—having achieved freedom—that freedom now conveys its own demands:

1. For a life of service in the three worlds, so familiar and now so completely transcended.

2. An overshadowing sense of outgoing love towards those who are, as yet, seeking liberation.

3. A recognition of the essential triangle which has now become the centre of the conceptual life of the soul:

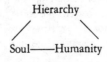

                              Hierarchy

                      Soul———Humanity

The soul now vibrates between the two points or pairs of opposites and acts as an invocative and evocative centre.

None of the above realisations may be registered in the brain consciousness or in the mind of the illumined personality. Theoretically, some dim vision of the inherent possibilities may be sensed, but the consciousness is no longer that of the serving disciple in the three worlds, using mind, emotions and physical body to carry out behest and hierarchical intent, as far as may be. That has disappeared with the death of the personality consciousness. The consciousness is now that of the soul itself, aware of no separation, instinctively active, spiritually obsessed by the plans of the Kingdom of God, and completely free from the lure or the faintest control of matter-form; the soul is, however, still responsive to and immersed in substance-energy, and its higher correspondence is still functioning on the levels of the cosmic physical plane—the buddhic, atmic, monadic and logoic planes.

What then must take place if the life of the soul is to be full and complete and so thoroughly inclusive that the three worlds form part of its area of awareness and its field of service? The only way in which I can make clear to you what the soul must do after the third initiation, is to sum it up in two ways:

First: The soul now becomes a conscious creator because the third aspect—developed and mastered through experience in the three worlds during the long cycle of incarnations—has reached a point of perfected activity. Putting it technically: the energy of the knowledge petals and the energy of the love petals are now so actively fused and blended, that two of the inner petals, surrounding the jewel in the lotus, are no longer acting as veils to that jewel. I am here speaking symbolically. Because of this happening, the death or the elimination of the personality is the first activity in the drama of conscious creation, and the first form created by the soul is a substitute for the personality. Thus an instrument for service in the three worlds is created. This time, however, it is an instrument with no life, no desire, no ambition and no power of thought of its own. It is only a sheath of substance, animated by soul life, but—at the same time—responsive to and suited to the period, race and the environing conditions wherein the soul chooses to work. Think this statement out and emphasise the words "suited to".

Second: The soul then prepares itself for the coming fourth initiation. This is basically a monadic experience and results—as you know—in the disappearance or destruction of the soul vehicle or causal body, and the establishment, therefore, of a direct relation between the Monad on its own plane and the newly created personality, via the antahkarana.

These two points are given to you for the first time in the sequential giving out of the occult teaching; hints have, however, prepared the way for these two facts. Information has also been given anent the mayavirupa through which the Master works and contacts the three worlds and which He deliberately creates in order to serve His purposes and plans. It is a definite substitute for the personality and can only be created when the old personality (built and developed during the cycle of incarnation) has been eliminated. I prefer the word "eliminated" to the word "destroyed". The *structure*—at the time of elimination—persists, but its separative life has gone.

If you will think clearly about this statement, you will see that a very complete integration is now possible. The personality life has been absorbed; the personality form is still left, but it persists without any real life of its own; this means that it can now be the recipient of energies and forces, needed by the working initiate or Master in order to carry on the work of salvaging humanity. . . .

The disciple who has eliminated (in the technical sense as well as in the mystical sense) the hold of the personality, has now the "freedom of the Ashram" as it is called; he can move at will among his fellow disciples and initiates. There will be nothing in his vibratory life or his quality which can disturb the rhythm of the Ashram; there will be nothing to call forth the "calming intervention" of the Master, as is frequently the case during the earlier stages of discipleship; nothing can now interfere with those higher contacts and spheres of influence which have hitherto been sealed to the disciple because of the intrusion of his personality. (17-515/20)

(f) THE FOURTH INITIATION

1. At the fourth Initiation of Renunciation, the destroying aspect of the Law of Sacrifice brings about the destruction of the causal body, the soul body, in order that the unified soul-infused personality may function directly under the inspiration of the Spiritual Triad—the triple expression or instrument of the Monad.   (6-398)

2. Students would do well to learn that this process of building the antahkarana is one of the means whereby man, the trinity, becomes a duality. When the task is completed and the antahkarana is definitely built—thus producing perfect alignment between the Monad and its expression upon the physical plane—the body of the soul (the causal body) is completely and finally destroyed by the fire of the Monad, pouring down the antahkarana. There is then complete reciprocity between the Monad and the fully conscious *soul on the physical plane.* The "divine intermediary" is no longer required. The "Son of God Who is the Son of Mind" dies;

the "veil of the temple is rent in twain from the top to the bottom"; the fourth initiation is passed, and there then comes the revelation of the Father.

This is the final and far-reaching result of the building of the bridge which is, in reality, the establishing of a line of light between Monad and personality, as a full expression of the soul—between spirit and matter, between Father and Mother. It is evidence that "spirit has mounted on the shoulders of matter" to that high place from whence it orginally came, plus the gain of experience and of full knowledge, and of all that life in material form could give and all that conscious experience could confer. The Son has done His work. The task of the Saviour or of the Mediator has been completed. The unity of all things is known to be a fact in consciousness, and a human spirit can say with intention and with understanding : "I and my Father are one." (18-475/6)

3. The Great Renunciation : One tremendous experience is vouchsafed to the initiate at this time; he realises (because he sees and knows) that the antahkarana has been successfully completed, and that there is a direct line of energy from the Spiritual Triad, via the antahkarana, to his mind and brain. This brings to the forefront of his consciousness the sudden and appalling recognition that the soul itself, the egoic body on its own level, and that which for ages has been the supposed source of his existence, and his guide and mentor, is no longer needed; his relation, as a soul-infused personality, is now directly with the Monad. He feels bereft and is apt to cry out—as did the Master Jesus—"My God, my God, why hast Thou forsaken me?" But he makes the needed renunciation, and the causal body, the soul body, is relinquished and disappears. This is the culminating renunciation and the climaxing gesture of ages of small renunciations; renunciation marks the career of all aspirants and disciples—renunciation, consciously faced, understood and consciously made. (18-695)

4. This Initiation of Renunciation is of supreme importance to humanity and to the individual initiate who is, of course, a member of the fourth kingdom. First of all, this great act of renunciation marks the moment when the disciple has nothing in him which relates him to the three worlds of human evolution. His contact with those worlds in the future will be purely voluntary and for purposes of service. (18-696)

61. THE REVELATION OF THE "PRESENCE"

1. Right through the later periods of the cycle of incarnation, wherein the man is juggling with the pairs of opposites, and through discrimination is becoming aware of reality and unreality, there is growing up in his mind a realisation that he himself is an immortal Existence, an eternal God, and a portion of Infinity. Ever the link between the man on the physical plane and this inner Ruler becomes clearer, until the great revelation is made. Then comes a moment in his existence when the man stands consciously face to face with his real Self and knows himself to be that Self in reality and not just theoretically; he becomes aware of the God within, not through the sense of hearing, or through attention to the inner voice directing and controlling, and called the "voice of conscience". This time the recognition is through *sight and direct vision.* He now responds not only to that which is heard, but also to that which he sees.   (1-113)

2. The medium of the inner sight has ever existed, and that which can be seen is always present, but the recognition of the majority as yet exists not.

This "recognition" by the initiate is the first great step in the initiation ceremony, and until it has transpired all other stages must wait. That which is recognised differs at the different initiations, and might be roughly summarised as follows:

The Ego, the reflection of the Monad, is in itself a triplicity, as is all else in nature, and reflects the three aspects of divinity, just as the Monad reflects on a higher plane the three aspects—will, love-wisdom, and active intelligence—of the Deity. Therefore:

At the *first initiation* the initiate becomes aware of the third, or lowest, aspect of the Ego, that of active intelligence. He is brought face to face with that manifestation of the great solar Angel (Pitri) who is himself, the real Self. He knows now past all disturbance that that manifestation of intelligence is that eternal Entity who has for ages past been demonstrating his powers on the physical plane through his successive incarnations.

At the *second initiation* this great Presence is seen as a duality, and another aspect shines forth before him. He becomes aware that this radiant Life, Who is identified with himself, is not only intelligence in action, but also is love-wisdom in origin. He merges his consciousness with this Life, and becomes one with it so that on the physical plane, through the medium of that personal self, that Life is seen as intelligent love expressing itself.

At the *third initiation* the Ego stands before the initiate as a perfected triplicity. Not only is the Self known to be intelligent, active love, but it is revealed also as a fundamental will or purpose, with which the man immediately identifies himself, and knows that the three worlds hold for him in the future naught, but only serve as a sphere for active service, wrought out in love towards the accomplishment of a purpose which has been hid during the ages in the heart of the Self. That purpose, being now revealed, can be intelligently co-operated with, and thus matured.

These profound revelations shine forth before the initiate in a triple manner:

As a radiant angelic existence. This is seen by the inner eye with the same accuracy of vision and judgment as when a man stands face to face with another member of the human family. The great solar Angel, Who embodies the real man and is his expression on the plane of higher mind, is literally his divine ancestor, the "Watcher" Who, through long cycles of incarnation, has poured Himself out in sacrifice in order that man might BE.

As a sphere of radiant fire, linked with the initiate standing before it, by that magnetic thread of fire which passes through all his bodies and terminates within the centre of the physical brain. This "silver thread" (as it is rather inaccurately called in the Bible, where the description of its loosing of the physical body and subsequent withdrawal is found) emanates from the heart centre of the solar Angel, linking thus heart and brain—that great duality manifesting in this solar system, love and intelligence. This fiery sphere is linked likewise with many others belonging to the same group and ray, and thus it is a literal fact in demonstration that on the higher planes we are all one. One life pulsates and circulates through all, via the fiery strands. This is part of the revelation which comes to a man who stands in the "Presence" with his eyes occultly opened.

As a many tinted Lotus of nine petals. These petals are arranged in three circles around a central set of three closely folded petals, which shield what is called in the Eastern books "The Jewel in the Lotus". This Lotus is a thing of rare beauty, pulsating with life and radiant with all the colours of the rainbow, and at the first three initiations the three circles are revealed in order, until at the fourth initiation the initiate stands before a still greater revelation, and learns the secret of that which lies within the central bud. In this connection the third initiation differs somewhat from the other two, inasmuch as through the power of a still more exalted Hierophant than the Bodhisattva, the electrical fire of pure Spirit, latent in the heart of the Lotus, is first contacted.

In all these words, "solar angel", "sphere of fire", and "lotus", lies hid some aspect of the central mystery of human life, but it will only be apparent to those who have eyes to see. The mystic significance of these pictorial phrases will prove only a snare or a basis for incredulity to the man who seeks to materialise them unduly. The thought of an immortal existence, of a divine Entity, of a great centre of fiery energy, and of the full flower of evolution, lies hidden in these terms, and they must be thus considered.

At the *fourth initiation,* the initiate is brought into the Presence of that aspect of Himself which is called "His Father in Heaven". He is brought face to face with his own Monad, that pure spiritual essence on the highest plane but one, which is to his Ego or higher Self what that Ego is to the personality or lower self.

This Monad has expressed itself on the mental plane through the Ego in triple fashion, but now all aspects of the mind, as we understand it, are lacking. The solar Angel hitherto contacted, has withdrawn himself, and the form through which he functioned (the egoic or causal body) has gone, and naught is left but love-wisdom and that dynamic will which is the prime characteristic of Spirit. The lower self has served the purposes of the Ego, and has been discarded; the Ego likewise has served the purposes of the Monad, and is no longer required, and the initiate stands free of both, fully liberated and able to contact the Monad, as earlier he learned to contact the Ego. For the remainder of his appearances in the three worlds, he is governed only by will and purpose, self-initiated, and creates his body of manifestation, and thus controls (within karmic limits) his own times and seasons. The karma here referred to is planetary karma, and not personal.

At this fourth initiation he contacts the love aspect of the Monad, and at the fifth the will aspect, and thus completes his contacts, responds to all necessary vibrations, and is master on the five planes of human evolution.

Further, it is at the third, the fourth, and the fifth initiations that he becomes aware also of that "Presence" which enfolds even that spiritual Entity, his own Monad. He sees his Monad as one with the Planetary Logos. Through the channel of his own Monad he sees the self-same aspects (which that Monad embodies) on a wider scale, and the Planetary Logos, Who ensouls all the Monads on His ray, is thus revealed. This truth is well-nigh impossible to express in words, and concerns the relation of the electrical point of fire, which is the Monad, to the five-pointed star, which reveals the Presence of the Planetary Logos to the initiate.

This is practically incomprehensible to the average man for whom this book is written. . . .

Thus by a graded series of steps is the initiate brought face to face with Truth and Existence. It will be apparent to thoughtful students why this revealing of the Presence has to precede all other revelations. It produces within the mind of the initiate the following basic realisations:

His faith for ages is justified, and hope and belief merge themselves in self-ascertained fact. Faith is lost in sight, and things unseen are seen and known. No more can he doubt, but he has become instead, through his own effort, a *knower*.

His oneness with his brothers is proven, and he realises the indissoluble link which binds him to his fellow men everywhere. Brotherhood is no longer a theory, but a proven scientific fact, no more to be disputed than the separateness of men on the physical plane is to be disputed.

The immortality of the soul and the reality of the unseen worlds is for him proven and ascertained. Whereas, before initiation, this belief was based on brief and fleeting vision, and strong inner convictions (the result of logical reasoning and of gradually developing intuition) now it is based on sight and on a recognition past all disproving, of his own immortal nature.

He realises the meaning and source of energy, and can begin to wield power with scientific accuracy and direction. He knows now whence he draws it, and has had a glimpse of the resources of energy which are available. Before, he knew that that energy existed, and used it blindly and sometimes unwisely; now he sees it under the direction of the "open mind", and can co-operate intelligently with the forces of nature.

Thus, in many ways, does the revelation of the Presence produce definite results in the initiate, and thus it is judged by the Hierarchy to be the necessary preamble to all later revelations.   (1-114/9)

62. THE KINGDOM OF SOULS

1. It is perhaps a new thought to some that the soul is organising itself for effort, reorienting its forces, and preparing for a fresh and powerful impulse, but so it is. All forms of life under the force of evolution pass from initiation to initiation, and the soul is not exempt from the process. Just as the soul of animal-man became united with another divine

principle (during individualisation), and so brought into being the fourth kingdom in nature, so the soul in humanity is seeking contact with another divine aspect. When that contact is made, the Kingdom of God will come on earth; the physical plane will thereby be transformed, and that peculiar period, presented symbolically under the term millennium, will come.

The Knowers of God in that era will preponderate over those who are simply aspiring to that knowledge, and their contact and the results of the force they transmit, will be felt in all the kingdoms of nature. Dominion over all forms, and the power to act as transmitters of that spiritual energy we call love, is the promised reward of the triumphant solar Angels, and the prized goal of their meditation work. The Sons of God will triumph on earth in full incarnated expression, and will bring light (therefore life) to all manifested forms. This is the "life more abundant" of which the Christ speaks.   (4-89/90)

2. I, who have entered somewhat into an understanding of the life of the solar Angel, seek to assure my fellow pilgrims that the passing things of the senses are but trivial and of no value, compared to the rewards, here and in this life, to the man who seeks to merge his everyday consciousness with that of his own soul. He enters then into the community of souls, and stands not alone. The only lonely periods are the result of wrong orientation and the holding on to that which hides the vision, and fills the hands so full that they cannot grasp what has been called "the jewel in the lotus".   (4-90)

3. Observers of times and seasons can make rapid progress in intuitional growth if they persevere in their meditation, train their intellects, and endeavour always to think in terms of universals. Let them look at the historical retrospect as part of the emerging preparation which will inaugurate the future. Let them take heart of grace as they recognise the fact that the kingdom of souls is steadily becoming a physical plane phenomenon (do I speak paradoxically?) and will be known eventually as a kingdom of nature and considered so by the scientists before two centuries have passed away. Those "Organised Observers" form the outer circle of the New Group and their keynote is synthesis, the elimination of non-essentials and the organising of human knowledge. Working in the many fields of human awareness, they are distinguished by a non-sectarian spirit, and by an ability to deal with foundational essentials and to link up varying departments of human investigation into one organised and unified whole. (4-606)

4. I wonder whether you have ever considered the widespread effect of all the reflective thinking, the aspirational prayers and the meditation work —untrained or as the result of training—done by people in their millions down the ages through the entire planet? Its quality is altering; its strength is increasing; its livingness is producing changes in the human organism. The tide of spiritual life is today so strong and striving that the next one hundred and fifty years will demonstrate the factual nature of the Kingdom of Souls or of God. This, as you surely can appreciate, will produce fundamental changes also in the immediate objectives before human progress and in the Masters' plans, in the teaching given, and in the training presented. (6-296)

5. Initiation is *par excellence* a series of graded steps or awakenings which enable the human being to become eventually a member, or a point of light, in the Kingdom of God. When an adequate number of members of the fourth kingdom have undergone the process of initiation (technically understood), *then* the fifth kingdom will come into exoteric manifestation. The method of making this hitherto subjective kingdom a factual entity, is rapidly nearing, and the proof of this is—for the first time in history —*group initiation.* This can now be undertaken, and it is for this that the Hierarchy is working today, where aspirants and disciples are concerned. (6-381)

6. The Kingdom of God or of Souls, distinguished by the potency and therefore, by the aura and radiatory emanation of love, is definitely anchored on Earth, and is penetrating ever more fully and successfully into the three worlds of strictly human endeavour. There have always been outposts of this kingdom among men; there have ever been individuals in all parts of the world—in the world religions or in other constructive groups—who were linked consciously to their souls, and consequently linked to the Hierarchy. There have always been those in every land who developed and expressed the Christ consciousness; this is loving understanding, and intelligent, living service, no matter by what words or terminology they expressed the tremendous spiritual event of which they were aware. But—from the standpoint of the world populations—the fourth kingdom in nature dominates in every field of thought and of activity, and not the Kingdom of God or of Souls.

Today, as a result of a spiritual awakening which dates from A.D. 1625, and which laid the emphasis upon a wider, general education and upon a revolt from the imposition of clerical authority, the radiation from the world of souls has greatly intensified and the Kingdom of God is becoming a corporate part of the outer world expression, and this for the first time in the long, long history of humanity.

The effect of this radiation or magnetic aura is now so extensive, that we need no longer talk in terms of bringing in the kingdom or of its manifestation on Earth. *It is already manifesting,* and its aura is co-mingled with the mental, astral and etheric auras of mankind. Recognition only is required, but (and this is a factor to be noted) recognition is being withheld until the Kingdom of Souls can be safeguarded from the narrow claims of any church, religion or organisation; many will claim (as they have ever done) that admittance into the Kingdom of God is to be found through their particular separative group. The Kingdom of God is *not* Christian, or Buddhist, or to be found focused in any world religion or esoteric organisation. It is simply and solely what it claims to be: a vast and integrated group of soul-infused persons, radiating love and spiritual intention, motivated by goodwill, and rooted in the human kingdom, as the kingdom of men is rooted in and is a break-away from the animal kingdom.   (6-406/8)

7. The outposts of that Kingdom and the vanguard of disciples and initiates is already here.

The work or the radiatory activity of the Hierarchy is today more potent than at any time in human history. The Masters and Their disciples (under the guidance of the World Teacher of that period) were physically present on Earth in early Atlantean times, and the radiation emanating from Them was protective, guarding and nurturing. Later, the Hierarchy withdrew into a subjective expression and humanity was—under the Law of Evolution—left to its own devices, thus to learn the Way and tread the Path of Return through individual experiment and experience. The Masters (in this long interim) have not come forth to contact humanity on any large or group scale; many of Their senior disciples have, however, emerged at varying intervals and when needed; the World Teacher has also come forth to sound the key or note for each new civilisation, and to express the results of the passing civilisation. Men have had, therefore, to find their way alone to the Hierarchy; in silence that Hierarchy has waited, until the number of "enlightened souls" was so great that their invocative appeal and their magnetic radiation reached a potency which could not be denied; the balance of equilibrium, attained between the Kingdom of God on Earth and the Kingdom of God in Heaven (to use Christian phraseology) became such that the "Gates of Return" could be opened and free intercourse established between the fourth and the fifth kingdoms of nature. The gates (and I am still speaking in symbols) are already opening, and soon will stand wide open to admit the passing of the "Son of Man, the perfected Son of God", back to the place—our Earth—where He earlier demonstrated perfect love and service. But—as you know—this time He will not come alone, but will bring with Him the Heads of certain of the Ashrams, as well as a trained group of initiates and disciples.

These happenings are taking place *today* before the eyes of all men, even though much that is going on remains totally unrecognised over vast areas of the world of thought, and by many millions of men. However, brother of mine, there are enough initiates and disciples working upon the physical plane at this time to ensure a recognition so extensive, that the steady, consistent arousing of human expectation is guaranteed. Ponder on this and learn to recognise on every side the signs of human anticipation, and the pronounced indication of the approach of the Hierarchy. (6-408/ 10)

8. The objective of the Plan is to reproduce upon the plane of Earth the inner Kingdom of the Soul. This has the Master of the Masters long foretold. Prepare the Way. (6-596)

9. Christ taught also that the Kingdom of God was on Earth and told us to seek that Kingdom first and let all things be of secondary importance for its sake. That Kingdom has ever been with us, composed of all those who down the ages have sought spiritual goals, liberated themselves from the limitations of the physical body, emotional controls, and the obstructive mind. Its citizens are those who today (unknown to the majority) live in physical bodies, work for the welfare of humanity, use love instead of emotion as their general technique, and compose that great body of illumined minds" which guides the destiny of the world. The Kingdom of God is not something which will descend on Earth when man is good enough! It is something which is functioning efficiently today and demanding recognition. It is an organised body which is already evoking recognition from those people who do seek first the Kingdom of God, and discover thereby that the Kingdom they seek is already here. Christ and His disciples are known by many to be physically present on Earth, and the Kingdom which They rule, with its laws and modes of activity, is familiar to many and has been throughout the centuries. (8-50/1)

10. From stage to stage, from crisis to crisis, from point to point, and from centre to centre, the life of od progressed, leaving greater beauty

behind it as it moves through one form after another, and from kingdom to kingdom. One attainment leads to another; out of the lower kingdoms man has emerged, and (as a result of human struggle) the Kingdom of God will also appear. The bringing in of that Kingdom is all that truly concerns humanity today, and all living processes in mankind are bent towards preparing each individual human being to pass into that Kingdom. The knowledge that there may be greater manifestations than even the Kingdom of God may be inspiring, but that is all. The manifestation of the Kingdom of God on Earth, the preparing of the way for its great Inaugurator, the Christ, the making possible the externalisation of the Hierarchy upon Earth, give us each and all a fully adequate task and something for which to live and work, to dream and to aspire.   (18-738)

63.   CONCLUSION

1. All these ideas and concepts are of value only in so far as they produce within the Thinker a more intelligent appreciation of the grandeur of the divine Plan, and appropriation of the energy and force which is his by right of participation in the processes of manifestation, and a wise co-operation in the furtherance of the evolutionary plan as it affects him individually and his groups.   (3-503)

2. When energy from the Ego controls, or imposes its rhythm upon the various sheaths via their respective major centres, when the triple fire is mounting in orderly fashion via the triple channel, and when the three head centres are united in triangular fashion, then we have illumination or the irradiance of the entire personality life, darkness gives place to light, and the Sun of Knowledge arises and dispels the darkness of ignorance. . . . The man becomes a burning and a shining light, radiating forth a light which burns from within.

When the next step is accomplished, and the energy of the Monad, focused through the jewel, makes itself felt also on the physical plane, passing through the triple egoic lotus, via the channels already utilised by the Ego, we have a man who is "inspired", who is a spiritual creator, and who is himself "a Sun of Healing Radiance".

These are the objectives before all those who tread the Path and the goal ahead for those who follow the necessary discipline of life, and the stages of unfoldment through meditation. . . . The usual method, a lengthy and laborious one, is to let the pupil find out each step of the way for himself, to teach him the constitution of his own body, the nature of the sheaths, and the function and apparatus of energy, and so let him gradually become aware of the forces latent in himself. What is meant by the "three periodical vehicles" and the seven principles or qualities of force, is slowly revealed to him, and through experience, experiment, frequent failures, occasional success, mature reflection and introspection, and frequent incarnation, he is brought to the point where he has produced a certain measure of alignment through self-induced and continuous effort. He is then taught how to utilise that alignment, and how to manipulate energy consciously so that he can bring about on the physical plane *results in service* that for many lives have been probably a dream or an impossible vision. When he is proficient in these two things—stabilisation and manipulation—then, and only then, are committed to him the words and secrets which produce the demonstration on the physical plane of spiritual, or monadic energy by means of the soul or egoic energy, utilising in its turn the energy of the material forms in the worlds, or what we might call bodily energy. This has been expressed in the following mystical and occult phrase:

> "When the jewel sparkles as does the diamond under the influence of the rays of the blazing sun, then the setting likewise gleams and rays forth light. As the diamond shines with increasing brilliance, the fire is generated which sets on fire that which (is) held and enclosed". (3-1130/2)

3. The great need at this time is for experts in the life of the soul and for a group of men and women who, undertaking the great experiment and transition, add their testimony to the truth of the statements of the mystics and occultists of the ages. (4-41)

4. The Hierarchy, through the Group of World Servers now in process of formation, is seeking to externalise itself, and to restore the mysteries to humanity to whom they truly belong. If the attempt is to succeed, it is basically necessary that all of you who have sensed the vision or seen a part of the intended Plan, should re-dedicate yourselves to the service of humanity, should pledge yourselves to the work of aiding to the utmost of your ability (ponder those words and search out their significance) all world servers, and should sacrifice your time and give of your money to further the endeavour of the Great Ones. Rest not, above all, from your meditation work; keep the inner link; think truth at all times. The need

and the opportunity are great, and all possible helpers are being called to the forefront of the battle. All can be used in some way, if the true nature of sacrifice is grasped, if skill in action is developed, and if work without attachment is the effort of each and all of you. (4-521)

5. To you, who live and work in this interim period and in this cycle of transition, with all its resultant, outer chaos and upheaval, is given the task of expressing steadfastness, service and sacrifice. . . . You need to absorb and to act upon the information you already have, before there is evoked from you that basic demand for further light which necessitates response from those of us who work within the limits of the Hierarchy. For that demand, we patiently wait.   (9-146)

6. I have told you much, had you the awakened intuition to read the significance of some of my comments.   (18-66)

7. And so, from stage to stage the disciple passes, going from light to light, from perception to perception, from force to energy, from personality focus to soul integration, and then from soul to spirit, from form to life. He has explored all the avenues of knowledge; he has descended into the depths, into hell and into the valleys; he has climbed the mountain top of initiation, and from there has swung out beyond space and time; he has lost all self-interest and is a focused point of thought in the mind of God. Can I say more than this? I think not, my brothers. And so I bring to an end this series of instructions, and my responsibility in this connection is ended. Yours now begins.   (5-772/3)

*

*   *

Training for new age
discipleship is provided
by the *Arcane School*.
The principles of the
Ageless Wisdom are
presented through esoteric
meditation, study and
service as a *way of life*.

Write to the publishers for information.